From Mother to Son

RELIGIONS IN TRANSLATION

SERIES EDITOR
Anne Monius, Harvard Divinity School
A Publication Series of The American Academy of Religion and Oxford University Press

Religion of Reason
Out of the Sources of Judaism
Hermann Cohen
Translated, with an Introduction
by Simon Kaplan
Introductory essays by Leo Strauss
Introductory essays for the second edition by
Steven S. Schwarzchild and Kenneth Seeskin

Durkheim on Religion
Émile Durkheim
Edited by W. S. F. Pickering

On the Glaubenslehre
Two Letters to Dr. Lücke
Friedrich D. E. Schleiermacher
Translated by James Duke and
Francis Fiorenza

Hermeneutics
The Handwritten Manuscripts
Friedrich D. E. Schleiermacher
Edited by Heina Kimmerle
Translated by James Duke and Jack Forstman

The Study of Stolen Love
Translated by David C. Buck and
K. Paramasivam

The Daoist Monastic Manual
A Translation of the Fengdao Kejie
Livia Kohn

Sacred and Profane Beauty
The Holy in Art
Gararrdus van der Leeuw
Preface by Mircea Eliade
Translated by David E. Green
With a new introduction and bibliography by
Diane Apostolos-Cappadona

The History of the Buddha's Relic Shrine
A Translation of the Sinhala Thūpavamsa
Stephen C. Berkwitz

Damascius' Problems & Solutions Concerning First Principles
Translated with Introduction and Notes by Sara Ahbel-Rappe

The Secret Garland
Āṇṭāḷ's Tiruppāvai *and* Nācciyār Tirumoḻi
Translated with Introduction and Commentary by
Archana Venkatesan

Prelude to the Modernist Crisis
The "Firmin" Articles of Alfred Loisy
Edited, with an Introduction by C. J. T. Talar
Translated by Christine Thirlway

Debating the Dasam Granth
Robin Rinehart

The Fading Light of Advaita Ācārya
Three Hagiographies
Rebecca J. Manring

The Ubiquitous Śiva
Somānanda's Śivadṛṣṭi and His Tantric Interlocutors
John Nemec

Place and Dialectic
Two Essays by Nishida Kitarō
Translated by John W.M. Krummel and Shigenori Nagatomo

The Prison Narratives Of Jeanne Guyon
Ronney Mourad and Dianne Guenin-Lelle

Disorienting Dharma
Ethics and the Aesthetics of Suffering in the Mahābhārata
Emily T. Hudson

The Transmission Of Sin
Augustine and the Pre-Augustinian Sources
Pier Franco Beatrice
Translated by Adam Kamesar

To my children, Bobby, Frankie, Johnny, and Aggie

AMERICAN ACADEMY
of RELIGION

From Mother to Son

*The Selected Letters of
Marie de l'Incarnation to
Claude Martin*

Translated and with introduction and notes by
MARY DUNN

OXFORD
UNIVERSITY PRESS

OXFORD
UNIVERSITY PRESS

Oxford University Press is a department of the University of Oxford.
It furthers the University's objective of excellence in research, scholarship,
and education by publishing worldwide.

Oxford   New York
Auckland   Cape Town   Dar es Salaam   Hong Kong   Karachi
Kuala Lumpur   Madrid   Melbourne   Mexico City   Nairobi
New Delhi   Shanghai   Taipei   Toronto

With offices in
Argentina   Austria   Brazil   Chile   Czech Republic   France   Greece
Guatemala   Hungary   Italy   Japan   Poland   Portugal   Singapore
South Korea   Switzerland   Thailand   Turkey   Ukraine   Vietnam

Oxford is a registered trademark of Oxford University Press
in the UK and certain other countries.

Published in the United States of America by
Oxford University Press
198 Madison Avenue, New York, NY 10016

© Oxford University Press 2014

All rights reserved. No part of this publication may be reproduced, stored in a
retrieval system, or transmitted, in any form or by any means, without the prior
permission in writing of Oxford University Press, or as expressly permitted by law,
by license, or under terms agreed with the appropriate reproduction rights organization.
Inquiries concerning reproduction outside the scope of the above should be sent to the
Rights Department, Oxford University Press, at the address above.

You must not circulate this work in any other form
and you must impose this same condition on any acquirer.

Library of Congress Cataloging-in-Publication Data
Marie de l'Incarnation, 1599-1672.
[Correspondence. Selections. English]
From mother to son : the selected letters of Marie De l'incarnation to Claude Martin /
translated by Mary Dunn.
pages cm. — (AAR religions in translation)
Includes bibliographical references.
ISBN 978–0–19–938657–4 (hardcover : alk. paper) — ISBN 978–0–19–938658–1 (ebook)
1. Marie de l'Incarnation, 1599 1672—Correspondence.   2. Martin, Claude, 1619–1696
Correspondence.   3. Mothers and sons—Correspondence.   4. Spiritual life—Catholic Church.
5. Mysticism—Catholic Church.   I. Martin, Claude, 1619–1696.   II. Title.
BX4705.M36A4 2014
271'.97402—dc23
2013049355

1 3 5 7 9 8 6 4 2
Printed in the United States of America
on acid-free paper

Contents

Acknowledgments ix

Introduction 1

Letters 41

Index 225

Acknowledgments

I AM GRATEFUL to the many people who have aided me in bringing this book into being. I owe especial thanks to Carla Zecher of the Newberry Library in Chicago, whose careful and meticulous editing of my translations and footnotes made this book a volume worth publishing. I am also indebted to my colleague Bill O'Brien, who offered me many valuable suggestions when it came to my questions about seventeenth-century French spirituality, and to my former research assistant Kyle Schenkewitz, who diligently executed a number of discrete research projects that enhanced the annotations in the present work. I am thankful, too, for the time and effort given to reading through and commenting on this volume by Dominique Deslandres and the anonymous reviewers for Oxford University Press. Finally, I am deeply appreciative of Anne Monius, who encouraged me (even through some rough patches) in this endeavor and who saw the project through from its start to its finish.

Top billing, however, goes to my family: first, to my mother, without whose loving and reliable assistance with my own children this project would never have been completed; then, to my husband Bobby, who has tolerated many a dinner date engaging with me over this or that interpretative detail about Marie de l'Incarnation and who continues to be an exemplary father to Bobby, Frankie, Johnny, and Aggie; and finally, to these four children themselves. They have, collectively, provided the initial and ongoing inspiration for my work on Marie de l'Incarnation, whose complicated relationship with her only son attracted my attention some years ago. It is to you that I dedicate this book.

From Mother to Son

Introduction

Are you not glad, my very dear son, that I abandoned you to his holy direction in leaving you out of love for him? Have you not found a boon therein which cannot be expressed? Know, then, once more, that when I separated myself from you, I died while still alive and that the spirit of God, who was unmoved by the tender feelings I had for you, gave me no rest until I had delivered the blow.... This divine spirit who saw my struggles had no sympathy for my feelings, saying to me in the depths of my heart, "Quickly, quickly, it is time, delay no longer. There is no longer anything good left for you in the world." Then he opened the door to religion for me... You came with me and in leaving you, it seemed to me that my soul was being sundered from my body with extreme pains.[1]

THUS WROTE MARIE de l'Incarnation, renowned French mystic and founder of the Ursulines in Canada, to her son Claude just two years before her death in 1672. By this time, Claude was a mystic in his own right and a professed religious himself, a Benedictine of the order of Saint-Maur. The event to which Marie alluded—as she had time and again both in her previous letters to Claude and in her spiritual autobiographies, the *Relations* of 1633 and 1654—was her decision to abandon Claude at the tender age of eleven in favor of consecrated religious life among the Ursulines.

In 1639, Marie migrated to the struggling and inchoate French colony at Quebec to found the first Ursuline convent in the New World, where she would pursue an active apostolate among the indigenous peoples and French settlers in the Saint Lawrence valley. Over the course of the next thirty-one years, the relationship between Marie de l'Incarnation and Claude Martin would take shape by means of a trans-Atlantic correspondence in which mother and son shared advice and counsel (both temporal and spiritual), concerns and anxieties, joys and frustrations. The letters sent by Marie to Claude reveal much about the

---

1. Letter 247, my translation. All translations from the original French that follow are my own. Unless otherwise noted, all citations to the letters in this introduction reference letters included in this volume.

early history of New France, an early modern anthropology of the Amerindian Other, and the spiritual itinerary of one of the most celebrated mystics of the seventeenth century. Uniting these letters into a coherent whole is, however, the distinctive relationship between an absent mother and her abandoned son, a relationship reconfigured from one of flesh and blood to one of the written word exchanged between professed religious united in Jesus Christ as members of the same spiritual family. Read over the *longue durée*, the letters give the impression of an increasing intimacy and identity between mother and son as Marie comes to reveal to Claude the confidences of her interior life with growing candor, to acknowledge the mutuality of her personal spiritual experiences and Claude's own, and to accept her material, social, and spiritual dependence on Claude as a priest of considerable status with the Order of Saint Benedict.

The following translations of forty-one of the eighty-one extant full-length letters written by Marie de l'Incarnation to her son, Claude Martin, from 1640 to 1671 are based on Dom Guy Oury's 1971 critical edition of the entire corpus of Marie's known correspondence, numbering 277 letters.[2] It is to Claude himself, however, that we owe the preservation of the majority of Marie's surviving (albeit heavily edited) letters. In 1681, Claude published 221 of Marie's letters under the title *Écrits spirituels et historiques*, selecting from among the letters his mother had sent to him and those he had managed to solicit from other family members, the Ursulines of Tours, Saint-Denis, and Dijon, and the Jesuit Joseph Poncet, among others.[3] Although Claude claims to have edited his mother's letters only in the interests of modernizing her outdated prose and making more linear her narrative style (which was marked by unfinished thoughts and accidental repetitions), comparisons between Marie's few remaining original letters and Claude's edited versions reveal that these editorial interventions extended far beyond mere aesthetic modifications. Moreover, in his attempt to separate his mother's letters into the categories of historical, on the one hand, and spiritual, on the other, Claude in some cases went so far as to alienate portions of a single letter

---

2. *Marie de l'Incarnation: Correspondance*, ed. Dom Guy-Marie Oury (Sablé-sur-Sarthe: Solesmes Abbey, 1971), hereafter, *Correspondance*. Other editions of Marie's letters exist, the best-known of which are those of Abbé Richaudeau (1876) and Dom Albert Jamet (1935, 1939). Richaudeau's edition largely reproduces Claude's 1681 text, with the addition of several letters discovered in the archives of the Ursulines of Mons and two letters addressed to the abbess of Port-Royal. Jamet's edition is an excellent scholarly one, carefully annotated with notes of historical and doctrinal interest, but remains regrettably incomplete, covering Marie's correspondence only up to 1652.

3. Extracts of a number of the letters published in the *Écrits* had been previously published as part of Claude's 1677 biography of his mother, *La Vie de la Vénérable Mère Marie de l'Incarnation* (Sablé-sur-Sarthe: Solesmes Abbey, 1981), hereafter, *Vie*.

deemed historical from those considered spiritual, and to cobble together into a composite text sections from multiple letters. Shortcomings notwithstanding, the 1681 *Écrits* remains the only record of the majority of Marie's extant letters and it is thus on Claude's edition that Oury principally relies, supplementing the *Écrits* where possible with the original texts or extracts of the letters published in Claude's 1677 *La Vie de la Vénérable Mère Marie de l'Incarnation*. Consequently, it is primarily the work of Claude Martin that this collection, too, reproduces in English translation.[4]

In this volume, I seek to make accessible to an English-speaking audience a representative selection of Marie de l'Incarnation's correspondence with her son, Claude. In determining which among the eighty-one extant letters to include in this volume, I gave priority to those that communicated a sense of both the nature and evolution of Marie's relationship with Claude and the range of their conversation in which spiritual concerns and historical context are mutually implicated. I have taken the liberty of modernizing the spellings of certain personal names and place names, breaking up cumbersome sentences, and simplifying punctuation in some instances, and I have attempted to capture (to the extent possible) the unstudied and rustic character of Marie's original prose. By means of extensive annotations, moreover, I have labored to contextualize the correspondence both within the broader cultural, historical, intellectual, and theological currents of the seventeenth century and within the body of contemporary scholarship on Marie de l'Incarnation and seventeenth-century New France.[5]

---

4. To my knowledge, letters written by Claude to his mother have not been preserved and we are, unfortunately, left with only one side of the epistolary exchange.

5. Until the 1990s, scholarship on Marie de l'Incarnation was dominated by the Benedictines (building on the legacy of their confrère Claude Martin). It is the Benedictines—particularly, Dom Albert Jamet and, later, Dom Guy-Marie Oury—to whom we owe gratitude for the painstaking work of producing and publishing critical editions of the bulk of Marie's writings. With the solid foundation provided by Jamet's and Oury's critical editions, scholarship on Marie de l'Incarnation began to flourish in the 1990s. This scholarship has tended to focus on Marie de l'Incarnation's spirituality, her mysticism, and her experience among and perspective on the Amerindians of the New World. A focus on Marie de l'Incarnation's spirituality has especially captured the attention of Francophone scholars. See, for example, Robert Michel, *Vivre dans l'Esprit: Marie de l'Incarnation* (Montreal: Bellarmin, 1975); Maria-Paul del Rosario Adriazola, *La connaissance spirituelle chez Marie de l'Incarnation, la Thérèse de France et du nouveau monde* (Paris: Cerf, 2001); and Pierre Gervais, *Marie de l'Incarnation: Études de théologie spirituelle* (Namur: Vie consacrée, 1996). Other scholars have trained their lenses more particularly on Marie's mysticism. See for example: Raymond Brodeur, ed., *Femme, mystique et missionnaire: Marie Guyart de l'Incarnation* (Quebec: Presses de l'Université Laval, 2001); and Marie-Florine Bruneau, *Women Mystics Confront the Modern World: Marie de l'Incarnation (1599–1672) and Madame Guyon (1648–1717)* (Albany: State University of New York Press, 1998). For work that focuses on Marie de l'Incarnation's location in colonial New France and among

On account of its selectivity, this volume necessarily presents the reader with a partial—both incomplete and prejudiced—perspective on Marie de l'Incarnation. Given both the number and the diversity of Marie's correspondents indicated by Oury's edition alone, it is not difficult to imagine that a different volume focused on a group of letters addressed to another set of correspondents would have offered the reader a very different picture of Marie de l'Incarnation.[6] Here, however, I have elected to train my lens exclusively on the letters exchanged between this absent mother and her abandoned son as a means of offering my own reader not only a critical and arresting source for understanding an often overlooked chapter in the early history of European North America (which, in Anglophone scholarship anyway, is all too heavily weighted in favor of Plymouth Rock and the Puritans), but also a window onto one of the more

---

the Amerindian populations, see Dominique Deslandres, "Altérité, identité et rédemption," in *Femme, mystique et missionnaire*, ed. Raymond Brodeur, 55–68 (Quebec: Presses de l'Université Laval, 2001); Dominique Deslandres, "Marie de l'Incarnation et la femme Amérindienne," *Recherches Amérindiennes au Québec* 13, no. 4 (1983): 277–85; Mary Dunn, "When 'Wolves Become Lambs': Hybridity and the 'Savage' in the Letters of Marie de l'Incarnation," *The Seventeenth Century* 27, no. 1 (Spring 2012): 104–20. More recently, scholars like Anya Mali and Rebecca Wilkin have attempted to tie these themes together, suggesting ways in which Marie's location in colonial New France might have impacted her mystical spirituality and vice versa: see Anya Mali, *Mystic in the New World: Marie de l'Incarnation (1599–1672)* (Leiden: E. J. Brill, 1996); Rebecca Wilkin, "L'Algonquin par abjection: Une mystique aborde le Nouveau Monde," in *L'Autre au XVIIème siècle: Actes du 4e colloque du Centre International de Rencontres sur le XVIIème siècle*, ed. Ralph Heyndels and Barbara Woshinsky, 31–46 (Tübingen: Gunter Narr Verlag, 1999). Few among the scholars at work on Marie de l'Incarnation, however, have given sustained attention to the relationship between the seventeenth-century mystic and the son she abandoned in favor of religious life. Where analyses have been undertaken of the relationship between Marie and Claude, these have been mostly within the context of Francophone scholarship; see for example, Chantal Théry, "L'Écho est le fils de la voix: Les rapports mère-fils," in *Femme, mystique, et missionnaire*, ed. Brodeur, 253–64; Jacques Maître, "Claude Martin, fils de Marie de l'Incarnation: essai de psychanalyse sociohistorique," in *Femme, mystique, et missionnaire*, ed. Brodeur, 265–76; Marie-Florine Bruneau, "Le sacrifice maternel commun alibi à la production de l'écriture," *Études littéraires* 27, no. 2 (Fall 1994): 67–76; Yvette Côté, "L'accompagnement d'une mère," in *Marie de l'Incarnation, entre mère et fils: Le dialogue des vocations*, ed. Raymond Brodeur, 143–52 (Quebec: Presses de l'Université Laval, 2000); Sophie Houdard, "Le cri public du fils abandonné ou l'inexprimable secret d'une mère," *Littératures classiques* 68 (2009): 273–84.

6. As, indeed, does Joyce Marshall's *Word from New France: The Selected Letters of Marie de l'Incarnation*, trans. and ed. Joyce Marshall (Toronto: Oxford University Press, 1967). Whereas the present volume aims to elucidate the contours of the complicated and richly textured relationship between Marie and the son she abandoned in favor of religious life, Marshall's collection (which includes at least twenty-four letters addressed to correspondents other than Claude) was intended to "provide a narrative of the life of the time" (*Word from New France*, 32). Oury's edition includes letters written to fifty-seven different correspondents, from the archbishop of Tours and various Jesuits to Marie's relatives back home and the governor of New France, among others.

intriguing and complicated stories of maternal and filial affection in the early modern Christian West.

Biographical Background

Marie de l'Incarnation was born Marie Guyart just before the turn of the seventeenth century on October 28, 1599, in Tours, France. The fourth of Florent Guyart's and Jeanne Michelet's eight children, Marie felt herself from an early age drawn to the liturgy and the sacraments and inclined to conversation with God the Father, the Blessed Virgin Mary, and the crucified Jesus Christ. Marie's attraction to Jesus Christ would remain a central theme in her religious itinerary, from her vivid dream of Jesus at the tender age of seven to her conversion experience of 1620, to her mystical marriage with the Incarnate Word in 1627, to her vocation as an Ursuline in the New World conceived in imitation of Christ.

Against her own inclinations, but in obedience to her parents, Marie married Claude Martin, a master silk worker, in 1617 and within two years the marriage had produced a son, Claude, born April 2, 1619. Whatever comfort Marie might have taken in her new role as wife and mother was, however, short-lived. A mere six months after the birth of their son, Claude (the elder) died, leaving the nineteen-year-old widow with the prospect of raising her infant son alone and the daunting task of handling the debts and lawsuits that had brought her husband's small factory to the brink of bankruptcy.[7]

Shortly after her husband's death, Marie experienced a dramatic vision of the crucified Christ, which she would later identify as the moment of her conversion and which left her with an enduring impression of the reality of sin, her personal need for redemption, and the burden of Christ's sacrifice.[8] After a brief stay in her father's house, toward the end of 1621 Marie moved into the home of her sister and brother-in-law, where she had been invited to help manage the house and the kitchen and where she continued to cultivate a rich interior life. The young Claude, who had recently returned to his mother's side after some two years under the care of a nursemaid, came with her. By her own account, Marie's relationship with her only son in these early years was not one marked by warmth. Although "I loved him dearly," Marie confessed in the *Relation* of 1654, "I...never caressed

---

7. Neither Marie de l'Incarnation nor her son reveals the direct cause of Claude Martin's business problems. Based on allusions in the *Vie*, however, Guy-Marie Oury suggests that the problems might have been instigated by a woman who had been infatuated with but rebuffed by Marie's husband.

8. Martin, *Vie*, 30.

him as one does children."⁹ Claude, for his part, describes his mother's demeanor toward him as one of benign lack of disinterest: "Her manner toward me was one of gentle seriousness and I acted likewise toward her, as much as my childishness allowed me... [But] just as she never caressed me, so also did she never treat me badly."¹⁰ For Marie, her son seems principally to have been the final—and most intractable—obstacle to her entry into religious life, which from the moment of her widowhood was "delay[ed]... only because of my son."¹¹

Finally, in 1631, Marie entered the Ursuline monastery in Tours. The eleven-year-old Claude accompanied her to the end. "Leaving our lodging to enter into the house of God," Marie writes in her *Relation* of 1633, "this child came with me totally resigned. He dared not admit his affliction to me, but I saw tears fall from his eyes. He caused me to feel such compassion that I felt as if my soul was being ripped apart."¹² Marie's decision to abandon her son had not been an easy one. Elsewhere she relates how, before joining the Ursulines, she had been tormented by concern for her son, "who was then not yet twelve years old and without any means of support... The Devil pushed me hard on this point, trying to convince me that I was wrong to have neglected my own interests by doing nothing either for myself or for my son, and that leaving him in this condition would be to ruin him and endanger my conscience."¹³ Claude's resistance to his mother's decision did not make matters any easier. Shortly before her departure, Claude ran away from boarding school. Although he was discovered at the port of Blois a short three days later, Marie experienced the event as "a heavy cross" and imagined that Claude's actions were the work of the devil who was trying to "trouble my soul by insinuating that I was the cause of this loss."¹⁴ The censure of her neighbors did nothing to alleviate Marie's uncertainty. Everyone, wrote Marie

---

9. Martin, *Vie*, 182.

10. Martin, *Vie*, 178.

11. Martin, *Vie*, 155–6.

12. Martin, *Vie*, 179.

13. Martin, *Vie*, 128.

14. Martin, *Vie*, 174–5. Marie and Claude explain the motivations for Claude's flight differently. While Marie seems to have been convinced that Claude ran away from home in order to follow a Feuillant priest to Paris with the intention of becoming a religious, Claude reveals in the *Vie* that, instead, his departure had been provoked by a "profound melancholy... which was like a presentiment and a prediction of the misfortune that was about to befall him." In Claude's own words, "He saw that his relatives who had knowledge of his mother's plan looked at him fixedly with eyes of pity without saying anything to him, then turning back around they conferred together in low voices about this affair... Seeing nothing but sadness and gloom," he could stand it no longer and ran away to Paris to stay with the friend of his uncle (Martin, *Vie*, 174–5).

reflecting on the episode in the *Relation* of 1654, took the opportunity "to offer new objections [to my entering religious life,] protesting that I would endanger my conscience for leaving [my son] while he was still so young, that what had happened to him would happen again, and that I would be guilty of the loss, and that what I deemed a virtue would become my chastisement."¹⁵

Indeed, even after she had stepped over the convent threshold—a moment she describes as one of inexpressible delight—Marie continued to doubt whether she had done the right thing, doubts that could only have been aggravated by Claude's persistent (and poignant) efforts to win his mother's attention. Throughout the early months of Marie's novitiate, Claude continued to agitate his mother's conscience, crying for her outside the convent gates, regularly entering the enclosure, going "to the parlor and beg[ging]...that I be given back to him or that he be allowed to enter with me," sometimes crawling into the convent choir or throwing his coat and hat there in view of his mother (which "spectacle...renewed all her pains"), on one occasion showing up in the refectory just as the community was about to sit down for a meal. Claude presented to his mother, too, some verses composed by his uncle who "had a particular talent for French poetry" on the subject of her withdrawal written in the voice of the abandoned son, "[a]nd all this in terms so tender and with such animated affections."¹⁶

Although Marie admits that all this "pierced my heart with compassion," she ultimately acquiesced to God's will that she abandon her son and accepted—with equanimity—God's promises that he would take care of Claude.¹⁷ As Marie would explain later, in leaving Claude for religious life she was not—all appearances to the contrary—depriving him of parental care, for not only had God given her "rest in the conviction that His loving and paternal Goodness would not destroy the one whom I had abandoned out of love for him," but she had placed him "in the hands of the Mother of goodness, trusting that since I was going to give my life for the service of her beloved Son, she would take care of you."¹⁸ Understood theologically, then, the abandonment was not what it seemed. In abandoning

---

15. Martin, *Vie*, 169.

16. Martin, *Vie*, 186. See also Letter 247.

17. Martin, *Vie*, 181.

18. Letter 56. Claude, recalling a speech delivered to him by his mother on the eve of her departure, remembers Marie making the point even more strongly: "My son, today you are losing your mother but you are not losing anything because I am giving you another in my place who will be much greater for you than me and who has much more power to do well by you. It is the Holy Virgin to whom I am recommending you. Be her good devoted one, calling her your mother and in your needs address yourself to her with confidence, reminding her that you are her son and that she must take care of you" (Martin, *Vie*, 177–8).

Claude, Marie had not abnegated her maternal responsibilities but had simply transferred them to a superior set of (divine) parents whose protection and care would far surpass that which she was capable of providing for Claude.

Even if we dismiss Marie's theologically inspired reimagining of the abandonment, it is worth considering to what extent (despite the unambiguous language that marks the correspondence) Marie's decision to leave the eleven-year-old Claude to enter consecrated religious life counted as abandonment when measured against the standards of maternal care in seventeenth-century France.[19] The expectations placed upon seventeenth-century French mothers included that of breastfeeding their own offspring. Religious and secular manuals alike advised maternal breastfeeding on a variety of grounds, including the presumption that moral character was transmitted by breast milk, the conviction that a nursemaid's affection could never match a mother's love, and the potential for emotional and physical abuse from hired help.[20] Published handbooks also urged parents to see to the education of their children, charging them with the responsibility of protecting their progeny from bad influences and inculcating within them a sense of morality, teaching them prayer and forming their souls. It was on the shoulders of mothers that seventeenth-century French society placed most of the educational burden for sons and daughters alike, although typically a mother's pedagogical responsibilities toward her son were transferred to others when the son began a more formal education away from home at the age of seven.[21] Finally, parents were expected to have some hand in arranging the futures of their children, a duty that began with the strategic selection of godparents and continued with the placement of teenaged children as apprentices and servants away from home.

However wanting we might find the relationship between Marie and Claude today, Marie does not fall measurably short of the mark of good maternal practice in seventeenth-century France. It is true that Marie did not breastfeed Claude, but neither did the majority of her peers. Despite formal recommendations to the contrary, statistics suggest that only a minority of mothers (particularly in urban areas and among the upper classes) actually complied. Moreover, Marie did not leave Claude for the Ursulines until he was eleven, well beyond the age at which most boys would have begun formal education away from home and just slightly

---

19. See, generally, Yvonne Knibiehler and Catherine Fouquet, *L'histoire des mères, du moyen-âge à nos jours* (Paris: Montalba). See also Jean-Louis Flandrin, *Families in Former Times: Kinship, Household and Sexuality* (Cambridge, UK: Cambridge University Press, 1979).

20. Shulamith Shahar, *Childhood in the Middle Ages* (New York: Routledge, 1990), 56.

21. Knibiehler and Fouquet, *L'histoire*, 106–16. Some churchmen even went so far as to warn about the consequences of an excess of maternal affection (*L'histoire*, 113).

earlier than most of Claude's peers from the ranks of the artisans would have entered into apprenticeships.[22] Even after entering religious life, Marie continued to maintain an active interest in Claude's education, providing for his instruction among the Jesuits in Rennes and seeing to his spiritual formation by means of their trans-Atlantic correspondence. Marie, too, assiduously sought to secure Claude's future, writing in 1640 "to several of our friends on your behalf to try to find you a suitable situation in case your plans do not work out."[23]

To what extent affection—the lack of which Claude complains about repeatedly over the course of his thirty-year correspondence with his mother—was part of the mix of maternal expectations in seventeenth-century France remains a matter of debate. Although Philippe Ariès, whose 1960 *L'Enfant et la vie familiale sous l'Ancien Régime* (translated into English as *Centuries of Childhood*) set the terms of the scholarly conversation about childhood, did not go so far as to deny that parents felt affection for their children, others did.[24] Edward Shorter, for example, argued that before the eighteenth century parents were largely indifferent to the happiness and development of their very young children. For Shorter, the popularity of wet-nursing (despite the considerably higher mortality rate of infants cared for by wet-nurses) provided eloquent testimony of the affective distance between parents and their children in preindustrial Europe. More recently, however, scholars like Linda Pollock have proposed that the history of childhood is one more of continuity than change, that parents have always felt affection for their children, and that rather than "search for the existence or absence of love

---

22. Early modern Europeans imagined childhood as a series of stages, the third of which began at age seven. It was at seven years of age that boys received their first pair of trousers and the child's initiation into the adult world began. As teenagers (most commonly between the ages of fifteen and nineteen), many children worked as apprentices or domestic servants away from home. André Burguière and François Lebrun, "Priest, Prince, and Family," in *A History of the Family*, vol. 2, ed. André Burguière et al., trans. Sarah Hanbury Tenison, 146–58 (Cambridge, MA: Harvard University Press, 1996).

23. Letter 41. The following year, however, Marie admitted that she had *not* accepted (against convention) the help of her powerful allies to place Claude, explaining that she had "thanked Madame the Duchess d'Aiguillon for the good that she wanted to do for you, but the thought that came to me then was that if you were advanced in the world, your soul would be in danger of ruin [which] made me resolve to leave you a second time in the hands of the Mother of goodness, trusting that since I was going to give my life for the service of her beloved Son, she would take care of you" (Letter 56).

24. Philippe Ariès, *Centuries of Childhood: a Social History of Family Life*, trans. Robert Baldic (New York: Knopf, 1962). Among those studies of the family faithful to the historiography of Ariès are: David Hunt, *Parents and Children in History: the Psychology of Family Life in Early Modern France* (New York: Basic Books, 1970); Edward Shorter, *The Making of the Modern Family* (New York: Basic Books, 1975); and Lloyd DeMause, *The History of Childhood* (New York: Harper & Row, 1975).

in the past...[historians] should investigate what love meant in a given culture and era, and how it was expressed."[25] The prosperity of the wet-nursing industry, argues Pollock, does not necessarily give evidence of parental neglect, but might in fact give indication of parents' solicitude for their children's well-being. Indeed, some parents carefully chose wet nurses or paid for them at great personal sacrifice. Wet-nursing, concludes Pollock, "existed so long not because of widespread indifference to the welfare of infants but because the combination of habitual practice and the structure of female employment ensured that a viable alternative to maternal breastfeeding was wanted and there was no other viable option."[26]

Even if, as most contemporary scholars do, we side with Pollock in recognizing affection between parents and their children as a constant in the history of childhood, one thing maternal love certainly did not mean in seventeenth-century France was the persistent presence of the mother at her child's side. The reality of premature death in early modern Europe—where the morality rate of infants under age one exceeded 25 percent and where one in four marriages was a remarriage—meant that, not uncommonly, it was on the shoulders of uncles, stepfathers, grandmothers, and others that the burden of parental responsibilities fell.[27] Within the context of a seventeenth-century French family marked by its fluidity rather than its stability, maternal love was not—and could not have been—expressed by a mother's commitment to assume the role of exclusive caregiver vis-à-vis her children. Indeed, that Claude lived with his maternal aunt and uncle after his mother entered religious life would have been far from unusual in seventeenth-century France, where the guardianship of orphans was typically assumed by the brother of the deceased.[28]

If anything, where Marie seems to have fallen short of contemporary standards of maternal affection was not so much in depriving Claude of her loving presence but in depriving Claude—and voluntarily, at that—of his rightful patrimony. Recent studies on the early modern French family draw attention to the

---

25. Linda Pollock, "Parent-Child Relations in Europe, 1500–1800," in *Family Life in Early Modern Times*, ed. David I. Kertzer and Marzio Barbagli, 191–220, 219 (New Haven: Yale University Press, 2001). See also Shahar, *Childhood*; Knibiehler and Fouquet, *L'histoire*; and Linda Pollock, *A Lasting Relationship: Parents and Children over Three Centuries* (Hanover, NH: University Press of New England, 1987).

26. Pollock, "Parent-Child Relations," 195.

27. André Burguière and François Lebrun, "The One Hundred and One Families of Europe," in *A History of the Family*, ed. Burguière et al., 14–15.

28. Christopher Corley, "Gender, Kin, and Guardianship in Early Modern Burgundy," in *Family, Gender, and Law in Early Modern France*, ed. Suzanne Desan and Jeffrey Merrick, 183–222 (University Park: Pennsylvania State University Press, 2009), 198.

priority of matters of inheritance in the regulations concerning widows and the guardianship of orphaned children. Edicts prohibiting the remarriage of widows were not, it seems, motivated by a concern for the emotional well-being of a widow's children, but rather by a concern for their financial well-being. Widows who did choose to marry again lost legal guardianship of their children, the presumption being that the widow would divert the resources rightfully belonging to the children of her first marriage to those of her second and her new husband.[29] Even Francis de Sales, whose disciple Jeanne de Chantal famously stepped over the prostrate body of her youngest son to enter religious life, did not go so far as to advise widows to relinquish their material responsibilities toward their children: "The widow with children in need of her skill and guidance, especially as regards their soul and the establishment of their life, *cannot and should not abandon them* in any way."[30]

And yet, notwithstanding what historians have noted about the fluidity of the French family and the priority of its economic interests, Marie's letters to Claude (coupled with her *Relations* and the 1677 *Vie*) give evidence that good mothering in seventeenth-century France meant something more than educating and protecting the patrimony of one's children. Not only do the young Claude's repeated (and wrenching) efforts to persuade Marie to leave the convent suggest something of Claude's own expectations of maternal affection, but the reaction of her contemporaries provides eloquent testimony of the degree to which Marie's decision to abandon her son "at so tender and weak an age" and to deprive him of the "little comforts mothers give their children" rendered Marie unworthy—in the eyes of her peers—to be called a mother.[31] Even Marie herself seems to have been only too aware that a mother's love expressed itself not just in an assiduous

---

29. See Claire Dolan, "L'an de deuil et le remariage des veuves. Loi et tradition au XVIe siècle en Provence," in *Veufs, veuves et veuvage dans la France d'Ancien Régime*, 47–70 (Paris: Honoré Champion, 2003). See also Sylvie Perrier, "Rôles des réseaux de parenté dans l'éducation des mineurs orphelins selon les comptes de tutelle parisiens (XVIIe–XVIIIe siècles)," *Annales de démographie historique* (January 1995): 125–35.

30. My emphasis. François de Sales, *Introduction à la vie dévote*, ed. André Ravier with the collaboration of Roger Devos (Paris: Gallimard, 1969), 247.

31. Martin, *Vie*, 185–7. See also Letter 247. Marie's decision to abandon Claude does seem—even within the context of what Barbara Diefendorf calls the extreme spirituality and penitential fervor of seventeenth-century France—somewhat exceptional. While Marie was not alone of her sex in seventeenth-century France in practicing mortification, seclusion, and self-abnegation, she does stand apart from her *dévote* peers—who, like Barbe Acarie, chose not to relinquish their maternal responsibilities but instead to focus them on the cultivation of Christian virtues in their children—in her apparent conviction about the incompatibility of spiritual development and maternal practice. See Barbara Diefendorf, *From Penitence to Charity: Pious Women and the Catholic Reformation in Paris* (New York: Oxford University Press, 2004), 7, 71–6.

attention to her child's future, but in physical caresses, embraces, and a unique maternal tenderness that could not be replicated by an uncle, a stepfather, or even a grandmother.[32]

Shortly after Marie made her profession among the Ursulines in 1633 she experienced a vision that would inspire her vocation in Canada. One night, Marie reports in the *Relation* of 1654:

> I dreamed that I was with a secular lady whom I had met...we came to a beautiful place...Advancing within, I saw at some distance to my left a little church of wrought white marble, on top of which was the Blessed Virgin, seated on the pinnacle. She was holding the Child Jesus on her lap. This place was very elevated, and below it lay a majestic and vast country, full of mountains, of valleys, of thick mists which permeated everything except the little building which was the church of this country. The Blessed Virgin, Mother of God, looked down on this country, as pitiable as it was awesome...It seemed to me that she spoke about this country and about myself and that she had in mind some plan which involved me.[33]

The dream, Marie claims, remained incomprehensible until she confessed what had happened to her to the Jesuit Jacques Dinet, then serving as her spiritual director. Dinet identified for Marie the "pitiable" and "awesome" country of her dream as Canada. Around the same time, Marie received her first copy of the Jesuit *Relations* from Joseph Poncet, who had been teaching Claude in the humanities at the Jesuit school in Orléans. Poncet, unaware of Marie's dream and Dinet's interpretation, had enclosed along with the *Relation* a letter announcing his own eagerness to join the mission in New France and inviting Marie herself to join him.

---

32. For an extreme example of maternal affection in seventeenth-century France, see Madame de Sévigné, *Correspondance*, ed. Roger Duchêne (Paris: Gallimard, 1972–8). Although the letters written by Madame de Sévigné to her daughter between the years 1669 and 1696 can hardly be said to be representative of seventeenth-century maternal practice, they nonetheless give evidence of an emerging ideology of motherhood premised on the expectation of intimate and intense affective ties between mothers and their children. For an analysis of Madame de Sévigné's relationship with her daughter and the ways in which their correspondence "enact[ed] and inscrib[ed] the maternal figure and the relational posture prescribed for women by male authorities in manuals on 'feminine' comportment and 'feminine' writing during her time," see Michèle Longino Farrell, *Performing Motherhood: The Sévigné Correspondence* (Hanover, NH: University Press of New England, 1991).

33. Martin, *Vie*, 229.

From 1634 until her departure for the colony in 1639, Marie set herself to finding a way to get to New France. By 1638, she had made contact with Madeleine de la Peltrie, a wealthy widowed laywoman whose financial support would make possible the foundation of the Ursulines in Quebec, and on May 4, 1639, Marie finally set sail from Dieppe, together with three additional Ursulines, de la Peltrie, and some others. After a nearly three-month journey across the Atlantic, they arrived in Canada toward the end of July. To Marie and her companions, Quebec—which counted only about 250 settlers—"must have seemed less prepossessing than the meanest provincial village."[34] The Ursulines took up temporary residence in the lower town in a small house consisting of just two rooms, a cellar, and an attic.

It was here, then, that Marie began to write to Claude and many others, typically—like her seventeenth-century peers—on single sheets of paper that had been folded in half to create four pages and which were then doubled over to create their own envelope and sealed shut with wax. As a literate woman, Marie did not rely on scribes but wrote her letters by her own hand, sometimes recording her thoughts, advice, greetings, and requests deep into the night, constrained by the imminent departure of the ships and the press of her temporal responsibilities. Never before, wrote Marie to a fellow Ursuline in Tours in 1652, "have I stayed up at nights so much as during these past four months. I have had to because the urgency of our business concerns and of our rebuilding leaves me no free time through the day to take care of correspondence."[35] To Claude, Marie expressed the same, admitting her fatigue, begging him to excuse her written errors, and apologizing for the inadequacies of her responses. The first ships (whether merchant vessels, frigates, or fishing boats) bearing letters from France would typically have arrived in Quebec's port in July or August and the last would have left late in the fall just when the Saint Lawrence River was beginning to freeze over. This "rigid seasonality," as Jane Harrison puts it, allowed Marie just a few short months in which to draft the hundreds of letters she was obligated to write to her former confessor, her sisters in Tours, her immediate family, and others, although she sometimes took the opportunity of the slower winter and spring months to respond at greater leisure to the more difficult spiritual questions Claude put to her.[36] When the last ship left in November at the latest, she would have to

---

34. Dom Guy-Marie Oury, *Marie Guyart (1599–1672)*, trans. Miriam Thompson (Sablé-sur-Sarthe: Solesmes Abbey, 1978), 268, 270.

35. Oury, *Marie Guyart*, 312, citing Lettre CXLVII, *Correspondance*, 497.

36. Jane Harrison, *Until Next Year: Letter Writing and the Mails in the Canadas, 1640–1830* (Waterloo, ON: Wilfrid Laurier University Press, 1997), 56.

wait almost a whole year more before receiving any response, if indeed the letters reached their intended recipients in the first place. So conscious was Marie of the uncertainties of the voyage across the Atlantic that she pledged to write Claude "as long as I shall live, by two different ships, so that if one is lost or captured by pirates, the other will bring you my news" and admonished her son to do the same.[37]

A History of New France?

The letters exchanged between Marie and Claude included in this volume constitute a rich source of the history of colonial North America, tracing the evolution of the colony from an underdeveloped, poorly organized, thinly populated outpost to a secure, ordered, and thriving province under the control of the French king. When Marie arrived in Quebec in 1639, "[t]he religious orders…were responsible for what little development there was." The colony was managed by the Compagnie des Cents Associés, and the population stood at less than 500.[38] The missions, recently made the exclusive privilege of the Jesuits, had not yet begun to bear fruit; there was, as yet, no system of education, no regular parish life, no resident bishop. By the time of Marie's death in 1672, however, much had changed—and most of it after 1663 when authority over the colony was transferred from the Compagnie des Cents Associés to King Louis XIV. The king's minister Jean-Baptiste Colbert had initiated a comprehensive (although not wholly successful) program of economic reform, the government had been restructured to include a governor, an Intendant, a Sovereign Council, and a system of law courts, and the colonial population had reached 6700 (an increase that depended in large part on a sustained campaign to grow the colony).[39] The Iroquois had finally been subdued, thanks to regular shipments of troops from

---

37. Letter 73.

38. William Eccles, *The Canadian Frontier, 1534–1760* (New York: Holt, Rinehart and Winston, 1969), 38. For a discussion of Marie de l'Incarnation as a witness to the early history of New France, see Dominique Deslandres, "French Catholicism in the era of exploration and early colonization," Stephen J. Stein, dir. *Cambridge History of Religions in America (CHRA)*, vol. 1 (Cambridge: Cambridge University Press, 2012), 200–18.

39. Beginning in 1663, the crown sent soldiers, laborers, livestock, and single women (the *filles du roi*) for the purpose of encouraging the settlement and sustainability of the colony. Whether it was the ready availability of marriageable women, the opportunity for land ownership, or the promise of temporary support from the crown, the incentives offered for settlement in New France proved, by all accounts, successful. For a brief and concise survey of the development of the colony in Canada, see Allan Greer, *The People of New France* (Toronto: University of Toronto Press, 1997).

France.[40] The missions had succeeded in converting vast numbers of Hurons, Algonquins, Montagnais, and others, and were beginning to make inroads among the Iroquois. And the Church in New France finally had a bishop and a regular system of tithes.[41] To this skeletal account of the history of seventeenth-century New France, Marie's letters to Claude add color, detail, and nuance, revealing her anxieties (and astounding equanimity) within the context of the Iroquois crisis, her thoughts about the progress of the missions, and her intimate reflections on the character of colonial officials from Bishop de Laval to Governor d'Argenson to Lieutenant General de Tracy.

As a source for the early history of New France, Marie's letters testify to the distinct intersection of commercial, political, and religious interests in the seventeenth-century colony. From the beginning, the religious and the commercial enjoyed something of a symbiotic relationship in New France as the Christian

---

40. For a discussion of colonial perspectives on the war against the Iroquois, see Louise Dêchene, *Le Peuple, l'état et la guerre au Canada sous le Régime français* (Paris: Boréal, 2008).

41. Seventeenth-century New France was home to two major Amerindian linguistic groups— the Algonquins and the Iroquoians. Among the Iroquoian people were the warring confederacies of the Huron (composed of the Attigneenongnahac, Arendarhonon, Attignawantan, and Tahontaenrat peoples) and the Iroquois (composed of the Mohawk, Oneida, Onandaga, Cayuga, and Seneca peoples). For a clear and concise presentation of the state of the Amerindian nations at the time of the arrival of the French colonists, see Allan Greer, *The Jesuit Relations: Natives and Missionaries in Seventeenth-Century North America* (Boston: Bedford/St. Martin's, 2000), 6–9. Although the history of conflict between the two confederacies predates the arrival of European colonists, hostilities between the Huron and the Iroquois intensified over the course of the seventeenth century as commercial interests augmented traditional blood-feuds and as firearms became readily available. Conflicts between the Huron (allied with the French) and the Iroquois (allied with the Dutch and the English) reached a fever pitch in the 1640s, following French refusal of an offer of peace from the Iroquois. Following a series of devastating attacks waged by the Iroquois on French settlements along the Saint Lawrence River, the two parties successfully negotiated a peace treaty at Trois-Rivières in July 1645. This peace, however, was short-lived, undone by the favoritism the French continued to show their Huron trading partners. Finally, with the arrival of the Carignan-Salières Regiment from France in 1665, the French and their Huron allies began to subdue the Iroquois, and in 1667 the French and Iroquois agreed to a peace that would endure for about a decade. Lasting peace between the two sides, however, would not be achieved until 1701 with the Great Peace of Montreal. See J. A. Brandao and William A. Starna, "The Treaties of 1701: A Triumph of Iroquois Diplomacy," *Ethnohistory* 43, no. 2 (Spring 1996): 209–76; and Matthew Dennis, *Cultivating a Landscape of Peace: Iroquois-European Encounters in Seventeenth-Century America* (Ithaca: Cornell University Press, 1993). For more detailed surveys of early encounters, see: Bruce G. Trigger, *Natives and Newcomers: Canada's "Heroic Age" Reconsidered* (Montreal: McGill-Queen's University Press, 1986) (on the Huron); Daniel K. Richter, *The Ordeal of the Longhouse: The Peoples of the Iroquois League in the Era of Colonization* (Chapel Hill: University of North Carolina Press, 1992) (on the Iroquois); and Denys Dêlage, *Bitter Feast: Amerindians and Europeans in Northeastern North America, 1600–64*, trans. Jane Brierley (Vancouver: University of British Columbia Press, 1993).

missions were understood as a means of at once saving infidel souls and cementing economic relationships between the French traders and their indigenous counterparts. Political interests, too, intersected with religious ones as the achievements of the former aided and enhanced those of the latter. Not only was the campaign against the Iroquois—financed and supported by the king of France—conceived of as a "holy war" and their defeat as a triumph for both church and state, but Marie's letters provide corroborating evidence for the argument that Christian baptism was appreciated—on both sides—as a means of forging alliances between native populations and French colonists.[42]

The confluence of the commercial and the political, on the one hand, and the religious, on the other, suggests that Marie was not alone in making sense of the early history of New France as one of enchantment. For Marie, magic and marvels, angels and saints, demons and the divine shaped and colored the colonial experience in ways that resonate with what Moshe Sluhovsky has argued about the obsession with possession in seventeenth-century Europe more broadly.[43] Just as she understood the campaign against the Iroquois as a holy war waged by devoted soldiers among whom "God has agreed to work miracles," so also did she conceive of the mission field itself as the battleground between the devil and Christ.[44] If it was God who proved the active agent behind the conversion of the Amerindians, it was the devil (closely allied with the Iroquois) who stood in the way of the Church's progress and sought to obstruct the salvation of souls at every turn. It was, moreover, by means of visions, portents, and miracles that God sought to communicate with the faithful on earth. Repeatedly throughout the correspondence, Marie makes much of the revelation, omens, and extraordinary cosmological phenomena that both anticipated and gave meaning to natural disasters and other events, reading the earthquake of 1663 as God's punishment

---

42. Letter 220. Not only was the political stability of the colony enhanced by the defeat of the Iroquois, but it was coincident with this turn of events that the Jesuit missions began to achieve successes among the Iroquois (in part because the terms of the peace treaties concluded with the various groups obliged the Iroquois to accept Christian missionaries and, incidentally, to send at least some of their daughters to receive an education among the Ursulines).

43. See, generally, Moshe Sluhovsky, *Believe Not Every Spirit: Possession, Mysticism, & Discernment in Early Modern Catholicism* (Chicago: University of Chicago Press, 2007).

44. Letter 220. See, Dominique Deslandres, *Croire et faire croire: les missions Françaises au XVIIe siècle (1600–1650)* (Paris: Fayard, 2003), 228–305, 408–45; Deslandres, «*Exemplo aeque ut Verbo*: the French Jesuits' Missionary World», in *The Jesuits: Culture, Learning and the Arts*, ed. John O'Malley, 258–73 (Toronto: University of Toronto Press, 1999); and Deslandres, «Le diable en mission: Rôle du diable dans les missions en France et en Nouvelle France», in *Les missions intérieures du 16e au 20e siècles, France, Italie*, ed. C. Sorrel et F. Meyer, 247–62 (Chambéry: Institut d'études savoisiennes-Université de Savoie, 2001).

upon Canada "for the sins committed there and above all for the contempt in which the ordinances of the Church are held" and comets, specters, and disembodied voices as the "awful portents" of the massacres and atrocities of the Iroquois.[45]

Marie's letters are, indeed, a valuable source for early colonial history, containing information useful to contemporary historians interested in reconstructing a history of seventeenth-century New France. But can we consider Marie's epistolary corpus a history itself? Marie's intentions in chronicling this or that colonial event were not, of course, like the intentions of Marc Lescarbot or François du Creux in composing their epic histories of New France.[46] Unlike Lescarbot and du Creux, Marie was not interested in charting the development of the nascent colony, measuring the advancements of the Christian missions, or making an inventory of colonial lands and peoples. Instead, motivating the bulk of Marie's letters to political dignitaries, religious officials, and even relatives back home were her commitments to justifying the Ursuline mission in the New World and securing financial support for her religious community and its work. Motivating the body of her correspondence with Claude, in particular, were interests of a more personal nature. In the letters she wrote to the son she had abandoned in favor of religious life, Marie was concerned not only to defend the colonial vocation of the Ursulines but to legitimate her own religious vocation more generally.

The body of Marie's correspondence, then, does not share a common orientation with Lescarbot's *Histoire de la Nouvelle-France* or du Creux's *Historia Canadensis*. To deny Marie the status of historian, however, is to overlook the important contributions of Natalie Zemon Davis and others to the discipline of history. Denied access to sources, education, and public office, early modern women wrote histories that might have differed in scope and audience from those produced by their male counterparts, but "[i]t would be a mistake to assess the achievement of these early female historical writers only in terms of some hierarchy of genres, in which general or national history is at the top and particular history is at the bottom."[47] Marie-Florine Bruneau,

---

45. Letters 204, 196, and 277.

46. Marc Lescarbot, *Histoire de la Nouvelle France* (originally published in 1609), ed. Edwin Tross (Paris: Librairie Tross, 1866); François du Creux, *History of Canada or New France*, ed. and trans. James B. Conacher (Toronto: Champlain Society, 1951). Other early histories of New France include: Chrestien LeClercq, *First Establishment of the Faith in New France*, trans. John Gilmary Shea (New York: John Shea, 1881); and Gabriel Sagard, *Le Grand voyage du pays des Hurons*, ed. Edwin Tross (Paris: Librairie Tross, 1865). For discussions of the early historiography of New France, see: Brian Brazeau, *Writing a New France, 1604–1632: Empire and Early Modern French Identity* (Aldershot, UK: Ashgate, 2009); and Allan Greer, "National, Transnational, and Hypernational Historiographies: New France Meets Early American History," *Canadian Historical Review* 91, no. 4 (December 2010): 695–724.

47. Natalie Zemon Davis, "Gender and Genre: Women as Historical Writers, 1400–1820," in *Beyond Their Sex: Learned Women of the European Past*, ed. Patrician Labalme, 153–82

following Davis, insists that Marie de l'Incarnation, "alone of her sex did contribute to the rich corpus of historical publications produced...on the beginnings of New France."[48] The kind of history Marie produced in her correspondence with Claude and others did, indeed, differ from the histories composed by Lescarbot, Du Creux, and even the Jesuits—all of whom, unlike Marie, had unrestricted contact with the outside world, the advantages of formal education, and ready access to channels of publication, and none of whom, like Marie, labored under cultural restrictions against women's writing. But it was—and is—a history nonetheless.

The kind of history offered to readers of Marie's letters is one decidedly feminine in terms of both content and style. In a way that finds no precedent in the histories penned by Marie's male contemporaries, the correspondence accounts for the presence and activities of women in the colony. In her letters to Claude, Marie details the daily activities of the Ursulines (which, she explains in a letter not included in this volume, merits no mention in the Jesuit *Relations* because "our cloister covers everything and it is hard to talk about what cannot be seen"), from the structure and administration of the early community in Quebec, to the challenge of securing novices with a genuine vocation for life in Canada, to the tasks of teaching, catechizing, and civilizing girls both French and Indian.[49] The correspondence recognizes the roles played by other women in the seventeenth-century colony, as well, including the Hospitaller nuns (who had arrived in Quebec at the same time as the Ursulines) and those women whose industry contributed much to the colonial economy reorganized under Intendant Jean Talon.

If the letters exchanged between Marie and Claude between 1640 and 1671 tell a woman's history of New France in terms of their content, so also do they betray a decidedly feminine rhetorical style. While what Alison Weber has called a "rhetoric of femininity" in the writings of Teresa of Ávila more markedly characterizes Marie's contributions to the Jesuit *Relations* and her own *Relation* of 1654, protestations of humility, incompetence, and obedience find a place within her epistolary correspondence as well.[50] Repeatedly throughout the correspondence, Marie draws

---

(New York: New York University Press, 1980). See also Davis, *Women on the Margins: Three Seventeenth-Century Lives* (Cambridge, MA: Harvard University Press, 1980).

48. Bruneau, *Women Mystics*, 77.

49. Lettre CCXXXV, *Correspondance*, 803.

50. In her 1990 study of Teresa of Ávila, Alison Weber develops the notion of a "rhetoric of femininity." Weber argues that the remarkable transformation of Teresa of Ávila from an object of Inquisition inquiry to a candidate for sanctity depended in part on her deliberate exploitation of the stereotypes of female ignorance, timidity, weakness, modesty, and incompetence; see Alison Weber, *Teresa of Avila and the Rhetoric of Femininity* (Princeton: Princeton University Press, 1990). Gillian Ahlgren makes a similar case for Teresa's success as a female mystic in the precarious context of Counter-Reformation Spain, contending that Teresa deployed strategies

attention to her ignorance and the lowliness of her sex, underscoring her passivity as the vessel of God whose spiritual achievements are owed not to personal effort but to divine inspiration alone. She professes ignorance of finer theological points, refusing to classify certain communications from God as "anagogies, for I don't focus on these distinctions."[51] Marie, too, deflects attention from her own authorial agency by attributing her written works to God or rendering them the consequence of obedience to her spiritual director "who holds [God's] place for me on earth."[52] Whether Marie consciously modeled her rhetorical style on that of Teresa of Ávila, whose writings she had read (and who, by the middle of the seventeenth century, had become widely popular in France), or whether she had simply absorbed contemporary cultural stereotypes about the nature and status of women, the rhetoric of femininity apparent in her correspondence surely went some way toward authorizing Marie as a woman writing in a world in which authorial status was the privilege of men alone.

Aiding the reception of Marie's published correspondence in seventeenth-century France must also have been the prevailing cultural conviction in the natural affinity of women for the epistolary genre.[53] Hand in hand with the

---

of humility and obedience, among others, as a means of surviving in a religious environment particularly hostile to both women and mysticism; see Gillian Ahlgren, *Teresa of Avila and the Politics of Sanctity* (Ithaca: Cornell University Press, 1996). Scholars working on Marie de l'Incarnation have noted similar rhetorical strategies in both those of Marie's writings included within the Jesuit Relations and her own spiritual autobiography of 1654. Bruneau, for example, contends that, just as "[t]he Jesuits represented Marie de l'Incarnation as they wanted women to be: obscure, serving, humble, and silent[, so]…when writing for the Relations, Marie de l'Incarnation complied with their desire" (Bruneau, *Women Mystics*, 86). Similarly, Anya Mali argues that in her *Relation* of 1654 Marie adopts a rhetoric of humility and passivity even as she claims to be "no less than the mystical bride of God [and gives] formal expression to the realization of her own spiritual goals" (Mali, *Mystic in the New World*, 57). See also, Dominique Deslandres, "Qu'est-ce qui faisait courir Marie Guyart? Essai d'ethnohistoire d'une mystique d'après sa correspondence", *Laval théologiques et philosophiques*, 53 no. 2 (June 1997): 285–300; Deslandres, "La religieuse et ses livres. Le cas de Marie Guyart de l'Incarnation au début de la Nouvelle-France", in *Ad Libros ! Mélanges d'études médiévales offerts à Denise Angers et Claude Poulin*, ed. Jean-François Cottier, Martin Gravel et Sébastien Rossignol, 345–74 (Montréal: Presses de l'Université de Montréal, 2009); and Jodi Bilinkoff, "Navigating the Waves (of Devotion): Toward a Gendered Analysis of Early Modern Catholicism," in *Crossing Boundaries: Attending to Early Modern Women*, ed. Jane Donawerth and Adele Seeff, 161–72 (Newark, DE: University of Delaware Press, 2000).

51. Letter 274.

52. Letter 155. Similarly, Teresa of Ávila repeatedly and deliberately claimed incompetence in matters of scripture and theological scholarship, thereby insulating herself from the exacting and technical standards imposed by clerical authorities intent on separating heresy from orthodoxy; see Weber, *Teresa of Ávila*, 98–122.

53. "Over and over again," argues Elizabeth Goldsmith, "we read that the female writing style is somehow particularly adapted to the epistolary form"; see Elizabeth C. Goldsmith, "Authority, Authenticity, and the Publication of Letters by Women," in *Writing the Female Voice: Essays on*

transformation of the letter from a formal composition based on the medieval *ars dictaminis* to an ideally informal medium of communication that aimed to give unstudied expression to the intimate interior of the writer was the emergence of women as letter writers par excellence. Precisely because of their comparative lack of formal education, women could supposedly compose naturally and easily the sorts of missives it would cost men untold effort and energy to replicate (and never perfectly, at that). And yet, as Elizabeth Goldsmith astutely observes, even as women's letters are celebrated as the masterpieces of seventeenth-century epistolarity, the integrity of those letters depended on the denial of the authorial agency of women letter writers themselves.[54] Instead, repeatedly throughout the course of the course of the seventeenth century, the role of author is claimed by the men who edited and published women's letters—as Claude did with his mother's letters in 1681

An Anthropology of the "Savage" Other

Despite the rule of enclosure, Marie de l'Incarnation's colonial experience permitted her substantial contact with and encouraged prolonged reflection on the indigenous peoples of New France.[55] The letters from mother to son suggest that Marie, like other European colonists, struggled to fit the native populations within a biblical worldview imported from France in which the place of the Amerindian (noble savage or ignoble brute?) was subject to debate. For European colonists throughout the New World, the existence of native peoples gave rise to a series of questions: Were the Amerindians irrational beasts or human beings included within the sphere of biblical revelation? Did the Amerindians represent an earlier stage in human development? A degenerate race? Were they, like the Europeans themselves, sons of Noah? And if so, from which of Noah's three sons had they descended? And how did they get to the New World?[56]

Epistolary Literature, ed. Elizabeth C. Goldsmith, 46–59 (Boston: Northeastern University Press, 1989). See also Farrell, *Performing Motherhood*, 27–56.

54. Goldsmith, "Authority, Authenticity," 55.

55. Letter 80.

56. See Deslandres, "Altérité, identité et rédemption," 56–7. For a seventeenth-century discussion of these and other questions, see Lescarbot, *Histoire*, and Jean Bodin, *Method for the Easy Comprehension of History*, trans. Beatrice Reynolds (New York: Octagon Books, 1966). For recent studies of seventeenth-century Canadian colonial anthropologies, see: Marie-Christine Pioffet, "Marc Lescarbot et la littérature géographique de la Renaissance," *XVIIe siècle* 222 (February 2004): 91–103; and Pioffet, "Le gai savoir ou la quête épistémologique de Marc Lescarbot au Nouveau Monde," *La Revue française*, June 2013, http://revuefrancaise.free.fr/Pioffet.htm. See also Réal Ouellet with Mylene Tremblay, "From the Good Savage to the

Though the official view of the Catholic Church (pronounced by Pope Alexander VI in 1493 and confirmed by Pope Paul III in 1537) affirmed the humanity of the indigenous Americans and the possibility of their conversion to Christianity, the debate over the place of the Amerindian within the biblical universe continued as the notions of the noble savage and ignoble brute competed for pride of place—and sometimes coexisted in uncomfortable tension—in the colonial discourse of the seventeenth century.[57] This bifurcated view of the indigenous American courses through Marie's thirty-year correspondence with Claude, sometimes made apparent within the context of a single passage in which the preternaturally pious convert confronts (or is confronted by) the barbarous and brutal infidel. If the noble savage merits admiration as "courageous," "docile," and "zealous," his ignoble and brutish counterpart proves cruel, barbarous, and "insolent."[58]

Curiously, convictions about the nature, temperament, or character of the indigenous Americans could be used to support either the image of the Amerindian as noble savage or ignoble brute. The perceived absence of government, money, and writing within Native American cultures (to which Marie alludes in a letter to Claude from 1670), for example, might provide evidence of innocence, on the one hand, or bestiality, on the other.[59] Similarly, chauvinistic opinions about the intellectual inferiority of the indigenous American saw proof, alternately, of the child-like virtue of the zealous "neophyte" (and at the same time justification for a colonial paternalism) and the naive gullibility of "brutes"

Degenerate Indian: The Amerindian in Accounts of Travel to America," in *De-centring the Renaissance: Canada and America in Multidisciplinary Perspective, 1500–1700*, ed. Germaine Warkentin and Carolyn Podruchny, 159–70 (Toronto: University of Toronto Press, 2001). At the same time that Europeans were struggling to assimilate indigenous Americans into their received worldview, so also were the Amerindians attempting to get a sense of the Europeans within their own cultural framework. Cornelius Jaenen points out that Amerindians perceived Europeans as, *inter alia*, dirty, hairy, and intellectually inferior, and European men, in particular, as weak, depraved, cowardly, and feminine; see Cornelius Jaenen, "Amerindian Views of French Culture in the 17th c.," *Canadian Historical Review* 55, no. 3 (1974): 261–91.

57. For an analysis of the bifurcated image of the Amerindian native in the Jesuit Relations, see Pierre Hurtubise, "Le Bon et le mauvais sauvage," *Église et Théologie* 10 (1979): 223–37. For a more general discussion of European conceptualizations of the New World and its people, see: Anthony R. Pagden, *European Encounters with the New World: From Renaissance to Romanticism* (New Haven: Yale University Press, 1993); and Robert F. Berkhofer, Jr., *The White Man's Indian: Images of the American Indian from Columbus to the Present* (New York: Knopf, 1978).

58. Letters 179 and 235; Letters 80 and 142.

59. Olive Patricia Dickason, *The Myth of the Savage and the Beginnings of French Colonialism in the Americas* (Edmonton: University of Alberta Press, 1984), 52–3.

lacking in reason.⁶⁰ The Amerindian's proximity to nature, likewise, might support either benign or deprecating comparisons with the animal world: Marie, for example, describes Amerindians receptive to the Gospel as "lambs" but renders the enemy Iroquois as untamed beasts who "run like deer" and track down their enemies like a predator its prey.⁶¹ Finally, the perceived difference between French and Indian could produce either damning assessments or salutary appraisals of the New World native, who emerge in some instances as perfidious and pitiless vis-à-vis their French counterparts and in others as more submissive, more zealous, and "generally speaking... more devout than the French."⁶²

Attempting to account for this dichotomous view of the Amerindian—at the same time courageous and perfidious, submissive and insolent, innocent and deceitful—Pierre Hurtubise (observing the same in the Jesuit Relations) suggests that the bifurcated image of the native American is owed, in part, to the way in which the mission field in New France was imagined as a battleground between the divine and the demonic.⁶³ Within this ideological context the indigenous populations functioned as pawns, alternately victims of Satan's empire or the converted children of God; it was the sacrament of baptism that made possible the transition from the former to the latter, transforming the ignoble brute into the noble savage. Indeed, whether conceived of as ignoble brute or noble savage, the Amerindian of Marie's correspondence permits the condition of alterity against which an articulation of French identity takes shape. Marie's letters dramatize, in other words, a separation between self and other that discursively produces the identity of the self by means of an articulation of difference from the other. Within the rhetorical context of Marie's letters, it is the ignobility of the Amerindian brute that proves the faith of the missionary and provides the opportunity for martyrdom; it is the nobility of the Amerindian savage that gives evidence of the efficacy of the missionary effort and legitimates the Ursuline apostolate's educating and catechizing indigenous girls.⁶⁴

To this colonial discourse bifurcated between images of the indigenous American as noble savage and ignoble brute, Marie contributes an especial

---

60. Letters 97 and 80.

61. Letters 110 and 179; Letters 183 and 196.

62. Letter 80.

63. Hurtubise, "Le Bon et le mauvais sauvage." For an analysis of the same in colonial discourse more generally, see Homi Bhabha, "The Other Question...Homi Bhabha Reconsiders the Stereotype and Colonial Discourse," *Screen* 24, no. 6 (November–December, 1983): 18–36.

64. On this point, see Dunn, "When 'Wolves become Lambs.'"

sensitivity to gender, alluding to virile women and feminine men in ways that render the Amerindian so radically Other as to defy received categories of male and female.[65] Writing to Claude just five years after her arrival in the colony, Marie maintains that on the basis of physical appearance alone, "one could hardly distinguish the men from the women, for their faces are similar."[66] More telling, however, are her descriptions of native women's political and economic activities and her anecdotal accounts of the virile women of the New World who deliberate in the councils, canoe like the men, and prove valiant assassins and courageous heroines possessed of astonishing physical strength and superhuman endurance. On several occasions, too, Marie alludes to the ways in which indigenous Christian women assumed tasks and responsibilities that seventeenth-century French culture had rendered the prerogatives of men (preaching publicly, for example, to mixed-sex crowds against both authority and tradition).

In the process of her ongoing contacts with the native populations of New France Marie was not—despite the cloister—impervious to the influence of Amerindian norms and practices.[67] For one, the Ursulines, like their Jesuit counterparts, conformed to the linguistic practices of their charges, proving adept at learning native languages; in her correspondence with Claude Marie herself describes studying Algonquin, Montagnais, and Huron and composing "a big Algonquin book about sacred history and holy things, along with a dictionary and an Iroquois catechism [and]…a big Algonquin dictionary in the French alphabet. I have another one in the Indian alphabet."[68] The Ursulines also adopted certain food practices typical to the surrounding native cultures, providing (in conformity with Amerindian custom) the catechumens with "a feast of peas or sagamite of Indian corn with some prunes" and offering gifts and foodstuffs to visiting Iroquois families as a means of persuading them to give their daughters

---

65. For a discussion of the ways in which traditional gender roles are subverted in the stories of (European) holy men and women in early modern Canada, see Allan Greer, "Colonial Saints: Gender, Race, and Hagiography in New France," *William and Mary Quarterly* 57 (2000): 323–48. See also Davis, *Women on the Margins*, 63–139.

66. Letter 80.

67. See Claire Gourdeau, *Les délices de nos coeurs: Marie de l'Incarnation et ses pensionnaires amérindiennes, 1639–1672* (Sillery, QC: Septentrion, 1994), 74–84. Gourdeau argues that although all instances of cultural contact necessarily implicate some degree of reciprocity, the Ursulines' Amerindian students tended to adapt to the French way of life more than the other way around, at least in part because the isolation of the cloister allowed the Ursulines to recreate, more or less, the conditions of European culture and society within the convent. See also Dominique Deslandres, "Les femmes missionnaires de Nouvelle-France," in *La religion de ma mère: Les femmes et la transmission de la foi*, ed. Jean Delumeau, 211–14 (Paris: Cerf, 1992).

68. Letter 235.

over to the Ursulines for a Christian education.[69] More profoundly, Marie's own identity as an Ursuline in the New World seems to have taken shape under the influence of the virile Amerindian woman so central to her correspondence, as she and her sisters engaged in the play of gender reversal within the context of the American colony. To the indigenous men who came to their parlor to discuss "what weighs on their hearts," the Ursuline sisters commanded "punctual obedience" and served as spiritual directors of sorts, a role that would primarily have belonged to male ecclesiastics in a European context.[70] In one instance a Huron chief even confessed his sins to Mother Marie de Saint Joseph in the absence of his (presumably male) confessor, permitting the nun a sacramental power she surely did not possess.[71]

The Spiritual Itinerary of a Mystic

The correspondence exchanged between Marie de l'Incarnation and her son also provides an intimate first-hand account of the spiritual itinerary of one of the most celebrated mystics of the seventeenth century. Representative in some ways of the Catholic Reformation, heiress in others to the French School of Spirituality, Marie nonetheless stands on her own as the reality of life in New France encouraged the articulation of a spirituality marked by the harmonization of action and contemplation and gave new meaning to the practice of *anéantissement*, abnegation, spiritual poverty, and suffering as a means of sharing in the experience of Christ.

Although some scholars have contested the depiction of Marie de l'Incarnation as "an exemplary type, reflecting the moods and aims of the Catholic Reformation", the verdict of historians who do identify a compatibility between the Ursuline mystic and the post-Tridentine agenda of the Church in Rome is not wholly without foundation. Marie, after all, conceived of her (albeit cloistered) religious career as one intimately engaged in the activity of mission, pursued a vocation oriented toward the active apostolate of teaching, and played a leading role in the "mystic invasion" of the seventeenth century.[72] Like Teresa of Ávila before her, Marie found herself drawn from childhood to missionary work. Even as a cloistered Ursuline submitted to the dictates of the Council of Trent, Marie

---

69. Letter 73.

70. Letter 80.

71. Letter 97.

72. Mali, *Mystic in the New World*, xiv; see also Bruneau, *Women Mystics*, 37.

(again, like Teresa before her) was convinced that she played no small part in the missions so fundamental to a reformed Catholicism. In addition to her active teaching apostolate among the native peoples of New France and her responsibility for the education of catechumens of both sexes who sought instruction at the Ursuline's parlor, Marie imagined that her prayers within the monastery had some effect on the progress of the mission beyond the cloister wall.

As a woman religious engaged in the active apostolate of teaching, Marie also found inspiration in and contributed to the Catholic Reformation objectives of catechesis and conversion—together with women of other newly emergent active orders like the Filles de Notre Dame, the Order of the Visitation, and the Hospitallers.[73] Faced with the threat of Protestantism in Europe and pressed by the exigency of converting the infidel abroad, a Reformed Catholicism depended on the work of women—both religious and secular—in order to shore up the boundaries of its beleaguered church. Like her *dévote* peers in seventeenth-century France, moreover, Marie imagined a fundamental complementarity between the twin impulses toward contemplation and activity, understanding "the state of union with God as a spur to action and not retreat."[74]

Finally, together with Marie de Valence, Barbe Acarie, and others, Marie's spiritual experience as a mystic warrants her place within the historiography of the Catholic Reformation.[75] While strictly speaking, as Marie-Florine Bruneau reminds us, the mystic invasion in which women played key roles was not a direct or intended outcome of the Catholic Reformation, the culture of reform encouraged a religious enthusiasm that inspired spiritual innovation by both men and women, clerics and laymen. Like the seventeenth-century mystics described by Michel de Certeau, Marie's mysticism did not give expression to a particular set of religious or philosophical doctrines, but rather unfolded as a heterogeneous set of lived practices reducible neither to verbalization nor to psychosomatization.[76] Beyond both language and the body, Marie's mysticism was primarily one of experience.[77]

---

73. For a study of active female religious orders in seventeenth-century France, see Elizabeth Rapley, *The Dévotes: Women and Church in Seventeenth-Century France* (Kingston, ON: McGill-Queen's University Press, 1990).

74. Diefendorf, *From Penitence to Charity*, 86.

75. For a study of mysticism in seventeenth-century France, see Sophie Houdard, *Les invasions mystiques. Spiritualités, hétérodoxies et censures au début de l'époque modern* (Paris: Les Belles Lettres, 2008).

76. See Michel de Certeau, *The Mystic Fable*, trans. Michael B. Smith (Chicago: University of Chicago Press, 1992).

77. Henri Brémond and María-Paul del Rosario Ariadzola, respectively, draw attention to the experiential emphasis of Marie de l'Incarnation's spiritual life. See Henri Brémond, *Histoire*

Closely connected to Marie's emphasis on the experience of mysticism, is her repeated insistence on the inexpressibility of such experience—de Certeau's *l'indicible*. No matter what one writes, Marie asserts to Claude in 1661, "one can never describe what happens in the soul when it is united in its depths to this divine object...the spirit comprehends inexplicable things and [t]he soul experienced in the ways of the spirit understands it to the extent of its grace."[78] Indeed, Marie's inability to express her spiritual experiences only intensified as she aged. The older one grows, she explained to Claude in 1653, "the more one is incapable of writing about such things because the spiritual life simplifies the soul in a consuming love such that one can no longer find the words to describe it."[79] So powerless did Marie find herself to articulate her interior dispositions that by the end of her life, she was unable even to pray "except to say by a sort of breath in this interior depth, 'My God, my God, my great God, my life, my love, my all, my glory.'"[80] Yet even while Marie invokes the inexpressibility of the mystical experience, her correspondence with Claude reveals her indebtedness to the received language of mysticism which de Certeau designates "the central point of the mystic in her novelty."[81] The letters from mother to son for example, as Paul-Eugène Couture points out, abound with oxymoron, a recognized characteristic of mystical language. Not only does Marie insist on the inadequacy of language to capture mystical experience as she proceeds to attempt just that, but she speaks of a fire that burns "without consuming," loving Claude so much that she wishes he was "worthy to spill your blood for Jesus Christ," and more.[82]

If Marie de l'Incarnation's association with the Catholic Reformation is warranted, so is her affiliation with the French School of Spirituality.[83] Admittedly,

---

littéraire du sentiment religieux en France depuis la fin des guerres de religion jusqu'à nos jours, vol. 2, tome 6 (Grenoble: J. Millon, 2006), 727–9; and María-Paul del Rosario Ariadzola, *La Connaissance spirituelle chez Marie de l'Incarnation: "la Thérèse de France et du Nouveau monde"* (Paris: Cerf, 1989), 368.

78. Letter 195.

79. Letter 153.

80. Letter 267.

81. Certeau, *Mystic Fable*, 103; cited in Sylvie Robert, "La relation indicible," in *L'Itinéraire mystique d'une femme: Rencontre avec Marie de l'Incarnation, ursuline*, ed. Jean Comby et le Laboratoire de recherche de la Faculté de théologie de Lyon, 195–221 (Paris: Cerf, 1993).

82. Paul-Eugène Couture, "L'oxymore dans la lettre LXVIII de Marie de l'Incarnation à son fils Claude Martin," in *Marie de l'Incarnation, entre mère et fils: Le dialogue des vocations*, ed. Raymond Brodeur, 93–8 (Quebec: Presses de l'Université Laval, 2000); Letter 68.

83. See, Yves Krumenacker, *L'école française de spiritualité: des mystiques, des fondateurs, des courants et leurs interprètes* (Paris: Cerf, 1998).

evidence for direct influence is absent—nowhere in her writings does Marie admit to having read the works of Pierre de Bérulle, Jean Eudes, Jean-Jacques Olier, and others. Nonetheless, Marie's spirituality took shape within the context of a seventeenth-century France in which the Christocentric theology of Bérulle played a critical role.[84] For Bérulle, the father of the French School, the spiritual life revolved around the twin poles of *exitus* and *reditus*—the recognition that the human person came from God and to God the person must return. To this basic Dionysian schema, Bérulle added a distinctive Christological emphasis, insisting that "our emanation reflects Christ, our wounding it through sin deepens our need for Christ, and our return to God is through the mediation of Christ."[85] The spiritual states through which the Christian passes on her way to the destination of salvation, insisted Bérulle, replicated those through which Christ himself passed, rendering the religious life not just of one's modeling oneself after Christ, but sharing in the person of Christ, which Bérulle fundamentally understood as a life of poverty and self-emptying or annihilation (*anéantissement*). For Bérulle, the Incarnate Word proved "an irruption of adoration and servitude in history." Christian living, then, consisted of a radical servitude (in communion with Christ) by means of which the Christian person might achieve *anéantissement*, becoming "mystically passive and receptive to Christ in the depths of being and in all one's actions" and capable of adoration together with Christ.[86]

Charles de Condren and Jean-Jacques Olier would later develop the Bérullian notion of *anéantissement* in the direction of a sacrificial theology; in the writings of both Condren and Olier, the ideals of immolation, oblation, and victimhood (echoes of which reverberate in Marie's letters) orient the Christian experience. Drawing attention to the fundamental corruption of human nature, Olier insisted that only through concerted effort toward self-annihilation might the human person participate in the life of Christ and achieve regeneration by the grace of God. Jean Eudes, too, whose theology bears the mark of a distinctive devotion to the heart of Jesus, likewise called for a death to self and a commitment to servitude, concluding that "[t]he greatest of all practices...the greatest of all

---

84. A Bérullian Christocentrism and emphasis on the abnegation of the will likewise characterizes the spirituality of the *dévotes* described by Diefendorf, suggesting a loose sense of influence. Diefendorf, *From Penitence to Charity*, 82–8.

85. William M. Thompson, ed., *Bérulle and the French School* (New York: Paulist Press, 1989), 33. For an analysis of the spirituality of Bérulle and others associated with the French school, see also Brémond, *Histoire littéraire*, vol. 1, tome 3.

86. *Bérulle*, 41.

devotions...is to be detached from all practices...and to surrender to the Spirit of Jesus."[87]

The spirituality of Marie de l'Incarnation owes, it seems, much to the Christocentric theology of the French School. From the form of her letters (which typically open and close with reference to and praise for Jesus Christ), to the centrality of Christ to her understanding of both her missionary vocation and her relationship with Claude, to the way in which Christ's own life served as a model for her personal spiritual itinerary, to the emphases of her devotional practices on the Incarnation and the sacred heart of Jesus, Marie's interior life shares the spiritual commitments of Bérulle, Eudes, and others. To begin with, Marie conceived of her missionary vocation (and that of her Jesuit counterparts) as part of the war effort waged for the protection and extension of the "kingdom of Jesus Christ, to which the demons are furiously opposed."[88] "[P]erfect imitators of Jesus Christ," the missionaries of New France (herself included) were for Marie, in a sense, the personal army of Incarnation and the colonial mission field nothing less than territory over which Christ ought rightfully to exercise control.[89] Similarly, just as it was Jesus Christ who gave meaning to her missionary activity, so it was the second person of the Trinity who oriented Marie's relationship with Claude. Not only did Marie's love for her son originate "in the poverty of Jesus Christ in which all treasures are found," but the fact of their communication was made possible in the first instance by their shared union in Christ.[90]

The Christocentrism of the French School seems, in particular, to have made an impression on Marie's idealization of the spiritual life structured in imitation of Christ. Like Bérulle and others of the French School, however, Marie did not suppose that Christian living stopped at the imitation of Christ but rather intimated that spiritual development ought to culminate in an interior familiarity with the inner life of Jesus. Notably, too, as for Jean Eudes whose Christocentrism slipped easily into Marian devotion, Marie's zeal for Christ led to an affection for the Virgin Mary. Not only did Marie tend to address herself to Christ's mother

---

87. Jean Eudes, *Vie et royaume de Jésus*, part 6 (Paris: P. Lethielleux, 1924), 452. Devotion to the heart of Jesus, though typical of the seventeenth-century French school generally, is richly developed in the theology of Jean Eudes. See Paul Milcent, *Saint Jean Eudes* (Paris: Bloud & Gay, 1964), 48–51. See also: Brémond, *Histoire littéraire*, vol. 1, 1313–39; and John Abruzzese, *The Theology of the Hearts in the Writings of St. Francis de Sales* (Rome: Institute of Spirituality, Pontifical University of St. Thomas Aquinas, 1985).

88. Letter 68.

89. Letter 68.

90. Letter 56.

after expressing her devotion for Christ himself, but she also remained committed to Mary as a "powerful and lovable protector" of the colonial Church and the Ursuline community throughout her Canadian experience.[91]

Finally, the glimpses Marie offers Claude of her own devotional practices reveals a Christocentric piety if not indebted to, then at least coincident with, that associated with the French School. In a letter written to Claude in 1647, Marie reproduces a prayer she addressed to "the second person of the Holy Trinity" (in typical fashion, insisting that the prayer was inspired by "a light [that] filled my spirit" and recited "without reflection").[92] An unrestrained encomium to Christ, the prayer gives expression to the depths of Marie's passion for the Incarnate Word, as Marie addresses Christ as her "Beloved," "my love and my whole good," "my Divine Spouse." She waxes lyrical on Christ's "double divine and human beauty," in ways reminiscent of Bérulle's attention to the double features of Christ's humanity and divinity, references her "nothingness [which] loses itself in [the] bottomless abyss" of the Incarnate Word, and admits that she is "powerless, having been consumed in you by a love I can't express," echoing the sacrificial theology of Charles de Condren.[93] Elsewhere Marie reveals to Claude her devotion to the sacred heart of Jesus (*à la* Jean Eudes), detailing her habitual (and effectual) practice of offering to God her prayers "by the heart of my Jesus, my way, my truth, and my life."[94]

In her correspondence with Claude, Marie draws sustained attention to *anéantissement* as preparatory to a spiritual life lived in intimacy with Christ, urging Claude time and again to "empty yourself of everything to make room for the divine spirit."[95] For Marie, as for the leading lights of the French School, the impulse toward *anéantissement* was founded on an awareness of the nothingness of the human person and proved a prerequisite to a mystical union with Christ. Sounding a note that might have come from Bérulle himself, Marie renders self-love an impediment to the desired "return to the one for whom we were born" and the purgation of the self the essence of the ideal of *anéantissement*.[96]

---

91. Letter 243.

92. Letter 109.

93. Letter 109. For a treatment of Bérulle's attention to the double features of Christ's humanity and divinity, see Edward Howells, "Relationality and Difference in the Mysticism of Pierre de Bérulle," *Harvard Theological Review* 102, no. 2 (April 2009): 225–43.

94. Letter 195.

95. Letter 155.

96. Letter 81.

Anéantissement, as Marie understood it, would naturally lead to abnegation before God which she tends to articulate in the language of abandonment. Repeatedly, Marie urges Claude to "abandon yourself to [God's] guidance," spiritual advice she claims to have followed herself on a number of occasions, including those of the fire of 1650, the earthquake of 1663, and—most intriguingly—on the occasion of her own abandonment of the young Claude.[97] With her predecessors and contemporaries in the French School, too, Marie shared the conviction that from *anéantissement* and abnegation would follow not just the imitation of Christ, but a participation in Christ's own life. For Marie, as for Condren, sharing in the life of Christ seems to have implied the experience of victimhood.[98] So extensive are references to suffering (or "crosses") in Marie's correspondence with Claude that the reader can hardly fail to notice the centrality of suffering to Marie's understanding of mystical union, which meant not just the spiritual or abstracted experience of loving Christ, but the lived, ongoing, and concretized practice of sharing in the labors and sufferings of Christ.[99]

Even as it owes much to the influences of the Catholic Reformation and the French School, Marie de l'Incarnation's spirituality stands apart, distinguished by the ways in which her personal history encouraged the elaboration of certain theological themes and lived practices in unique and particular directions. Anya Mali persuasively argues that the New World exercised a decided influence on the development of Marie's distinct brand of spirituality.[100] In important ways,

---

97. Letter 68.

98. For an analysis of the spiritual life of Marie de l'Incarnation as one centered on the experience of victimhood, see Anya Mali, "L'état de victime et le 'petit discours' mystique," in *Femme, mystique et missionnaire*, ed. Brodeur, 211–20.

99. A genealogy of Marie de l'Incarnation's interior life ought also to consider, as Dominique Deslandres does, the possible influence of more marginal strands of seventeenth-century French Catholic piety and practice. Despite Marie's avowed affection for and close interaction with the Jesuits (against whom the Jansenists positioned their own theology throughout the course of the seventeenth century) traces of a spirituality nonetheless compatible with Jansenism—including Marie's decided aspiration to sanctity, her occasional allusions to predestination and grace, and her persistent emphases on corrupted human nature and the need for self-annihilation—are apparent in her correspondence with Claude. Likewise, although Marie predates the Quietist movement (which would not fully develop until the end of the seventeenth century), the reader familiar with the works of Madame Guyon and Archbishop Fénelon will not fail to notice in the letters from mother to son what Moshe Sluhovsky has identified as a "pre-Quietist" spirituality inclined toward quiet prayer, repose in God, and the abandonment of self. See Dominique Deslandres, "Augustinisme, quiétisme ou air du temps? Éléments d'une méthode historique pour aborder un texte religieux," in *Marie de l'Incarnation, entre mère et fils: Le dialogue des vocations*, ed. Raymond Brodeur, 29–41 (Quebec: Presses de l'Université Laval, 2000); and Sluhovsky, *Believe Not Every Spirit*, 97–136.

100. See Mali, *Mystic in the New World*, especially 164–73.

Mali acknowledges, Marie's mystical ascent imitates that of her Christian peers—unfolding according to discrete states which move the mystic progressively closer to union with God, reaching its apex in spiritual marriage, and finding its fulfillment in the transformation of the mystic in the divine image. Yet, for Marie—in contrast to her mystical counterparts—the mystical experience did not terminate in spiritual marriage (which was, after all, only the seventh among the thirteen states of prayer she identifies in her *Relation* of 1654), but continued to find expression in a flurry of activity compatible with her responsibilities as the founder and sometimes superior of the Ursulines in New France. Activity and contemplation were rendered, within the demanding context of the New World, not just compatible but complementary and mutually enriching as Marie gave new meaning to what it meant to live the life of a mystic united and transformed in the person of Christ. Although the confluence of the active and the contemplative in Marie de l'Incarnation's spiritual experience bears the traces both of a Catholic Reformation spirituality and of the French School (under the influence of de Sales), Mali contends that it was her experience in New France that forced Marie's elegant resolution of the tension between activity and contemplation.[101] In New France, Mali argues, Marie could reconcile the incongruity of "her contemplative state and active calling and the seeming paradox of being in a passive state of mystical repose while yet desiring to take an active part in the business of saving souls, because she saw the missionary call as an integral part of her mystical life."[102]

If (as Mali argues) the reality of life in New France encouraged the articulation of a spirituality marked by the harmonization of action and contemplation, so also did it give new meaning to—and facilitate—the practice of *anéantissement* and abnegation promoted by the likes of Bérulle, Condren, Olier, and Eudes. Canada—so distant from France and so vulnerable to the vicissitudes of both nature and man—provided unparalleled opportunity for the abandonment so critical to spiritual progress, forcing the *anéantissement* that amidst the comforts and security of home might otherwise have been more elusive. The colonial environment, too, seems to have informed Marie's understanding of what it meant to live the life of a mystic sharing in the poverty and suffering of Christ, both

---

101. Olier, for example, sought to develop a spiritual program in which an interior orientation toward Christ would be expressed exteriorly by means of corporeal acts, insisting that all those faithful in Jesus Christ (presumably regardless of their involvement in the secular world) are priests. See Jean-Jacques Olier, Ms. 11, Fols. 65–75, cited in Gilles Chaillot, *L'experience de Dieu avec Jean-Jacques Olier* (Montreal: Fides, 2000), 71.

102. Mali, *Mystic in the New World*, 98.

favorite themes of the French School, as Marie's understanding and practice of the ideal of spiritual poverty was sharpened by the material poverty of life in New France—which Marie witnessed among the indigenous populations, observed in the daily life of Bishop Laval, and experienced in the conditions of the colonial cloister, in the shortages occasioned by the hazards of the sea and the persecution of the Iroquois, and in the aftermath of the great fire of 1651, which reduced the Ursulines to a poverty of biblical proportions. For Marie, there was something of spiritual value in the material poverty of life in the colony as material poverty encouraged, even compelled, abnegation to divine Providence. As Rebecca Wilkin puts it, for Marie, Canada proved an inexhaustible source of abjection that enhanced her mystical itinerary oriented toward union with the divine.[103]

The Relationship between an Absent Mother and Her Abandoned Son

Indeed, Marie de l'Incarnation's seventeenth-century correspondence deserves attention for the ways in which it reveals much about the early history of New France, constructs an early modern anthropology of the Amerindian, and traces the spiritual itinerary of one of the most celebrated mystics of the seventeenth century. Equally compelling, however, is the window Marie's letters to Claude provide onto the distinctive relationship between an absent mother and her abandoned son. Over the course of some thirty-one years, the relationship between Marie and Claude transformed from one of flesh and blood to one of the written word exchanged between professed religious, united in Jesus Christ as members of the same spiritual family.

Giving shape and substance to the relationship that unfolds in the written correspondence between mother and son is the fact of Claude's (double) abandonment by his mother—for the first time at the age of eleven when Marie entered the Ursuline convent in Tours and for the second when she left for New France in 1639.[104] In at least eight of her eighty-one full-length extant letters to Claude, Marie alludes (sometimes at great length) to the abandonment, suggesting that for

---

103. Wilkin, "Algonquin par abjection," 38.

104. For an analysis of how the abandonment figures in the writings of both Marie and Claude (including the *Relations* of 1633 and 1654, the *Vie*, and the letters), see Mary Dunn, "'The Cruelest of All Mothers': Marie de l'Incarnation, Motherhood, and Christian Discipleship," *Journal of Feminist Studies in Religion* 28, no. 1 (2012): 43–62. See also Sophie Houdard, "Le cri public du fils abandonné ou l'inexprimable secret de la cruauté d'une mère," *Littératures classiques* 68 (Summer 2009): 273–84.

both mother and son, the event played a critical role in determining the dynamic between the two. As early as 1641, just two years after her arrival in the colony, Marie refers to the abandonment, attributing Claude's entry into religious life to her own decision to leave him at the convent threshold. Just three short years before her death, Marie would again draw Claude's attention to the abandonment and compel his approval for her decision as the precipitating factor of his spiritual success.[105] In both letters, too, Marie claims to have resisted the abandonment and displaces blame for the event on others, alternately her confessor at the time and God himself. These two letters, which, in a sense, bookend Marie's correspondence with Claude, reveal not only a marked consistency in Marie's interpretation of the event, but also the ways in which the abandonment remained a persistent undercurrent over the course of their thirty-year epistolary relationship.

A close look at the letter from 1641 (the first in which Marie makes mention of the abandonment and only the second in the collected correspondence) suggests that in Marie's eyes it was her decision to abandon her "beloved son" that guaranteed Claude's entry into religious life and inaugurated the reconfigured relationship between mother and son united as professed religious in a single spiritual family. In notable contrast to her letter of 1640, in which Marie tersely accuses Claude of negligence, immaturity, and cowardice for his apparent lack of direction and ambition, the letter of 1641, written on the occasion of the beginning of Claude's novitiate with the Benedictines at Vendôme, has a wordy, almost ebullient quality. In this letter, Marie sets the tone of correspondence to follow, detailing the activities of the Ursulines, reporting on the missions, dispensing spiritual advice, and alluding to the fact of Claude's abandonment as not a burden, but a "useful" benefit to Claude that made possible his entry into religious life.[106]

If Marie tended to invoke the abandonment in order to defend her decision—for which her friends and neighbors had categorically condemned her—as the exclusive cause of Claude's religious success, Claude himself appealed to the abandonment as the currency by means of which he sought access to his mother's writings. And indeed, Marie's ultimate acquiescence to Claude's persistent request for her spiritual autobiography indicates that Claude's repeated allusions to the abandonment touched a maternal nerve. As Natalie Zemon Davis puts it, the *Relation* of 1654 (heavily edited and published by Claude in 1677 as *La Vie de la Vénérable Mère Marie de l'Incarnation*) and the correspondence between mother

---

105. Letters 56 and 247.

106. Letter 56.

and son "constituted an act of forgiveness, Marie of herself and Claude of his mother for the abandonment."[107]

Whether understood as the primary cause of Claude's own religious conversion or the fuel that fired Marie's maternal guilt, the abandonment precipitated and made possible the transformation of his relationship with the mother who had voluntarily relinquished her biological ties with her son. The reconfigured relationship between mother and son—whether occasioned by the abandonment itself (as Marie would have it) or by Claude's manipulation thereof—proved no longer a relationship of flesh and blood, but one between spiritual companions united "in the heart of our lovable Jesus" and mediated by Christ and other sacred figures.[108] As early as 1641, Marie gave expression to this transfigured relationship in which the mother-son dyad gave way to a wider spiritual family consisting of a communion of personages both sacred and secular. It was only through Jesus—or, as Marie puts it more particularly in 1647, through a shared consecration to a single "divine master"—that Marie could communicate with Claude at all.[109] So central was the mediation of Jesus to Marie's conceptualization of her association with Claude that the relationship had become almost Trinitarian as the three distinct persons—Marie, Claude, and Christ—became (in Marie's eyes) united together as one. Concludes Marie in a letter written to Claude in 1660, "As I am united to you in all the good works that the Divine Goodness does through you, so also what I do in him, for without him I can do nothing, is likewise yours."[110]

If it was Claude's entry into religious life that made possible a reconfigured relationship with his absent mother as early as 1641, the relationship between mother and son nonetheless transformed over the course of their thirty-year correspondence. Geographical distance (paradoxically) led not to an increased estrangement, but to a spiritual and emotional intimacy between Marie and Claude. Over time, Marie came to reveal her interior life with progressively less reserve, to acknowledge the mutuality of their religious experiences, and to accept her growing dependence on Claude. It would seem on the basis of a plain reading

---

107. Davis, *Women on the Margins*, 103.

108. Letter 143. Repeatedly, throughout the correspondence Marie subordinates her biological relationship to Claude to a spiritual one. See also Letter 109.

109. Letter 109.

110. Letter 188. Marie's interpretation of her relationship with Claude as, in effect, a Trinitarian one draws attention to (and was, perhaps, informed by) the centrality of the Trinity in her own interior life. For an analysis of the Trinitarian focus of Marie's spirituality, see Ghislaine Boucher, "À la rencontre d'une théologienne d'"expériences,'" in *Femme, mystique et missionnaire*, ed. Brodeur, 119–26.

Introduction 35

of the letters—which repeatedly identify Claude as "my very dear and beloved son" and Marie as Claude's "very affectionate mother"—that Marie's relationship with Claude was, from the beginning, marked by a consistent and sincere maternal affection. The reader, however, would do well to beware that the sentiment expressed in the correspondence might better reflect rhetorical convention than a genuine emotional intimacy.[111] In an essay on the correspondence between a Renaissance noblewoman and her son-in-law, Christina Antenhofer makes the point strongly: expressions of affection in early modern letters "are to be looked at as a collective discourse pattern in the kinship group: they are not individual feelings but formalized expectations among kin."[112] In adopting the posture of an affectionate mother vis-à-vis her beloved son, then, it could be that Marie (who elsewhere casts herself as "the cruelest of all mothers") was not necessarily revealing the sincerity of her feelings for her son, but simply following seventeenth-century rhetorical conventions instead.[113] Indeed, the contrast between Marie's professed affection for Claude, on the one hand, and her pronounced affection for Christ, on the other, at least qualifies (if not belies) the depths of the intimacy she claims with her abandoned son. The prayer to Christ which Marie reproduces for Claude in the letter of 1647 provides powerful testimony of the affective and almost unbridled passion of which Marie was, in fact, capable and which, as it turns out, she shared with Christ alone. Thus, Marie-Florine Bruneau can conclude, remarking upon the tension between Claude's desire for his mother and Marie's own desire for God, that "[w]hile the son yearned to be the sole object of his mother's desire, indeed, to take God's place…he became the third party to a loving couple, which did not include him."[114]

Moreover, despite these explicit expressions of maternal affection, Marie's letters to Claude betray evidence of a persistent reserve. Even as she professes to want to hide nothing from Claude, Marie deliberately cultivates an emotional distance made possible by her geographical estrangement from Claude, frequently qualifying her desire for intimacy with an acknowledgement of the condition that

---

111. Letter 56.

112. Christina Antenhofer, "Letters across the Borders: Strategies of Communication in an Italian-German Renaissance Correspondence," in *Women's Letters across Europe, 1400–1700: Form and Persuasion*, ed. Jane Couchman and Ann Crabb, 103–22 (Aldershot, UK: Ashgate, 2005). See also Jennifer C. Ward, "Letter-Writing by English Noblewomen in the Early Fifteenth Century," in *Early Modern Women's Letter Writing, 1450–1700*, ed. James Daybell, 29–41 (New York: Palgrave, 2001).

113. Letter 109.

114. Bruneau, *Women Mystics*, 66.

renders it unfortunately but absolutely impossible. "If I had your ear," she writes to Claude in 1653, "there is no secret in my heart that I would not want to confide to you. I would willingly make my general and particular confessions to you... You see thus that I have no reserve toward you, and that only geographical distance impedes our commerce."[115] Here, it was the unbreachable expanse of the Atlantic that frustrated open communication in this instance; in other letters Marie alludes to the press of temporal business as the impediment to the liberal commerce for which she purported to yearn.[116]

Considered over the course of their thirty-year correspondence, however, the relationship between Marie de l'Incarnation and her abandoned son does suggest something of a deepening of spiritual and emotional intimacy. In notable contrast to the initial succinct and brusque letter of 1640, the letters that follow open for Claude a progressively wider window onto Marie's personal spiritual experiences in conjunction with Claude's own advancement in religious life. The following year, upon learning that Claude had begun his novitiate with the Benedictines, Marie offers her son extensive spiritual advice for the first time, alluding to her own interior experience on the occasion of Claude's abandonment. Two years later, Claude had professed his vows and Marie took the opportunity to compose an even wordier letter in which she warns Claude against self-love, superfluous reasoning, and an excessive love of solitude, inter alia. By the time Claude had taken sacerdotal orders some five years later, Marie saw fit to converse with her son about "the things of God" even more openly, as Claude's progress in the religious life compelled Marie to recognize an increasing affinity with her son, "with whom," she admits in 1647, "I feel I share the same spirit."[117]

The gradual weakening of Marie's reserve toward Claude proves apparent, too, in the drama of Claude's ongoing (and ultimately successful) efforts to obtain Marie's spiritual autobiography, the eventual *Relation* of 1654. As early as 1643, Claude had asked for Marie's papers, a request Marie defers until her death and then only "[i]f obedience permits."[118] Some four years later however, pressed by Claude's steadfast persistence, Marie resolves that "from now on I will conceal nothing of my present state from you."[119] Yet, Marie would later admit, she nonetheless continued to "keep... something back from" Claude.[120] Only after a delay of more than five years

---

115. Letter 153.

116. Letter 188.

117. Letters 153 and 109.

118. Letter 68.

119. Letter 109.

120. Letter 155.

Introduction 37

did she succeed in carrying out "this act of obedience" and even then she had "so much repugnance towards it that it had been necessary to command me to do so three times over."[121] Although Marie finally obeyed, the opportunity presented by the great fire that destroyed the Ursuline monastery in 1651 permitted Marie to yet again defer the satisfaction of Claude's request and to maintain her characteristic reserve toward him as she admits (without a trace of remorse) to having voluntarily let the papers burn.[122] Ultimately, however, Marie—moved by God and compelled by her director who had ordered her to "rewrite the same things that I had written before, and which had been burned with our monastery" and "even commanded" her to send the papers to Claude—shared with her son the intimacies of "the operations that [God] had worked upon me since calling me to the interior life."[123]

Indeed, by the last decade of her life Marie seems to have abandoned any inclination toward reserve with Claude. No longer revealing the secrets of her interior life out of compulsion—whether by Claude's own appeal or out of obedience to her confessor—Marie at last begins to share her religious experiences with Claude more freely, from her interior dispositions during the course of a "great illness," to her current method of prayer, the pattern of God's guidance upon her, and her fears and anxieties about the proximity of death and the state of her soul.[124] The penultimate letter sent from Marie to her son in 1671 just one year before her death testifies to the erosion of the last remaining vestiges of the mother's reserve toward her son as she openly invites him to inquire into her interior life. "If you want something from me," Marie writes to Claude, "I will not neglect to respond to you about it, if I am alive and in a position to do so." Indeed, Marie confesses, "If I was near to you, I would pour my heart into yours and take you for my spiritual director."[125]

Just as over the course of their correspondence Marie gradually becomes more open with Claude about her interior dispositions, so also, over time, does she come to acknowledge the mutuality of their religious experiences and to recognize Claude as a spiritual peer. Once again, it is the letter of 1641 (and again, in marked contrast to that of 1640, in which Marie adopts the position of a reproving

---

121. Letter 136.

122. Letter 136. Claude, unsurprisingly, interpreted Marie's decision to let the papers burn as yet another display of her chronic "lack of affection," an accusation his mother quickly dismisses, reminding Claude that "as I told you last year, [the] fire consumed them" (Letter 143).

123. Letter 153.

124. Letter 216.

125. Letter 274.

mother toward her misbehaving son) that sets the tone for the letters that follow, drawing attention to their shared status as children in the same spiritual family and the coincidence of their religious aspirations. For Marie, Claude's entry into religious life meant the inauguration of a new relationship with her son, one based not on the hierarchical ordering of parent and child but founded instead on the congruence of their spiritual experiences. Between spiritual peers united in communion with Christ, the vast expanse of the Atlantic mattered little. Marie imagined herself sharing with Claude in the recitation of the holy office; she imagined sharing with him the struggle to balance the demands of active responsibilities with the impulse toward contemplation; she imagined sharing with him in experience of the mystical life.

Marie's perception of her identity with her son seems only to have intensified over time as she gradually transforms from Claude's spiritual mentor to his spiritual equal. Whereas just four years after her arrival in New France, Marie describes the discernment of her vocation to Claude "for your consolation and instruction," by 1666 she had recognized that Claude had something to teach her himself, admitting (in a letter not included in this volume) that his "letter of confidence... [both] consoled and edified me."[126] In addition to the spiritual advice each shared with the other by means of their letters, Marie and Claude also exchanged more formal compositions. Marie finally sent her son the much-anticipated *Relation* of 1654 and Claude sent to his mother his book of *Meditations* for which the Ursulines in New France, Marie confesses, were profoundly grateful. By 1669, it was no longer Claude who was asking for Marie's writings, but Marie (on behalf of her community) who demanded as much from Claude, begging her son to compose a prayer for the octave of Saint Ursula for use in the community in New France.

Over time, Marie came to acknowledge her material, social, and spiritual dependence on her abandoned son. Writing to Claude in 1659 in the midst of the intensification of hostilities with the Iroquois, she attempts to placate his fears for her safety, affirming that "[i]f our affairs were in danger, I would be the first to warn you, so as to enable you to provide for our safety."[127] Isolated and at risk in the alien wilderness of New France, Marie seems to have recognized that it was upon Claude that she could ultimately rely in the event of material need. Similarly, Marie turned to Claude for assistance within the context of several delicate social situations, as well, asking him to disabuse the Ursulines in Tours

---

126. Letter 68; Lettre CCXXII, *Correspondance*, 764.

127. Letter 183.

of false beliefs about the Jesuits in New France, and later, to correct against the misrepresentations of the Ursulines themselves. Perhaps most poignantly, toward the end of her life Marie comes to acknowledge her spiritual dependence on her ordained Benedictine son. All along she had appealed to Claude (and his monastic companions) for spiritual help and prayers on behalf of the Canadian mission and the conversion of "infidel souls," the affairs of New France, her friends and acquaintances, and her own spiritual progress and "conversion. But by 1667 Marie had begun to actively solicit Claude's intercession for her soul at the moment of her death. Although his mother's request for masses offered for the salvation of her soul at the holy altar had begun as early as 1650 (two years after Claude had entered the priesthood), her almost desperate dependence on his sacerdotal authority reached fever pitch as she confronted an acute and ongoing illness just five years before her death in 1672:

> On account of my sincere affection for you and yours for me, I advise you to you procure as many masses as possible for me from the reverend Fathers of your holy congregation when you learn of my death…I will burn for a long time in purgatory unless divine mercy relieves me through the intercession of the Church. It seems to me that I am quite rich to have you and in you, all your good Fathers. Thus I expect that you will think seriously about this, so that by means of your sacrifices and theirs, I will soon be able to go and enjoy him whom my heart and my soul want to love and bless eternally.

"I will be rigorously punished unless you remember to obtain remission for me by means of your holy sacrifices at the holy altar," she repeats. "Obtain for me, again, the authenticity of this peace."[128]

In the translated correspondence that follows, Marie de l'Incarnation shares—in ways that sometimes converge with and at other times diverge from her male counterparts—her reflections on the religious, political, and economic development of seventeenth-century New France, her impressions of the Amerindians, and the idiosyncrasies of a mystical itinerary inflected by the realities of life on the Canadian frontier. As such, the forty-one letters included here constitute an important resource for understanding the early history of colonial North America, which is not just one of the Pilgrims and the Protestants, but equally one of Ursulines and Jesuits, Catholics and Animists, French and Iroquois. At the same time that they contribute to a broadened appreciation of North

---

128. Letters 174 and 234.

American history, however, these letters provide a window onto one very particular human relationship—that between Marie de l'Incarnation and Claude Martin, the son she abandoned when he was just eleven years old to enter religious life. It is my hope that English-speaking readers will find in this volume not only a much-needed supplement to colonial narratives weighted in favor of their (male) British forbears, but also a unique opportunity to listen to the voice of one seventeenth-century mother in whose life the conflicting demands of faith and family played out in intimate detail.

Letters

Jesus Mary Joseph

Letter 49: September 10, 1640

May the love and life of Jesus be yours.[1]

My very dear son,

I do not want to treat you as you have treated me. What! Did you have the audacity to let the fleet leave without giving me a word of consolation by a letter from you? Others did, otherwise I would not have known your news. I won't say what people are telling me about you. It is enough that I know your needs so I can offer them to our good God. All that's left is for me to beg you, since you were not fortunate enough to take advantage of your vocation, although at least you were not so unfaithful as to abandon it altogether, to make up by diligence what you have lost by negligence.[2] I am writing to several of our friends on your behalf to try to find you a suitable situation in case your plans do not work out.[3] It is time that you know yourself. You are old enough for that. You were helped mightily during your schooldays—now it's up to you to push yourself. It would be too shameful for a well-brought-up young man not to have courage. Therefore, get some spine, my dear son, and realize that you will gain nothing in this world without effort. Have you left off devotion to the Holy Virgin and her glorious spouse Saint Joseph? Don't make this mistake. You will not get ahead in the ways

---

1. This letter appears neither in Claude's 1677 *La Vie de la Vénérable Mère Marie de l'Incarnation* (Sablé-sur-Sarthe: Solesmes Abbey, 1981; hereafter, *Vie*) nor in the 1681 *Lettres historiques* or *Lettres spirituelles de la Vénérable Mère Marie de l'Incarnation*. It was, however, included in the dossier sent to Claude's cousin, Marie Buisson, after Claude's death in 1696 and preserved at the Ursuline monastery at Tours. The letter was reproduced by Dom Edmond Martène, who drew on the Ursuline archives in composing his 1697 *Vie de Dom Claude Martin*, and was later published in Dom Albert Jamet, ed., *Marie de l'Incarnation: Écrits spirituels et historiques* (Paris: Desclée-de Brouwer, 1929).

2. In 1639 and again in 1640, Claude was denied entrance among the Jesuits. See Dom Guy-Marie Oury, *Dom Claude Martin: Le fils de Marie de l'Incarnation* (Sablé-sur-Sarthe: Solesmes Abbey, 1983), 40–1.

3. See Letter 56.

of salvation without their help. Spend time with those who are their devotees and who imitate their virtues. By this means you will win God's good graces. Frequent the sacraments and flee from those who want to turn you away from them.[4] Pray for me and thank the Divine Goodness for the great grace he has given me in calling me to such a lofty vocation. Ask him that I be faithful to him and that he may give me the grace to persevere until death in his holy service in this blessed land of Canada in which I am so unworthy to live. Always maintain affection for the Jesuit Reverend Fathers and also give much of it to my brothers and sisters who wish to oblige you as much as possible. Farewell. I am, my very dear son, your very affectionate mother,

Sister Marie de l'Incarnation.
R[eligious] U[rsuline].

Letter 56: September 4, 1641

May the love and the life of Jesus be your heritage.
My very dear and beloved son,

Your letter brought me such great consolation that it's difficult to express it.[5] All year long, I had borne great crosses for you, my mind envisioning the snares into which you could stumble. At last, our good God gave me rest in the conviction that His loving and paternal Goodness would not destroy the one who had been abandoned out of love for him. Your letter confirmed this for me, my very dear son, and made me see that my hopes for you had been realized—even exceeded—since His Goodness placed you in such a holy order and one that I honor and esteem greatly. I had wished this grace for you at the time of the reform of St. Julien and of Marmoutier, but since vocations must come from heaven, I didn't say a word about it to you, not wanting to interfere in what belongs to God alone.[6]

---

4. See also Marie de l'Incarnation, *Relation de 1654*, vol. 2; Jamet, *Marie de l'Incarnation: Écrits*, 165. H. O. Evennett suggests that critical to the spirituality of the Counter-Reformation (or Catholic Reformation) was an emphasis on the frequent reception of the sacraments; see, H. O. Evennett, *The Spirit of the Counter-Reformation* (Notre Dame: University of Notre Dame Press, 1970), 23–42.

5. On January 15, 1641, Claude began his novitiate among the Benedictines of Saint-Maur at Vendôme; Oury, *Dom Claude Martin*, 50.

6. The reform of the monasteries of Saint-Julien and Marmoutier began in 1637 under the direction of the Maurists. The Maurists, taking their inspiration from the late sixteenth-century

You were abandoned by your mother and your relatives.[7] Hasn't this abandonment been useful to you? When I left you, you were not yet twelve years old and I did so only with strange agonies known to God alone. I had to obey his divine will, which wanted things to happen thus, making me hope that he would take care of you. I steeled my heart to prevail over what had delayed my entry into holy religion a whole ten years. Still, I had to be convinced of the necessity of delivering this blow by Reverend Father Dom Raymond and by ways I can't set forth on this paper, though I would tell you in person.[8] I foresaw the abandonment of our relatives, which gave me a thousand crosses, together with the human weakness that made me fear your ruin.

When I passed through Paris, it would have been easy for me to place you. The Queen, Madame the Duchess d'Aiguillon and Madame the Countess Brienne, who did me the honor of looking upon me with favor and who have again honored me with their commands this year, by their letters, wouldn't have refused me anything I desired for you. I thanked Madame the Duchess d'Aiguillon for the good that she wanted to do for you, but the thought that came to me then was

---

reform of the Abbey of Saint-Vannes in Lorraine, instituted reforms intended to restore Benedictine houses throughout France to an original conventual observance. For a discussion of the Maurist reforms, see Joseph Bergin, *Church, Society, and Religious Change in France, 1580–1730* (New Haven: Yale University Press, 2009), 95–104; Maarten Ultee, *The Abbey of St. Germain des Prés in the Seventeenth Century* (New Haven: Yale University Press, 1981); and Edmond Martène, *Histoire de la Congrégation de Saint-Maur* (Paris: A. Picard, 1928–43).

7. See also *Relation de 1654*, 272–5; Marie de l'Incarnation, *Relation de 1633*, vol. 1; Jamet, *Marie de l'Incarnation: Écrits*, 268–77; Letters 109, 155, 195, 211, 247, and 267. In choosing to abandon Claude in favor of the religious life, Marie de l'Incarnation found herself in the company of a whole host of mothers in Christian history, including (perhaps most famously) Perpetua and Felicitas. See *The Passion of Saints Perpetua and Felicity*, trans. W. H. Shewring (London: Sheed and Ward, 1931). See also L. Stephanie Cobb, *Dying to be Men: Gender and Language in Early Christian Martyr Texts* (New York: Columbia University Press, 2008), 92–123. For a collection of essays that examine some of these women, see Anneke B. Mulder-Bakker, *Sanctity and Motherhood: Essays on Holy Mothers in the Middle Ages* (New York: Garland, 1995). See also Clarissa Atkinson, *The Oldest Vocation: Christian Motherhood in the Middle Ages* (Ithaca: Cornell University Press, 1991).

8. The Feuillantine Dom Raymond had served as Marie's confessor and spiritual director from 1620 to 1631 or 1632. Marie's allusion here to the insecurity of the epistolary medium draws attention to the ways in which early modern letter-writing did not presuppose a simple binary relationship between addressor and addressee, but rather a more complex set of interactions between sender, scribe, bearer, recipient, and multiple readers. See James Daybell, "'I wold wyshe my doings might be…secret': Privacy and the Social Practices of Reading Women's Letters in Sixteenth-Century England," in *Women's Letters across Europe, 1400–1700: Form and Persuasion*, ed. Jane Couchman and Ann Crabb, 143–62 (Aldershot, UK: Ashgate, 2005). See also Daybell, Introduction, *Early Modern Women's Letter Writing, 1450–1700*, ed. James Daybell, 1–15 (New York: Palgrave, 2001).

that if you were advanced in the world, your soul would be in danger of ruin.⁹ What's more, the thoughts that had formerly occupied my mind, in wanting only spiritual poverty for your inheritance and for mine, made me resolve to leave you a second time in the hands of the Mother of goodness, trusting that since I was going to give my life for the service of her beloved Son, she would take care of you. Did you not also take her as your mother and spouse when you entered the congregation (the Day of the Purification)? Therefore, you could expect from her only a good like the one you possess. The advantages presented for you in Paris would have been something, but infinitely inferior to those you now possess. I believe, and your letter assures me of it, that you neither regret them nor the humiliating conditions of your birth to which you allude, and which were not at all inconsiderable. I don't know who told you about it; I would not have dared to talk to you about it. I have never loved you but in the poverty of Jesus Christ in which all treasures are found.

Indeed, you were not yet in the world when I wished these treasures for you. My heart felt such powerful impulses about this, I cannot express them. So, you are now in the militia, my very dear son. In the name of God, cherish the words of Jesus Christ and imagine that he says to you: "He who puts his hand to the plow and looks back is not fit for the kingdom of heaven."¹⁰ What he promises you is much greater than the advantages for which you were caused to hope and which you must esteem as mud and muck, so as to gain Jesus Christ for yourself.¹¹ Your glorious patriarch Saint Benedict gave you a great example of this. Imitate him, in the name of God, so that my heart may have this consolation by the first fleet, that the vows I have offered to His Divine Majesty, for twenty-one years without interruption, have been received in heaven. I see you engaged in holy resolutions, which gives me hope that God will give you perseverance. Not a day goes by that I don't sacrifice you to his love on the heart of his beloved Son. May it please His Goodness that you be a true holocaust totally consumed on this divine altar.¹²

---

9. By all accounts Marie Madeleine de Vignerot du Pont de Courlay, Duchesse d'Aiguillon and niece of Cardinal Richelieu, stands as an example of the seventeenth-century French *dévote* described by Elizabeth Rapley in *The Dévotes: Women and Church in Seventeenth-Century France* (Kingston, ON: McGill-Queen's University Press, 1990). Widowed after just two years of marriage, the childless Duchesse dedicated herself to charitable causes after following her uncle to the court of Louis XIII, funding a number of religious houses in Paris, and providing support to the foreign missions and institutions like the Hôtel-Dieu in Quebec.

10. Luke 9:62.

11. Philippians 3:8.

12. The language of sacrifice Marie employs here resonates with the theology of the French School and, in particular, the sacrificial theology of Charles de Condren. See Charles de Condren, *L'idée du sacerdoce et du sacrifice de Jésus-Christ* (Vitry-le-François: E. Hurault, 1849);

It is true what you say, my very dear son. I found Canada quite other than what I expected, but differently than you imagined. The labors are mild for me here and so easy to bear that I experience what our Lord said, "My yoke is easy and my burden light."[13] My efforts were not wasted in the thorny business of learning a foreign language, which is now so easy for me, I have no difficulty teaching our holy mysteries to our neophytes, of whom we had a great number this year—more than fifty seminarians and more than seven hundred visits from Indians, male and female, all of whom we assisted spiritually and temporally.[14] The joy my heart feels in the holy occupation that God gives me wipes away all the fatigues I feel on ordinary occasions. I am begging our Reverend Mother Françoise de Saint-Bernard to send you a copy of the account that I made for her on the progress of our seminary.

As for all of Christianity, there are now three nations that want to come and settle at Sillery.[15] Their daughters are destined for the seminary. All the Christians are doing very well. One Montagnais, a new Christian, served as an apostle to his nation and, with Reverend Father Le Jeune, rattled the three nations I told you about. The letters written by two of our seminarians to that Reverend Father when he was catechizing those nations elicited the admiration of all these good catechumens and made them want to give us their daughters, since they can achieve what the French girls can in terms of both salvation and learning, from which it seemed that their miserable condition of being born in barbarity would

---

see also José Pereira and Robert Fastiggi, *Mystical Theology of the Catholic Reformation: An Overview of Baroque Spirituality* (Lanham, MD: University Press of America, 2006), 208 and following; and Jean Galy, *Le sacrifice dans l'école française* (Paris: Nouvelles Éditions Latines, 1951). See also Letters 68, 135, 143, 188, and 195. For an analysis of the ways in which the realities of New France impacted Marie's understanding of sacrifice (as well as spiritual poverty), see Anya Mali, "L'état de victime et le 'petit discours' mystique," in *Femme, mystique et missionnaire: Marie Guyart de l'Incarnation*, ed. Raymond Brodeur, 211–20 (Quebec: Presses de l'Université Laval, 2001).

13. Matthew 11:30.

14. I have chosen to translate the French "sauvage" as "Indian" throughout this text to avoid the more pejorative implications of the English cognate, "savage." For a discussion of the meaning of the French "sauvage" and its closest English equivalents, see John DuVal and Kathleen DuVal, "Are Sauvages Savages, Wild People, or Indians in a Colonial American Reader?," *Translation Review* 79, no. 1 (Winter 2010): 1–16. See also Gordon M. Sayre, *Les Sauvages Américains: Representations of Native Americans in French and English Colonial Literature* (Chapel Hill: University of North Carolina Press, 1997), xv.

15. The Jesuits established Sillery as a settlement for converted Amerindians in New France in 1638 modeled on the Paraguayan *réduction*. For a study of *réductions* in New France, see Marc Jetten, *Enclaves amérindiennes: Les "réductions" du Canada, 1637–1701* (Quebec: Septentrion, 1994). See also Anya Mali, *Mystic in the New World: Marie de l'Incarnation (1599–1672)* (Leiden: E. J. Brill, 1996), 111–13.

exclude them.¹⁶ All of our new Christians have suffered greatly on account of the tyranny of the Iroquois, who have waged war against them as well as against our French.

Monsieur our Governor drove the Iroquois away in an offensive undertaken to save our good neophytes. The *Relation* will tell you about it.¹⁷ The Reverend Fathers of the Society of Jesus who are with the Hurons experienced unbelievable hardships in their missions this winter, given the extraordinarily severe cold and snows. In addition, the barbarity of this nation caused them to suffer excessively. The Reverend Father Chaumonot, whom you know, felt their blows. He is an apostle who is delighted to be found worthy to suffer for Jesus Christ. Almost miraculously, he learned the Huron language and with it performed marvels in a nation where he and the Reverend Father Brébeuf scattered the first seeds of the gospel. The Reverend Fathers Garnier and Pijart thought they would be killed, but our Lord protected them miraculously. The Reverend Father Poncet escaped the hands of the Iroquois, who were away when his canoe passed by quickly, piloted by some Hurons who feared the death that this great servant of God ardently desired.¹⁸

He is staying at Trois-Rivières. He helps the Algonquins with a zeal that you can imagine, and he is learned in the Algonquin language. This is also the one I'm

---

16. Over time, Marie would lose confidence in the possibility of "civilizing" Amerindian girls in the model of the French. By 1668, no longer convinced that native girls "can achieve what the French girls can," Marie despairs to Claude that "[i]t is...very difficult, if not impossible, to make them French or to civilize them." That same year, she admits that "[o]ver the course of the many years that we have been in this country, we have civilized only seven of our eight who became French; the great number of others have all returned to their parents" (Lettres CCXXXVII and CCXLIV, *Marie de l'Incarnation: Correspondance*, ed. Dom Guy-Marie Oury [Sablé-sur-Sarthe: Solesmes Abbey, 1971], 809 and 828 [hereafter, *Correspondance*]). All subsequent references to letters not included in the present volume are taken from Oury's French edition and are identified by letter number. The fruit of her experience with native American girls over the course of some thirty years, Marie's decided pessimism about their capacity to become French reflects what Peter Goddard calls an "Augustinian anthropology" characteristic of the early years of the Jesuit mission in seventeenth-century New France. Peter A. Goddard, "Augustine and the Amerindian in Seventeenth-century New France," *Church History* 67, no. 4 (December 1998): 662–81. See also, Dominique Deslandres, "Le jésuite, l'intoléré et le sauvage : la fabrication par omission d'un mythe," in *Primitivisme et mythes des origines dans la France des Lumières, 1680–1720*, ed. Ch.Grell et C. Michel, 87–99 (Paris: Presses de l'université Paris-Sorbonne, 1989).

17. Reuben Gold Thwaites, ed., *The Jesuit Relations and Allied Documents*, vol. 21 (Cleveland: Burrows, 1896–1901), 59–79. For a comprehensive study of the wars between the French and the Iroquois in seventeenth-century New France, see José António Brandão, *Your Fyre Shall Burn No More: Iroquois Policy Towards New France and its Native Allies to 1701* (Lincoln: University of Nebraska Press, 1997).

18. Thwaites, *Jesuit Relations*, vol. 21, 175–85.

studying, which serves me among the Algonquins and the Montagnais, as they are neighboring nations.[19]

Mother Marie de Saint-Joseph is studying the Huron language. We also have girls from that country, and she is succeeding quite well at it.

Nevertheless, we have more of a relationship with the Algonquins, and this is why everyone applies themselves to learning their language. A number of nations that speak this language were discovered near the northern coasts. They are being instructed and everyone wants to believe. It is thought that there could be some martyrs in the great labors that must be undertaken, for the devil, enraged that Jesus Christ stole from him the empire that he had dared to usurp so many years ago, always provokes some evil-doers for the purpose of harming gospel workers. I hope that you will see the *Relation*. I will try to arrange for someone to send you one once it is printed.

I am very deeply consoled by the good wish you made for me (namely, martyrdom). Alas, my very dear son, my sins will deprive me of this blessing.[20] I haven't done anything up to this point capable of winning God's heart, for—think about it—it is necessary to have worked hard to be found worthy to spill one's blood for Jesus Christ. I dare not have such high pretensions, but leave it to His immense Goodness, who has always informed me of so many of his favors that even absent my own merit, he still wants me to do that to which I dare not aspire; I beg him to do it. I give myself to him and I also give you to him, and beg him for the blessing that you ask of me, that he may satisfy you with the blessings he has dispensed to so many brave soldiers who have remained inviolably true to him.

---

19. For an analysis of the Jesuit missions among the Algonquin and Montagnais in seventeenth-century New France, see Emma Anderson, *The Betrayal of Faith: The Tragic Journey of a Colonial Native Convert* (Cambridge, MA: Harvard University Press, 2007), and Kenneth Morrison, *The Solidarity of Kin: Ethnography, Religious Studies, and the Algonkian-French Religious Encounter* (Albany: State University of New York Press, 2002). See also Alain Beaulieu, *Convertir les fils de Caïn: Jésuites et amérindiens nomades en Nouvelle-France, 1632–1642* (Quebec: Nuit Blanche, 1990), and Peter A. Goddard, "Converting the 'Sauvage': Jesuit and Montagnais in Seventeenth-Century New France," *Catholic Historical Review* 84, no. 2 (April 1998): 219–39.

20. See also Letters 68 and 142. Marie's emphasis on martyrdom resonates with the sacrificial theology of Charles de Condren and an early modern revival of martyrdom, and is suggestive of the ways in which New France (where the possibility of martyrdom was very real) might have shaped a spirituality imported from France. For a study of martyrdom in the early modern era across confessions, see Brad Gregory, *Salvation at Stake: Christian Martyrdom in Early Modern Europe* (Cambridge, MA: Harvard University Press, 1990). For an analysis of the ways in which Marie reworks traditional notions of martyrdom, see Katherine Ibbett, "Reconfiguring Martyrdom in the Colonial Context: Marie de l'Incarnation," in *Empires of God: Religious Encounters in the Early Modern Atlantic*, ed. Linda Gregerson and Susan Juster, 175–90 (Philadelphia: University of Pennsylvania Press, 2011); see also Ulrike Strasser, "Clara

If someone came to tell me, "Your son is a martyr," I think I would die of joy. Let's leave it up to God. He bides his time, this God full of love. Be faithful to him and rest assured that he will find you opportunities to become a great saint if you obey his divine movements, and if you take pleasure in dying to yourself and in following the example offered you by so many great saints of your order.[21] If our Lord gives you the grace to be professed, I beg you to let me know about it and to tell me how His Goodness called you and what measures you took to bring it about.

Finally, my very dear son, share your good news with me, which, as you can imagine, brings me a very great consolation. I believe that the Reverend Father Superior will let you do this. I give myself the honor of writing to him and thanking him for the honor of his affection and his solicitude for you. And pray hard to God for me. I visit you many times a day and I speak about you ceaselessly to Jesus, Mary, and Joseph.

It is possible that one of our Mothers from Tours will come over by this first fleet to find us. It isn't certain that this will happen yet, given that the matter depends on some circumstances that can only be resolved in France. This is Mother le Coq, *dit* St. Joseph, whom you knew as my novice mistress.[22] She is a great servant of God and is, at present, the superior at Loches. Nevertheless, we will ask for her from Tours, for she is professed there. Monsieur de Bernières wrote me about your happiness.[23] He is delighted about it. The Reverend Father

---

Hortulana of Embach or How to Suffer Martyrdom in the Cloister," in *Female Monasticism in Early Modern Europe: an Interdisciplinary View*, ed. Cordule van Wyhe, 39–58 (Aldershot, UK: Ashgate, 2008).

21. Marie's allusion here to the ideal of *anéantissement*, or annihilation, of self echoes a Bérullian emphasis on *anéantissement* as the means to a life lived in the service and for the glory of God. Henri Brémond, *Histoire littéraire du sentiment religieux en France*, 5 vols. (Grenoble: Jerome Millon, 2006), vol. 1, 977–1003, 1147–52; William M. Thompson, ed., *Bérulle and the French School; Selected Writings* (Mahwah, NJ: Paulist Press, 1989), 41–7; Jean-Jacques Olier, *Introduction à la vie et aux vertus chrétiennes* (Paris: Le Rameau, 1953), 131–5. The theme of annihilation, however, has deep roots in the history in medieval Christian mysticism. In *The Mirror of Simple Annihilated Souls*, for example, Marguerite Porete gives an account of what Bernard McGinn describes "a deeply apophatic form of mysticism involving the annihilation of the created will through the power of totally disinterested love." Bernard McGinn, *The Essential Writings of Christian Mysticism* (New York: Random House, 2006) 172.

22. Marie de Savonnières de la Troche, a professed Ursuline of Tours, accompanied Marie de l'Incarnation to New France in 1639. Her conspicuous presence in Marie's letters to Claude (see, for example, letters 80, 81, 97, 109, 142, 143, 153, and 173) suggests an intimacy between the two nuns elaborately expressed in the biography (hagiography?) Marie composed following Mother de Saint-Joseph's death in 1652. See Lettre CXL, *Correspondance*, 436–73; Thwaites, *Jesuit Relations*, vol. 38, 67–165.

23. Jean de Bernières (1602–59) occupies an important place in the history of seventeenth-century French spirituality. Born to a noble and pious family in Caen, Bernières founded l'Ermitage as a

Dom Raymond and all my relatives also wrote me about it, as well as our good Mothers of Tours, who love you very much.

Farewell, my very dear son. I will never tire of conversing with you. The Reverend Father Poncet greets you. He is delighted about your happiness, as is Mother Marie de Saint-Joseph, to whom God gives many graces and great talents for winning souls for him. Pray for her and for me who am,

My very dear and beloved son,
Your very humble and very affectionate mother

Sister Marie de l'Incarnation, r. urs. Ind. From Quebec, at the seminary (of St. Joseph) of the Ursulines
4th September 1641
Pray for me on the day of the feast of the glorious apostle St. Paul. I was professed on this day.

Letter 68: September 1, 1643

My very dear son,
The peace and love of Jesus. You complain that you haven't received the ample letters I wrote you last year. One thousand leagues of sea and more are prone to dangers, and each year, those that are brought to us and those that go back again to France run the same risk. I responded to all the points of your letter, and since you wish it, and because it is impossible for me to refuse you anything, I will make a short summary of it. But so that you don't lose everything, I have already written

---

house where *dévots* like himself—whether lay or religious—could dedicate themselves to lives of prayer and charity. Although Bernières never journeyed to New France himself, he played a critical role in early years of the nascent colony, enabling the passage of Madeleine de la Peltrie from France to New France (by means of a sham marriage) and contributing to the spiritual formation of Quebec's first bishop, François de Laval, who spent four years at l'Ermitage in Caen. Two posthumous publications—*Le Chrétien intérieur* and *Les Œuvres spirituelles*—allow us a sense of the content of Bernières's mystical spirituality. Echoes of Marie's own spiritual vocabulary resound in Bernières's texts as the mystic elaborates not only on the doctrine of abandonment, but also on "conflagrations" and "fires," "caresses" and "graces," "union" and "consolation," testifying if not to a mutual influence between the two correspondents then at least to a shared spiritual culture. For an overview of Bernières's spirituality, see Brémond, *Histoire littéraire*, vol. 2, 851–77. Much to his disappointment, Claude never succeeded in retrieving the letters written by his mother to Bernières, which were among her most extensive and dealt largely with the subject of prayer and other spiritual matters. See *Correspondance*, xi–xii, citing to Claude Martin, *Lettres*, Avertissement ii–iii. For Marie's own account of her relationship with Bernières, see *Relation de 1654*, 339–46.

you part of it by the first ship, which ought to reach France a month before the others, if it arrives safely.

You can believe that upon learning that you are completely God's by the holy vows of religion, my heart was more consoled by this news than by any other I have ever received in my life.[24] The infinite mercy of God gave me this grace in giving it to you. I had given you to him before you were born. When I was in the world, my heart sighed after him incessantly, that it might please His Goodness to accept you. You had hardly reached the age of thirteen when he promised me that he would take care of you, which gave my heart more peace than I can say.[25] When you were a bit older, and I was told that your life was a little too footloose, I bore crosses for you that made me appeal endlessly to God, although I knew well that he would not fail you. But you could by your failings thwart his plans or, rather, I could. It was then, as security for your soul, that I gave him the Holy Virgin and Saint Joseph through whom I offered you daily to His Divine Majesty. Do you think, my very dear son, that when I spoke to you about God, the benefits of religion, and the happiness of those who serve him, I did not clearly see that your heart was closed to my words? I did see it, and this was my greatest cross to bear, for it seemed to me that with each step you were going to fall into the abyss. But I always had an instinct in my heart that told me that God would give you the grace of calling you to serve him in a quite particular manner, in due time and in the manner in which he had called me. And, in fact, I see it pretty well described in what you tell me happened to you. Take heed, my very dear son, if you survive me you will know more about this, since you want me to give you my papers.[26] If obedience permits it then, I too wish it, so that you may know the excesses of the Divine Goodness on me, as well as on you.

By an excess of his love, our divine master burns our hearts without consuming them. Nevertheless, our own misery prevents his work from being completely effective. The agent does his part in full, but our own indifference stands in the way of the divine strokes and impedes the soul from achieving the perfect annihilation that transcends all imaginable purification. I have not stopped praying for you, my very dear son, and I don't neglect to offer you on the sacred altar of the very lovable heart of Jesus to his eternal Father. But how, you ask, am I sacrificed on the heart that casts fire everywhere, and yet I do not burn?[27] Do you think that

---

24. Claude pronounced his vows on February 3, 1642.

25. See also *Relation de 1654*, 281.

26. Claude's struggle for his mother's spiritual writings would be a protracted, but ultimately triumphant one. See Letters 109, 136, 143, 153, 155, 162, and 163 (written in 1654 to accompany "the papers that I had promised you").

27. Luke 12:49. Allusions to burning and conflagration, while typical to the vocabulary of Western Christian mysticism generally and to seventeenth-century French spirituality in

we always feel the fire that burns us? I am talking about this divine fire. We would never be humble if we were not conscious of our infirmities, and it's good that love prevents us from feeling his fire, so that we burn more purely.

It is, again, an excess of our misery to have in ourselves the saint of saints and not to be holy from the first moment we touch or receive him. O my very dear son, how far it is from him to us, although he is in us and united to us, since we received him in the very holy sacrament. If we wanted, once and for all, to follow and imitate our life and exemplary way, we would become saints upon our first communion. And yet, although we sometimes have good dispositions which this celestial spouse accepts—namely, those ordained by the Church and which make us worthy to take communion and produce in us the effects of sanctification—we are so weak and puny that we take back what we had given to him. Our miserable self-love is unable to undergo an annihilation as total as he, who wants only that souls resemble him, desires. Heed this point: our self-love makes us slaves and reduces us to nothing, for what is it if not leaving the whole in order to be in ourselves, who are but pure nothings?[28] Therefore look no further for the reason why we are not saints from the first time we make our communion. Meditating in the great silence to which God has called you will make you see more clearly into this matter than me. And what's more, you have so many saints among you consumed in the service of the great master that with their advice and examples, you will become holy if you want.

---

particular, resonate curiously within the renewed context of martyrdom in Reformation Europe as well as colonial New France, where torture by fire was a torment not infrequently visited upon missionary (and other) captives by their indigenous captors. See, for example, the accounts of the martyrdoms of René Goupil, Isaac Jogues, Jean de Brébeuf, and Gabriel Lalemant in Thwaites, *Jesuit Relations*, vol. 28, 115–35; vol. 31, 15–51; and vol. 34, 23–35. See also Letters 56, 142, and 153. For a discussion of the ways in which aboriginal culture shaped the experience and inscription of Jesuit martyrdom in seventeenth-century New France, see Timothy Pearson, "Becoming Holy in Early Canada: Performance and the Making of Holy Persons in Society and Culture" (PhD diss., McGill University, 2008), 60–112.

28. Marie's rendering of self-love as an impediment to spiritual progress fits squarely within a Christian tradition that imagines mystical union as one between a beloved and a lover who "renounces self-love, loves nothing but the beloved, and is wholly absorbed into the beloved." Charlotte Radler, "'In love I am more God': The Centrality of Love in Meister Eckhart's Mysticism," *Journal of Religion* 90, no. 2 (April 2010), 190. The theme of self-purgation is well developed in the writings Meister Eckhart; see Bernard McGinn, *The Mystical Thought of Meister Eckhart: The Man from whom God Hid Nothing* (New York: Crossroad, 2001), 131–47. Moshe Sluhovsky's overview of the new spirituality in early modern Spain, Italy, and France nicely illustrates the ways in which the struggle against the self would continue to play a major role in the writings of mystics like John of the Cross, Miguel de Molinos, and Benoît de Canfield. Moshe Sluhovsky, *Believe Not Every Spirit: Possession, Mysticism, & Discernment in Early Modern Catholicism* (Chicago: University of Chicago Press, 2007),

You say that you would like to say mass in the land of the infidels one day. If God gave you this honor, you can imagine how much joy it would bring me. Oh, how happy I would be if one day someone came to tell me that my son was a victim immolated for God. Never was Saint Symphorosa as content as I would be.[29] See how much I love you: I wish you to be worthy to spill your blood for Jesus Christ. I bless His Goodness for the desires he gives you, but take care not to hamper your spirit too much with superfluous reasoning, which would be a continual waste of your time. It would happen that you wouldn't be able to untangle yourself easily. For, passion, being moved by overly impulsive desires, blocks the light of the spirit and makes it difficult to correctly judge a vocation, which reveals itself more perfectly by a sweet and loving confidence, and by a long perseverance that does not affect the peace of the heart, than by means of a rapid boil and continual agitation that occur in the senses alone. It has seemed to me that since my childhood, God has disposed me to the grace I now possess, for I was more inclined to reflect spiritually on the generous actions of those who worked and persevered for Jesus Christ in foreign lands than in my own country.[30] My heart felt united to these apostolic souls in a wholly extraordinary way. I was sometimes so powerfully overtaken that had social niceties not held me back, I would have run after those whom I saw applying themselves zealously to the salvation of souls. I didn't know then why I had these impulses, for I had neither the experience nor the wit to recognize them, nor was it yet time, for he who arranges things smoothly wanted me to pass through various stages before revealing his will to the most unworthy of his creatures. Many things happened as time went on. You'll know about them one day, my very dear son. I have only told you in passing here about what happened to me in my childhood, for your consolation and instruction.

Regarding the ideas you propose to me, believe me, do not concern yourself with anything but following God. By this I mean that you must abandon yourself to his guidance with an easy confidence and wait with a peaceful heart to find out

---

102–36. See also Hélène Trépanier, "Entre amour-propre et anéantissement: Le 'je' des autobiographies mystiques féminines," in *La femme au XVIIe siècle*, ed. Richard G. Hodgson, 301–13 (Tübingen: Gunter Narr, 2002). Marie's focus on the dangers of self-love draws not only on the Christian tradition, but also on seventeenth-century French moral discourse in which self-love (or *amour propre*) played a leading role. For a discussion of self-love in French moral discourse, see Charles-Olivier Stiker-Métral, *Narcisse contrarié l'amour-propre dans le discours moral en France, 1650–1715* (Paris: Champion, 2007).

29. Saint Symphorosa, according to tradition, was martyred along with her seven sons during the reign of the Roman emperor Hadrian in the second century. *The Writings of Hippolytus, Bishop of Portus*, vol. 2, trans. Rev. S. D. F. Salmond (Edinburgh: T. & T. Clark, 1849), 191–4.

30. *Relation de 1654*, 168–9, 302–13.

what his plans for you will be.³¹ Don't worry about anything else. He will guide you by the hand, for it is thus that he behaves toward souls who seek to please him and not to satisfy themselves. Oh, how sweet it is to follow God! I am not telling you this so that you stifle his spirit but so that you serve it in a greater purity and breathe only in the realization of the plans he has for you, for the purpose of his glory and the sanctification of your soul. Exact obedience to your superiors will be the touchstone by which you will know if you are thus disposed.

Ah, my very dear son, how important it is to depend on God's plans for you! This is the secret to becoming a great saint and rendering oneself capable of benefitting others. I am delighted to see saints here—this is what I call the gospel workers—in an awful nudity of soul. Truly, these words of the apostle can be aptly applied to them: *You have died and your life is hidden with Jesus Christ in God.*³² I am at a loss for words to describe my experience of it. Meditate on this sentence and think about how far we are from resembling our divine master. What the creature can't do itself, God does here in ways one never would have imagined. Don't think that when you ask me what I endure and tell me to leave nothing out, I am speaking to you about the scarcity of temporal things, of the day-to-day poverty, of the privation of everything that can console the senses, of the troubles that can afflict them, of contradictions, adversities, and similar things. No, all these are sweet, and one doesn't think about them, although there is no end to them. These are roses amidst which one is too comfortable, and I assure you that the joy I feel here often gives me scruple.

Just now someone came to tell me that the ship that was bringing the majority of our provisions, and all the necessities for our community as well as our seminarians, is lost. What belongs to the Reverend Fathers and the Hospitaller Mothers was there, too. Despite all this, we are so much at peace that it's as if it didn't affect us, even though this loss means an extreme shortage for us. But blessed be our divine master, let him be infinitely blessed forever more. He feeds the birds of the sky and the animals of the earth. Would he let us die? Thus it is not these things that make one suffer, but a certain operation of God on the soul, which is more painful to nature than tortures and torments.³³ And when I tell you that the gospel workers are dead and their life is hidden in God, I mean that

---

31. The language of abandonment that Marie uses here to prescribe an ideal relationship between humans and God echoes that used to describe her relationship with Claude, whom she admits to having "abandoned" in favor of religious life. See for example, Letter 56.

32. Colossians 3:3.

33. Curiously, although the context of seventeenth-century Canada must have offered her ample opportunities for the practice of corporeal mortification, Marie had abandoned such exercises by this point in her religious vocation. A more traditional celebration of physical

they underwent this operation, even joining themselves to the worker and giving themselves up along with him, merciless toward themselves in order to cut this nature, which is so harmful to perfect imitators of Jesus Christ, to the quick.

It seems to me that you are anxious to know if I have suffered greatly. Yes, my heart cannot conceal anything from you, yet I have not suffered as much as I could, nor have I yet achieved the perfection of those of whom I was speaking. But obtain for me the grace to be able to achieve it. This will be my reward for what I endured for you.[34] For my fear that you would fall into the abysses toward which you ran in the world caused me to make an agreement with God that I would bear the punishment of your sins in this life, if he wouldn't punish you by depriving you of the good for which he had made me hope for you. After this compact, you wouldn't believe what great crosses I suffered for this reason. Even when you were about to make your profession, I once had to excuse myself from the table and withdraw to offer you to God. It was then that the crosses I suffered for you came to an end, as I noted, by comparing your letters with what had happened to me. I tell you this to make you see how much God loved you, drawing you to himself by ways full of his goodness, so that your whole life might burn in him as a continual offering of thanksgiving. As for me, this is my occupation, too, although I do it very imperfectly.

This sort of cross I'm telling you about is followed by the trials we suffer for the kingdom of Jesus Christ, to which the demons are furiously opposed. It is true, and I tell you this in my other letters, that we are greatly consoled by the conversions that take place, but the persecution of our new Christians and the constant turmoil this causes make us suffer and feel what it is to have adopted the interests of the Son of God as our own. I am going on at length, but I must do it because you want me to.

You tell me about your solitude. It is true that retreat is sweet, and one never converses better with God than in silence. This is what consoles me about the fact that His Goodness has called you to a holy order where this virtue reigns in its perfection, and where silence enables you to do more for yourself and others than you ever could by means of speech. The mixed life has its nuisances, but it is animated by the spirit of he who ordained it.[35] I never find myself more in God

---

suffering (which reads the physical exterior as a reflection of the spiritual interior) is not, however, absent from Marie's correspondence. See, for example, Letters 73 and 97 on the sufferings of Isaac Jogues and the martyrdoms of Anne de Noüe and Ennemond Massé.

34. *Relation de 1654*, 374–8.

35. See also Letter 128, 155, 163, and 177, inter alia. *Relation de 1633*, 234–6; *Relation de 1654*, 205–8. For her integration of the active and the contemplative—the "mixed life"—Marie has been called the "Teresa of Canada," not least of all by her son himself who writes that his mother "was a second Saint Teresa…the saint Teresa of the new World," (Martin, *Vie* 753). Anya Mali,

than when I leave my repose out of love for him, in order to speak with some good Indian and teach him how to do some Christian act. I take pleasure in doing this before God, for our Indians are so simple that I would tell them everything I have in my heart. I tell you this to make you see that this sort of mixed life gives me more vigor than I can say. Also, it is my vocation, which I must love above any other. And if I might have the benefit of no longer being superior and seeing myself relieved of my obligation to oversee the monastery that we're having built, I would be delighted to exist only for our neophytes. Perhaps my self-love is making me speak, but without regard for my inclinations, I desire that God's will be done.

As for you, your duty is to receive guests and be in a position to do charity. When one loves the cell too much, it is good to be a bit deprived of it for a while.[36]

---

however, takes issue with such a ready identification between Marie and Teresa, arguing that it "obscures the fact that this balancing act was a source of pain and bewilderment for Marie, who overcame institutional obstacles and the seeming dissonance of her inner callings to achieve religious goals which were not in keeping with her sex and situation." The influence of the New World, Mali contends, proved decisive in shaping the distinctive mixing of the active and contemplative that marked Marie's Canadian apostolate; see Mali, *Mystic in the New World*, xv, 91–107. For a study of the theology of the mixed life among early modern Catholic women, see Laurence Lux-Sterritt, *Redefining Female Religious Life: French Ursulines and English Ladies in Seventeenth-Century Catholicism* (Aldershot, UK: Ashgate, 2005); Dominique Deslandres, "In the Shadow of the Cloister: Representations of Holiness in New France," in *Colonial Saints: Discovering the Holy in the Americas*, ed. Allan Greer and Jodi Bilinkoff, 129–52 (New York: Routledge, 2003); and Rapley, *Dévotes*. The flowering of mixed apostolates among early modern Catholic women religious was, arguably, an outgrowth of the new, "secularized" mysticism of the later Middle Ages, which presumed that "God could be found in the secular realm and in the midst of everyday experience" (Bernard McGinn, "The Changing Shape of Late Medieval Mysticism," *Church History* 65, no. 2 [June 1996]: 198–201, 213–19). See also Karen Scott, "Catherine of Siena and Lay Sanctity in Fourteenth-Century Italy," in *Lay Sanctity, Medieval and Modern: The Search for Models*, ed. Ann W. Astell, 77–90 (Notre Dame: University of Notre Dame Press, 2000), and Scott, "Urban Spaces, Women's Networks, and the Lay Apostolate in the Siena of Catherine Beninscasa," in *Creative Women in Medieval and Early Modern Italy*, ed. E. Ann Matter and John Coakley, 105–19 (Philadelphia: University of Pennsylvania Press, 1994). Indeed, the theology of the mixed life was not the invention of early modern religious women. As early as the twelfth century, Richard of St. Victor insisted that in the highest degree of mystical union, the soul "descends from the lonely peaks of contemplation to practice charity in the lowly world of men" (Louis Dupré, "The Christian Experience of Mystical Union," *Journal of Religion* 69, no. 1 [January 1989]: 8). For a discussion of the ways in which the theology of the mixed life was developed by the French School, see Thompson, *Bérulle and the French School*, 10–11.

36. Shortly after he pronounced his vows, Claude was sent to the Benedictine abbey of Tiron where he was put in charge of an inn intended for visiting friends and families, a responsibility that no doubt consumed much of the young novice's time and energy and about which he seems to have complained to his mother. A subtle but persistent tension in Marie's correspondence

It will give me pleasure if you tell me about the progress of your holy order, which I honor and love as no other. I know about the great services it rendered to the Church in former times, and I hope it will return to its prior splendor. The significant progress that we see in its restoration bodes well for it. From our end of the world, I offer it to God. Although I am very poor and unworthy of being heard, my heart is thus moved and I can't hold it back.

I rejoice that your superior is training you in mortification. This is a sign that he loves you and wants good things for you. Let God and your superiors act as they desire and trust that His Goodness will put you where he wants, for his glory and for your sanctification. You would oblige me by sending me one of your sermons in writing. Don't I have the right to ask this of you, since you can imagine what a significant consolation I would have in seeing, at least, what I can't hear? If God wants you in the ministry of preaching, he will give you the necessary talent. In any case, you belong to him. I am content. Let us live and die in his holy service, my very dear son.

You ask me if we will see each other again in this world? I do not know, but God is so good that if his name is to be glorified by it, and if it's for the good of your soul and mine, he will make it happen. Let's leave it up to him. I would not want this less than you, but I don't want to want anything other than in him and for him. Let's lose our own wills out of love for him. I see you every day in him, and when I am at matins in the evening, I think that you are there, too, for we are in choir until eight-thirty or so and since your day is five hours earlier than ours, it seems that we find ourselves together singing the praises of God. It delights me that you love humility. Indeed, you needed it as much as I did, for the world had really made us prideful. Always preserve your love for this precious virtue; it is the solid foundation without which the whole edifice of the perfection that you want to erect in your soul would be ruinous and short-lived. Finally, remain in the consolation that we are both God's servants, which is the noblest of all qualities and what we ought to love most. Let us remain in Jesus and see each other in him.

Letter 73: September 30, 1643

My very dear and beloved son,

May the love and life of the king of nations consume your heart by the fire with which he ravishes the hearts of our neophytes. You should by now have received the letters I wrote you last July, in which I gave you a short account of what happened this year in our New France and in the new church of Jesus Christ. I had not yet received your letters, but my Mother Saint-Bernard had sent me the one in which you complained to her that you had not received any from me last year. I had written you much, but what one entrusts to the sea is subject to chance.

This is why such things are to be expected, my very dear son, but to remedy the situation somewhat, I have resolved to write to you, as long as I shall live, by two different ships, so that if one is lost or captured by pirates, the other will bring you my news. Do the same yourself, if obedience permits, for you can imagine that our contentment will be mutual in this regard.

But we must not waste time. Let's begin speaking about our neophytes. The first foundations of the Church were laid this year at Miscou, which is a French settlement, established only for the fur trade. Ten leagues beyond, a chapel was built and a great mission established for the Indians of the north coast, who were attracted to the faith by conversation with our Montagnais Indians from Tadoussac. This mission promises great fruits, for the subjects are well-disposed. This place is one hundred fifty leagues from here in your direction.

One hundred leagues from there is the mission of Tadoussac, where marvels were seen this year. A great number of Indians journeyed by land for more than twenty days, having come there in order to receive instruction and then baptism. They have such religious sentiments and perform such Christian actions that they shame us and surpass us in piety. These are the fruits of the zeal of our good sedentary Christians,[37] for they go here and there for the express purpose of winning souls for Jesus Christ. All these nations are from the north coast, and Tadoussac, where they gather, is forty leagues or so from here on the way to Miscou.

Sillery is located one league above Quebec, and we are in the middle. Some of our sedentary Indians are there and some are in Quebec, where trading goes on.[38]

Last year, the nation of the Attikameks came here in order to receive instruction, and more than half were baptized.[39] The first baptism was done in our church as well as the first wedding, for when the man and woman were baptized, they were married at the same time, in front of the church. After this, many were baptized and married. I must confess to you that the joy my heart feels when I see a soul washed in the blood of Jesus Christ is inexplicable. Every day, these good people received instruction in our chapel. Following mass, we provided them with a feast of peas or sagamite of Indian corn with some prunes, after which

---

with her son is that between what Marie deemed Claude's excessive enthusiasm for the solitary life and Marie's own conviction in the spiritual value of the active life—which, as Marie understood it, was in no way antithetical to the practice of contemplation. See, for example, Letters 217 and 267.

37. Sedentary Amerindians—in contrast to their nomadic counterparts—lived in permanent dwellings and were the primary targets of early Christian missionary efforts in New France.

38. Thwaites, *Jesuit Relations*, vol. 23, 302–18.

39. Thwaites, *Jesuit Relations*, vol. 24, 65–101.

they would stay practically all day at our grill in order to receive instruction or learn some prayer.⁴⁰ It was prodigious to see how quickly and easily they learned everything we taught them. One poor woman who was a bit more thick-headed than the others got angry at herself and said, while prostrating herself, "I will not get up from this day forward until I know my prayers." She remained all day with her mouth against the ground, and God so blessed her fervor that when she got up, she knew everything that she wanted to learn. The fervor is universal, and we are delighted to see great men eagerly coming to find us, so that we can teach them how to do interior acts and say jaculatory prayers, which they use in their meetings.⁴¹

The chief of this nation was a great sorcerer and the most superstitious man in the world. I heard him defending the virtue of his spells and superstitions, and shortly after, he came to find the Father with whom he had argued, and brought him his spells and the drum he used in his charms and protested that he never wanted to use them again. I am sending you this drum so that you can see how the devil entertains and seduces these poor people with a child's instrument, for you will know that it serves to cure illnesses, to foretell things to come, and to do similar extraordinary things. After this change, we had the consolation of seeing all the drums of this nation sacrificed to God in a single day.⁴² They have all returned to their country on the hunt, so that they will arrive there in spring.

---

40. Thwaites, *Jesuit Relations*, vol. 23, 313. The *Jesuit Relations* contain numerous references to and descriptions of sagamite, consisting of "cornmeal cooked in water, and seasoned with fat" to which meats, vegetables, and other ingredients were typically added; Thwaites, *Jesuit Relations*, vol. 49, 31.

41. Repeatedly throughout her correspondence with Claude, Marie alludes to the preternatural piety of indigenous Christians—and often as a foil to their French counterparts. See, for example, Letters 80 and 97. For a discussion of representations of the Amerindian as a critique of the Western, European self, see Robert F. Berkhofer, Jr., *The White Man's Indian: Images of the American Indian from Columbus to the Present* (New York: Knopf, 1978). See also Allan Greer, "Colonial Saints: Gender, Race, and Hagiography in New France," *William and Mary Quarterly* 57 (2000): 323–48, and Greer, *Mohawk Saint: Catherine Tekakwitha and the Jesuits* (New York: Oxford University Press, 2005). A symptom of the more general bifurcated representation of the "savage Other" in early modern colonial discourse, Marie's marveling praise of the devout convert contrasts with her unforgiving condemnation of the demonic infidel—and sometimes within the space of a single letter. See, for example, Letter 97. See also Letter 142. For an analysis of the split image of the Amerindian native in the *Jesuit Relations*, see Pierre Hurtubise, "Le Bon et le Mauvais Sauvage," *Eglise et Theologie* 10 (1979): 223–37. See also Réal Ouellet with Mylene Tremblay, "From the Good Savage to the Degenerate Indian: the Amerindian in Accounts of Travel to America," in *De-centring the Renaissance: Canada and America in Multidisciplinary Perspective, 1500–1700*, ed. Germaine Warkentin and Carolyn Podruchny, 159–70 (Toronto: University of Toronto Press, 2001).

42. Thwaites, *Jesuit Relations*, vol. 24, 71, 85–91. Marie's invocation of the devil here gestures toward the ways in which for Marie powers both divine and demonic were at work in New

And because they were newly instructed, one of our new Christian women from Sillery has gone with them, in the cold of a most horrible snow, to make them repeat their prayers daily lest they forget them.[43] We have learned that they are leading an admirable life.

It is a marvel to see the fervor of our good neophytes. They are not content to believe in Jesus Christ. Rather, zeal so overcomes them that they are not satisfied, and think that they only half-believe if everyone does not believe like them. The chief of the Abenakis left his country and his people to come settle here, so that he could receive instruction and then be able to attract his people to the faith of Jesus Christ.[44] He was baptized yesterday and married to one of our seminarians named Angelle, about whom the *Relation* spoke with praise last year.[45] His zeal will carry him much further, for he has resolved to bring the gospel to many other nations. "I will not be content," he told me, "with bringing my people and my youths to the faith and to prayer, but since I have been in many nations where I know the language, I will use this advantage to go visit them and lead them to belief in God."

The men are not the only ones afire with this zeal. A Christian woman traveled to a quite distant nation for the express purpose of catechizing those who lived there. She succeeded so well that she led them all here, where they were baptized. She must have had an apostolic courage to face the dangers to which she was exposed for the purpose of thus serving our Lord. We often see similar fervors in our good neophytes, who truly shame those born of Christian parents.

France. See Dominique Deslandres, "'Le Diable a beau fair...' Marie de l'Incarnation, Satan, et l'Autre," *Théologiques* 5 (1997): 23–41. Marie's apparently genuine conviction in the agency of the devil and the reality of demonic forces in New France contrasts with what Peter Goddard contends about the worldview of seventeenth-century Jesuits in Canada. For the Jesuits—members of France's educated elite, proponents of a rational neoscholasticism, close companions of the indigenous people among whom they lived and worked—native beliefs and practices were the consequences not of demonic manipulation but ignorance and superstition; see Peter A. Goddard, "The Devil in New France: Jesuit Demonology, 1611–1650," *Canadian Historical Review* 78, no. 1 (March 1997): 40–62. See also Hurtubise, "Le Bon et le Mauvais Sauvage." For a study of demonology in early modern Europe generally, see Stuart Clark, *Thinking with Demons: The Idea of Witchcraft in Early Modern Europe* (Oxford: Clarendon Press, 1997). For a recent discussion of demonology in the New World, see Jorge Cañizares-Esguerra, *Puritan Conquistadors: Iberianizing the Atlantic, 1550–1700* (Stanford: Stanford University Press, 2006).

43. This woman, an Algonquin named Angélique, merits mention as well in Thwaites, *Jesuit Relations*, vol. 24, 95.

44. Here, I follow Oury who identifies the Abnakiouois in this passage as the Abenakis.

45. Thwaites, *Jesuit Relations*, vol. 22, 113–23.

There is not a person of note among the Hurons who doesn't want to be Christian. Four chapels were built there this year, and before that, they had a difficult time tolerating even one. The Iroquois nevertheless singularly persecute this poor nation. They have captured and killed a great number of Hurons over the past two years, and fifteen days ago, they also defeated their fleet.[46] You know that last year they seized Reverend Father Jogues and some Frenchmen and some Hurons with one of our seminarians.[47] They killed the old ones and carried away the other captives. The Reverend Father was beaten black and blue and stripped naked upon arriving in their country. They cut off his thumb and bit off his index finger down to the knuckle, burned the tips of his other fingers, and then made him suffer a thousand other ignominies. They did the same to a Frenchman his servant, and another who also belonged to him had his head cracked open by a hatchet blow. The poor Father, believing that they would do the same to him, knelt to receive the blow and to offer his sacrifice, but they did nothing more to him. They did to most of the other captives as they had done to him, then let them live. They did nothing to our seminarian Thérèse, who throughout courageously professed the holy gospel and prayed out loud.[48] At present, the Reverend Father is preaching the gospel there. He is the first to have this honor, and God so blesses his work that he has already baptized more than sixty people during his captivity.

I must speak a bit about our sedentary seminarians, who give us all possible contentment. One said to me some time ago, "I speak often to God in my heart. I take great pleasure in saying the names of Jesus and Mary. Ah, how beautiful are these names!" We hear them sometimes speaking about God and having spiritual discussions. Among other things one day, they asked each other for what they felt most obliged to God. One said, "It is because he was made man for me and endured death to deliver me from hell." The other responded, "It is because he made me a Christian and placed me by baptism among the number of his children." A little one who is not more than nine years old and has been receiving communion for a year and a half raised her voice and said, "It is because Jesus gives himself to us as the meat of the Holy Sacrament at the altar."[49] Is this not delightful in girls born in barbarity?

They do not neglect to examine their consciences or accuse each other, which they do with an unparalleled ingenuity. They sometimes ask to be punished, in

---

46. Thwaites, *Jesuit Relations*, vol. 24, 269–95.

47. Thwaites, *Jesuit Relations*, vol. 23, 247–9; vol. 24, 279–81, 297–303.

48. Thwaites, *Jesuit Relations*, vol. 23, 295–7.

49. Thwaites, *Jesuit Relations*, vol. 23, 293–5.

order to already compensate God, while still in this world, for the pain of the sins they have committed. One, having been corrected, was asked what she had thought of her punishment, "I thought," she said, "that because I am loved, I am disciplined so that the spirit will come to me, for I do not have it. I, who have been instructed, am much guiltier than my companion, who did wrong and yet was not instructed."

You see what our tasks are. I beg you to take great care of the kingdom of Jesus Christ. Pray for the conversion of the Iroquois, who do great harm to it and block the way there, because they fear that the most distant nations might come to receive instruction. The nation of Iroquet has not ceased traversing the lands of these barbarians, who have shot at them more than a hundred times, but God has protected them so well that not a single one has been wounded.[50] I am writing you at night on account of the number of the letters and the ships that are about to leave.[51] My hand is so weary that I can hardly guide it, and because of this, I finish by begging you to excuse me if I do not reread my letter.

Letter 80: August 26, 1644

My very dear and beloved son,[52]

Your letters brought me an inexpressible consolation. I mean your two letters that I received in July. The ships arrived earlier than usual and brought us back the Reverend Fathers Quentin and Jogues, the latter, by a very particular providence of God, having been rescued by the Dutch who inhabit the coasts of the Iroquois country I told you about last year. They boarded him on a ship and sent him to France, which they had been strictly ordered to do by the queen. Thus, God has given us a true living martyr who bears on his body the wounds of Jesus Christ. The arrival of these Fathers brought us such joy as you might imagine. The poor Father would likely have been burned upon returning to his village if the Dutch, who were warned about it, had not rushed to the rescue. He told me about the

---

50. Thwaites, *Jesuit Relations*, vol. 24, 291–3.

51. Estimates of the number of letters Marie wrote over the course of her lifetime range from 3000 to 20,000, which would put the annual number of letters somewhere between 60 and 400 (an admittedly expansive range). Given that Marie had to pen most of her correspondence during the summer months, between the time the ships arrived (typically July) and when they departed (typically August)—and this in the midst of carrying out her active apostolate of teaching and fulfilling her responsibilities as superior, among other things—one can sympathize with the weariness to which she admits.

52. In 1644, Claude was sent to the abbey at Jumièges to begin his studies in philosophy and theology. He would remain at Jumièges until 1648.

very particular operations of God upon him during his captivity. There are thousands of martyrs who have died at less cost. Imagine the most ignominious things that a chaste person can be made to suffer—he suffered them. I don't know if the *Relations* made or will make mention of them. I'm going to tell you about just one episode of his travails.

After awful beatings, which made him look like a monster left for dead, after having chopped off two of his fingers and burned and bitten the others, they paraded him naked from village to village, theater to theater. In the midst of a great crowd, they hung him in the air by the thick of his arms, from two large and very high stakes, binding him as tightly as possible with willow ropes. He was in this torment for such a long time that it was greater and more painful to him than all the others, because of the weight of his body against such tight ropes. They tightened the ropes anew when they saw that this increased his torment. A barbarian from another quite distant village couldn't stand this and, moved by a natural compassion, untied him when he was nearly dead. See how God rewarded this man. After all the Father's torments, the Iroquois gave him to a family who took care of him and had affection for him (that is to say, they did him no harm) and allowed him to pray to God. (They call that magic, and a Frenchman who accompanied the Father was martyred for it.) Then these people took the Father everywhere they went, and by this means he baptized all the sick children and the adults, too. Thus, he sent many souls to heaven. While traveling, he passed through the village of the man who had untied him, and without thinking about him, he went into his cabin to see as usual whether he might do any good. When the Father was leaving, this poor man who was in a corner called to him and said, "And how, my brother, could you have no pity on me? Don't you know I saved your life, untying you from your torment? I am dying. Help me." The Father, as astonished as he was joyous, instructed him and baptized him, and he died right away. Thus he gained heaven on account of his natural compassion, and for the corporeal life he had given to the Father, he merited for his soul eternal life.[53] Is that not an admirable providence? He [Father Jogues] took advantage of a number of unforeseen opportunities to send a great number of souls to heaven. He is admirably humble, which reveals his great sanctity. And even when he was captive, his great modesty elicited the admiration of the barbarians, and they thought him more of a man.

To respond to what you want to know about this country, I will tell you, my very dear son, that there are houses of stone, wood, and bark. Our own is made of stone. It is ninety-two feet long and twenty-eight feet wide. It is the most

---

53. Thwaites, *Jesuit Relations*, vol. 31, 87–9.

beautiful and the biggest in Canada of its style. It includes the church, which is as long as the house is wide, and is itself seventeen feet wide. Perhaps you will think that this is small, but the extreme cold doesn't permit a more substantial space. There are times when the priests' hands and ears are in danger of freezing. Our choir, the seminary, and our quarters are together, I say, ninety-two feet long and twenty-eight feet wide. The fort is made of stone and its outlying houses are, too. Those of the Reverend Fathers, of Madame our foundress, the Hospitaller nuns and the sedentary Indians are of stone, those of the settlers, of *colombage pierrotté*.[54] Two or three also are of pure stone. Some of the Indians have portable houses made of birch bark, which they set up quite neatly with poles. In the beginning, we had one of the same kind for our classes. Do not think that our houses are made of big stones. No, only the cornerstones are big. The cornerstones are made of a type of stone like a variety of nearly black marble, which is extracted in blocks; these blocks are quite neatly cut, better than the rough stone of France. These cornerstones are very beautiful, but they cost a lot to cut because the stone is so hard. One man costs thirty *sols* a day, and we feed him on feasts and Sundays and bad weather.[55] We get our workers from France, and we engage them for three or more years.[56] We have ten of them who make all our stuff for us, except that the settlers furnish us with lime, sand, and brick. Our house has

---

54. "Madame our foundress" is Madeleine de la Peltrie, described by Dom Guy-Marie Oury as courageous, impractical, generous, and spirited, whose economic support made possible the foundation of the Ursulines in New France. For more on de la Peltrie, see Dom Guy-Marie Oury, *Madame de la Peltrie et ses fondations canadiennes* (Quebec: Presses de l'Université Laval, 1974). The *colombage pierrotté* architectural style to which Marie refers describes timber-frame constructions in which stones or rubble mixed with clay or lime plaster were packed between the posts.

55. In Marie de l'Incarnation's New France, one *sol* was worth twelve *deniers* and twenty *sols* were worth one *livre*. Although it is, of course, impossible to determine the exact value of the *sol* in today's currency, a comparison between the daily wages paid to an unskilled laborer in seventeenth-century Canada (about thirty *sols*) and those paid to his counterpart in twenty-first-century Canada (about one hundred dollars) is instructive.

56. Throughout the seventeenth century, the system of indentured servitude played a key role in the population of the nascent colony. Usually poor, male, and single, indentured servants (or *engagés*) typically bound themselves to their employers for three-year terms of service in exchange for food, clothing, shelter, and annual salaries of approximately sixty *livres*. At the expiration of their terms of service, many *engagés* opted to settle in New France (whether enticed to stay by liberal grants of land promised by the French king or deterred from leaving by the prohibitive cost of transatlantic travel). For discussions of labor conditions and the engagé system in seventeenth-century New France, see Allan Greer, *The People of New France* (Toronto: University of Toronto Press, 1997), 72–5; and Peter Moogk, "Reluctant Exiles: Emigrants from France in Canada before 1760," *William and Mary Quarterly* 46, no. 3 (July 1989): 473–88. See also Louise Dechêne, *Habitants and Merchants in Seventeenth-Century Montreal*, trans. Liana Vardi (Montreal: McGill-Queen's University Press, 1992).

three floors. Our cells are on the middle one and are made like those in France. Our fireplace is at the end of the dormitory in order to heat the corridor and the cells, which are separated only by pine wood. It is impossible to get warm there otherwise, for don't think that in the winter we can stay in our cells for long without heat. It would be too much to stay there even for an hour, and still we must keep our hands under wraps and our bodies well-covered. Apart from the observances, we ordinarily have to do our reading, writing, and studying next to the fire, which is an inconvenience and an extreme submission, particularly for me, who never warmed myself in France. Our beds are made of wood and close like an armoire. Although we line them with blankets or wool, it is difficult to get warm there. In the winter, our Indians leave their stone houses and go to live in cabins in the woods where it's not quite as cold. We light five or six logs at a time, for we burn only thick wood, and thus we warm ourselves on one side, but on the other we freeze. With four fireplaces, we burn 175 cords of wood during the year, six months of which is winter. Despite the severity of the cold, we keep choir all winter long, but we suffer there a bit. Our fence is not made of stones, but only of big stakes of whole trees ten feet high, brought together in a frame. Neither the country nor our poverty can yet permit such a great expense. In brief, the fences here are absolutely minimal, except that of the fort—which is so large that it is not yet finished even after six years.[57] The roofs of the houses are made of double planks or shingles with planks underneath.

The Indians are clothed.[58] In the summer they wear large moose skins, squared like a blanket and as large as the skin of an ox, which they throw over

---

57. Marie's description of her enclosure as "minimal" raises intriguing questions about the nature of the cloister in the New World, in particular, and about the enforcement of Tridentine norms and decrees abroad more generally. See Elizabeth C. Goldsmith, *Publishing Women's Life Stories in France, 1647–1720: From Voice to Print* (Aldershot, UK: Ashgate, 2001), 22–9. In 1563, the Council of Trent mandated the strict enclaustration of religious women. The degree to which the requirement of strict enclosure erected an impermeable boundary between the convent and the outside world, however, varied from place to place and from time to time. See, for example, Elizabeth Lehfeldt, *Religious Women in Golden Age Spain: the Permeable Cloister* (Aldershot, UK: Ashgate, 2005); Claire Walker: "'Doe not suppose me a well mortified nun dead to the world': Letter-writing in Early Modern English Convents," in *Early Modern Women's Letter Writing*, ed. Daybell, 159–76. The relative freedom afforded by the distance from Rome together with the practical benefits active religious women brought to nascent European colonies in the New World, in particular, meant a relaxation of the norms of enclosure in fact. See, Rapley, *Dévotes*, 100–12; Emily Clark, *Masterless Mistresses: The New Orleans Ursulines and the Development of a New World Society, 1727–1834* (Chapel Hill: University of North Carolina Press, 2007), 127–60; and Clark, "A New World Community: the New Orleans Ursulines and Colonial Society, 1727–1803" (PhD diss., Tulane University, 1998), 252–81.

58. Claude, like his contemporaries, seems to have labored under the conviction—or at least the suspicion—that the Amerindians of New France were naked. The curious fixation of early

their shoulders. They attach it with little pieces of leather, such that their arms are naked and exposed at the sides. They have only that and a girdle—their feet and heads are naked. When they are at their homes in the country, and when they fight against their enemies, they are as naked as one's hand, except for the girdle which hides them rather modestly. Their skin is the color of the habits of the Minims, because of the sun and the grease with which they rub themselves almost all over, and their faces are ornamented with red and blue stripes.[59] In winter, their robes consist of bed blankets adapted like those mentioned above, and they have sleeves of the same and leggings of leather or worn-out blankets, which go up to their waists. They have robes made of beaver, its fur serving as a coat. Those who cover their heads trade for red night caps in the commissary. Sometimes they also wear capots or hats with ear flaps. They have robes. When the Fathers forget, we give them some. So much for those who are well dressed. But there are some Indians who are nearly naked at all times, on account of their poverty. As for the women, they are quite modestly attired. They always have belts (for the men almost never have any and their robes blow open at the will of the wind). Their robes reach down to the middle of their legs and go up as high as their necks. Their arms and heads are almost always covered by a men's red night cap or a hat with ear flaps or a cap, their hair pulled down around their faces and bound up from behind. They are quite modest and discreet. We make little tunics for our seminarians and fix their hair in the French style. Were it not for the way they wear their robes, one could hardly distinguish the men from the women, for their faces are similar.[60] Their shoes are made out of moose hide, which is like that of a buffalo. They gather these up by the tips and put a square piece of hide at the

---

modern Europeans on the question of native dress or undress suggests an easy equation between clothing and civilization. See Tzvetan Todorov, *The Conquest of America* (New York: Harper & Rowe, 1984), 35; Berkhofer, *White Man's Indian*, 15, 28; Philippa Levin, "States of Undress: Nakedness and the Colonial Imagination," *Victorian Studies* 50, no. 2 (Winter 2008): 189–219; Louise Montrose, "The Work of Gender in the Discourse of Discovery," in *New World Encounters*, ed. Stephen Greenblatt, 177–217 (Berkeley: University of California Press, 1993). For a recent study of the centrality of material culture to discourses on race within the context of early modern French colonialism, see Sophie White, *Wild Frenchmen and Frenchified Indians* (Philadelphia: University of Pennsylvania Press, 2013).

59. Members of the Order of the Minimi, or Minims, founded by Francis de Paula in the fifteenth century, are known for their radical commitment to humility and their habit consisting of coarse black wool. See, P. J. S. Whitmore, *The Order of Minims in Seventeenth-Century France* (The Hague: Martinus Mijhoff, 1967).

60. Marie's effacement of gender distinctions in this instance—elaborated elsewhere by allusions to the virile native woman and the effeminate indigenous man—testifies to the persistence of an enduring trope of colonial discourse which renders the Amerindian so radically Other as to defy received categories of male and female. See, Robert J. C. Young, *Colonial Desire: Hybridity in Theory, Culture, and Race* (London: Routledge, 1995), 85–110; Sara

heel. Through this, they thread a small strap as one does with a purse. Thus do they make their shoes. The French wear the same kind in the winter, particularly because one can't go out except with snowshoes on one's feet for walking on the snow, and these don't accommodate French shoes. As for us, we have nothing to do with that. There you have what you desire to know on this score.

Is our community big? It's big enough for now. We have eight choir sisters and one converse.[61] There are four choir sisters from our house in Tours and four from the Congregation in Paris. The converse is from Dieppe. I will speak to you elsewhere about this. The Hospitaller Mothers have only five choir sisters and one converse.[62]

Are our Indians as perfect as I told you? When it comes to manners, they have no French *politesse*, which is to say that they don't know how to give compliments and aren't familiar with French customs.[63] We aren't concerned with that, but with thoroughly teaching them the commandments of God and the Church, all the points of our faith, all the prayers, how to examine their consciences properly and all other religious practices. An Indian makes his confession as well as a male or female religious. They are as artless as can be, making much out of the

---

Mills, *Discourses of Difference: An Analysis of Women's Travel Writing and Colonialism* (London: Routledge, 1991); and Cornelius Jaenen, "Amerindian Views of French Culture in the Seventeenth-Century," *Canadian Historical Review* 55, no. 3 (1974): 261–91. It is important to note, however, that the trope of the virile woman was a common one in Christian hagiography too. See Barbara Newman, *From Virile Woman to Woman Christ: Studies in Medieval Religion and Literature* (Philadelphia: University of Pennsylvania Press, 1995). The trope of the virile woman in Marie de l'Incarnation's epistolary corpus also presents an intriguing analogue to the figure of the *femme forte* in seventeenth-century French literature. See Letters 179, 183, and 246. For a discussion of the *femme forte* and an analysis of Marie de l'Incarnation as such, see Tamara Harvey, *Figuring Modesty in Feminist Discourse Across the Americas: 1633–1700* (Aldershot, UK: Ashgate, 2008), 113–40. See also Natalie Zemon Davis, *Women on the Margins: Three Seventeenth-Century Lives* (Cambridge: Harvard University Press, 1995), 117–22.

61. The distinction between choir nuns and converse nuns was one of function and privilege as well as, in most cases, age and social class. Choir nuns (who took solemn vows, sang divine office, and enjoyed the authority to vote on community affairs and hold leadership positions) tended to make their professions while still teenagers and to come from among the noblesse or emerging bourgeoisie. By way of contrast, converse nuns (bound by only simple vows and responsible for the domestic matters of the convent) entered religious life at an average age of 24.5 and were usually of much humbler origins. See Elizabeth Rapley, "Women and the Religious Vocation in Seventeenth-Century France," *French Historical Studies* 18, no. 3 (Spring 1994): 617, 621.

62. The Hospitaller sisters, members of the Augustinian order, founded Quebec's Hôtel Dieu in 1639. The *Jesuit Relations* discuss the activities of the Hospitaller nuns. See, for example, Thwaites, *Jesuit Relations*, vol. 36, 167.

63. For a discussion of the significance of politesse within the cultural context of seventeenth-century France, see Jean Starobinski, "Le mot civilisation," in *Le remède dans le*

littlest things, and when they have sinned, they do public penances with great humility. Here is an example. The Indians have no other drink except broth from their boiled sagamite, whether of meat or Indian corn or from boiled bones or water. The French having offered them brandy or wine to drink, they find they quite like it, but it takes only one drink to make them crazy and furious. This is because they eat only mild things and never salty ones. This drink is killing them, and this is what obliged Monsieur our governor to prohibit the French from giving it or trading it to them upon penalty of large fines.[64] Nevertheless, when the ships arrive, it is impossible to prevent the sailors from trading it to them in secret. The older Indians and the young of their families do not partake in any of this, nor do those who are good Christians, but only the youth. It happened this year that some of them got drunk.[65] The elders, together with the Father of this mission, fined them a certain number of beaver pelts to be used to buy something to adorn the chapel, and in addition barred them from entering the church for three days and ordered them, the innocent as well as the guilty, to go twice a day to say prayers at the church door in order that they might obtain mercy and appease he who made everything. Others are making a public confession in the church of the French and voicing their faults out loud. Still others are fasting for three days on bread and water. Since they rarely commit such excesses, so also are these penances rare.

The Indians are like the French—some are more or less devout than others, but generally speaking, they are more devout than the French. We do not settle them in the French villages lest they imitate the French, although the French are pretty sober in this country. No matter how respectable they are, however, the Indians are not capable of the liberty of the French.

Madame our foundress, who is extremely zealous, visited the mission of Tadoussac this year, which is thirty-five leagues from here and where the

---

Mal: Critique et légitimation de l'artifice à l'âge des Lumières (Paris: Gallimard, 1989), 11–59. See also Peter France, "Polish, Police, Polis," in *Politeness and its Discontents: Problems in French Classical Culture* (Cambridge University Press, 1992), 53–73.

64. The conflict over the brandy trade would prove a persistent one throughout the early history of the French colony, pitting ecclesiastic authorities (who found the trade disruptive to the missionary project) against merchants (for whom the trade eased and made more profitable commercial transactions) and sometimes civil authorities (whose interests were, in part, aligned with those of the merchants). For a recent study of the problem of alcohol among early modern Amerindians, see Peter C. Mancall, *Deadly Medicine: Indians and Alcohol in Early America* (Ithaca: Cornell University Press, 1995). For a discussion of the role of the Church in the conflict over the brandy trade, see Cornelius Jaenen, *The Role of the Church in New France* (Toronto: McGraw-Hill Ryerson, 1976), 77–82; W. J. Eccles, *The Canadian Frontier, 1534–1760* (Albuquerque: University of New Mexico Press, 1983). See also Letters 204 and 254.

65. Thwaites, *Jesuit Relations*, vol. 24, 145–7.

Christians lead quite exemplary lives. Many have also been baptized. Over there, our people found a great number of Indians who were living deep in the woods. They instructed them and made them capable of holy baptism. This good lady was delighted to see such great fervor in people who, from father to son, had been brought up in brutality. They had come for the sole purpose of being baptized. The French who were there (for this is where the fleet from France which brings us all the necessities for the country anchors and docks) cried with joy to see wolves become lambs and beasts children of God. Fathers incite their children and children their fathers to see who will be the most fervent. They are touched particularly by God and we frequently hear them at our grill discussing what weighs on their hearts. Here is an example. Before leaving to go to war against the Iroquois, the chief of the Indians of Sillery came to see me and said, "My mother, this is what I am thinking. I have come to see you to tell you that we are going to look for our enemies. It doesn't matter if they kill us. For a long time they have even been capturing and killing our friends the French and those who instruct us. We are going to war not because they are killing us but because they are killing our friends. Pray for us, for we have offended God and he is punishing us. The youth are not wise. I tell them, "You are angering God and he is punishing us, reform yourselves and he will be pacified. A certain N. (who had committed a moral wrong) committed such a wrong again. I begged the great chief of the French and the Father Superior to banish him from among us because he is attracting the devil here. This is where our misfortunes are coming from. They said to me, 'Wait until springtime and he will reform himself.' They are too good to have waited, because he didn't reform himself. Pray for us, all of you, for we do not know what will happen to us on account of our offenses." He is a true saint and the second to be baptized among all the Indians.[66] He is blameless. In a public speech he

---

66. Although we must remind ourselves that the heterogeneity and historical contingencies of colonial discourses belies the possibility of identifying a single "Jesuit" or "French" or "early modern" anthropology of the "Indian," in its broad strokes Marie's anthropology of the Amerindian resonates with that of her Jesuit peers and with her early modern counterparts, more generally. For a comparisons of representations of Amerindian women in the *Jesuit Relations* and in the writings of Marie de l'Incarnation, see Marie-Florine Bruneau, *Women Mystics Confront the Modern World: Marie de l'Incarnation (1599–1672) and Madame Guyon (1648–1717)* (Albany: State University of New York Press, 1998), 103–14; and Davis, *Women on the Margins*, 117–20. Allan Greer has written persuasively on the question of gender in early modern New France and the Christian missions; see Greer, "Colonial Saints" and *Mohawk Saint*. For more general studies of the ways in which gender impacted the composition of colonial narratives, see Shirley Foster, *Across New Worlds: Nineteenth-Century Women Travelers and their Writings* (New York: Harvester Wheatsheaf, 1990); Lisa Lowe, *Critical Terrains: French and British Orientalisms* (Ithaca: Cornell University Press, 1991); and Mills, *Discourses of Difference*.

made to his people in the church where the Reverend Father de Quen had remonstrated the youth, this good man raised his voice and made a general confession out loud (the Father was not aware of what he wanted to do) and mentioned all the wrongs he had committed over the past seven or eight years that he had been a Christian, adding, "My brothers, it is I who have attracted all the misfortunes that are happening to you. You see how ungrateful I am for God's graces—see the sins I have committed since I have been his child. But still he is good. Take courage, don't despair. If we serve him, he will have mercy on us...," and several other quite touching things.

A good woman who came to our grill begged Mother Marie de Saint-Joseph to instruct her about the holy sacrament, for, she said, it has been a long time since I last attended public prayers. And as someone was instructing her, she replied, "That's just what I had been taught and had forgotten. You oblige me by making me remember it." And then she said, "God is giving me many graces. In the past, the death of my children so afflicted me that nothing could console me, but now I am so convinced of the wisdom and goodness of God that if he took all of them away from me, I wouldn't be sad. I think to myself, if my child needed a longer life to better secure his salvation, he who made everything wouldn't refuse him this, given that he is so good and that nothing is impossible for him. But since he calls my child to himself, I must therefore say that since he knows everything, he sees that perhaps my child would stop believing in him and commit sins that would cast him into hell. I then say to him, 'Determine my fate, you who made everything, and the fate of all my children, too. No matter how you test me, I will never stop believing in you, loving you, and obeying you. I want what you want.' And afterwards, I say to my children whom I see dying, 'Go, my child, go to heaven to see he who made everything. When you are there, pray for me that I may go there, too. When you die, I will pray for your soul so that you will soon leave purgatory." This good woman once came to me to recite a long prayer she had composed for the warriors. The insistent words she said to God moved me. Her name is Louise. It seems that since her baptism, God is pleasing himself by taking away her children, one after another.

By these few words, you see the sentiments of our good Christians. Their consciences are quite tender. This winter, a young man and his wife took their child on the hunt, where he died. They were so afraid of displeasing God, by burying him in land that had not been blessed, that over the course of three or four months, his mother constantly carried him around her neck, by rocky chasms, through the woods, snow, and ice, with unparalleled effort. They came back, properly, to observe Easter and had their child buried bundled in a skin.

I told you in my earlier letter that the faith is taking deep root in the nations to the north and among the Hurons. I just received news of it from Reverend Father

Chaumonot, whom you saw in Paris with Father Poncet. Here is what he says: In the five principle Huron towns we have built chapels where one can always find our Fathers. If conversions continue for these next two winters as they have for the two previous ones, we hope that the Christians will become the majority in these five towns and that, in a short time, they will attract not only all their fellow townspeople, but the rest of the country as well, and even the entire Huron nation.

I told you in my previous letter how the Iroquois captured one of our Reverend Fathers and several Christians, French as well as Indians, of whom five were killed and two burned alive. Life is but a little thing, but the cruelty that these barbarians inflict upon their victims is horrible. Given the weakness to which the spirit is sometimes subject, we fear that our poor Christians will despair, for there is no one there to console and encourage them. In the name of God, recommend them to all my Reverend Fathers of your holy house. Three hundred fugitive Indians have taken refuge next to our little house this winter. They were instructed in our chapel, except those who were not yet ready to hear about God. Apart from this initial instruction, the women and girls came to our classroom and the men to our parlor and, after restoring their souls, we attempted to restore their bodies. Monsieur our Governor gave quite charitably to them at that time. He is the most charitable person one can ever imagine. All the poor people had thought they were going to die from hunger. These corporeal restorations we give them are like charms that attract them and tame them much, but our own needs and poverty don't permit us to do what we would like. This is what constrains me to ask for charity from our friends in France, not for us, but for the poor Indians, or rather for Jesus Christ. Sedentary nations have been discovered who, having heard about God and seen Christians in their country performing religious acts, do likewise and wish for gospel workers. But because the ways there have been blocked by the enemies of God, they are held back. Nevertheless three have risked going to the Hurons in order to go further up from there, for these nations are yet three hundred leagues beyond. Now, there are five hundred leagues between here and the Hurons, but if the way there was free, the distance would be half as long.

Never grow tired of prostrating yourself at the feet of the king of all the nations. He died for all and all do not yet live. Alas! My very dear son, if I was worthy of running about everywhere to try and win some soul for him, my heart would be satisfied. Is it not distressing to see the demons holding such an absolute authority over all the people? Let us go together in spirit and try to deliver someone from among them to our good master. You will do as much in your solitude as if you were actually present there.[67] The eternal Father has revealed to a certain someone that

---

67. In suggesting to Claude that, through contemplative prayer, he could contribute to the success of the missionary enterprise, Marie sounds a Teresian note. Although she accepted

if she asks him by the heart of his Son, he will give her everything she wants.[68] Let's ask him for souls for the amplification of his kingdom. I beg you, let us be jealous that his enemy possesses them. It is this enemy who animates the Iroquois who, at present, are the greatest impediment to his glory in this country, apart from my own wickedness. But on this point, find for me friends close to God, I beg you, especially among my Reverend Fathers, whom I greet with humility. I ask them for their holy blessing and to participate in their holy sacrifices and holy prayers. I am not worthy to belong intimately to them, or even to have a part of myself among them.

As for you, I am ever with you at God's side. Let us remain, therefore, in this vast ocean and live here below while waiting for the eternity in which we will truly see each other. Farewell.

Letter 81: August 30, 1644

Jesus, Mary, Joseph
My very dear and beloved son,
May the life and love of Jesus forever be your strength and your all!

If you have felt joy upon receiving the letters I wrote you, don't doubt that I felt likewise upon receiving yours, which reveal to me God's providence, love, and mercy upon you, for which I will praise him eternally. Yes, he wants you to love him. So begin now, and believe today that you didn't truly love him yesterday, since the stages of this holy torment are such that one only sees what is before oneself as perfect and what is behind as defective. Take good care and you will see this, my very dear son. Perhaps you will say to me, how can you walk in the footsteps and live in the cells of so many saints, if you don't imitate their examples? Good works follow the saints and they are all before you. Run, therefore, without stopping, my son, until you reach the king of the saints, who wants you more for himself than you want him for yourself. The saints are saints only because they have stubbornly insisted upon forgetting everything by willingly having contempt for themselves, in order to attach themselves to this divine prototype and true exemplary cause for his children.[69] I have sometimes wondered whether

---

enclosure, Teresa of Ávila envisioned her Carmelite vocation as one of an active apostolate of prayer and with very real effects in the world and, in particular, the mission field. See Jodi Bilinkoff, "Woman with a Mission: Teresa of Avila and the Apostolic Model," in *Modelli di Santità e modelli di comportamento*, ed. Marina Caffiero et al., 295–305 (Turin: Rosenberg & Sellier: 1994). Marie, likewise, seems to have imagined her own vocation similarly. See Letter 97 and *Relation de 1654*, 309–13.

68. *Relation de 1654*, 315.

69. The understanding of God as "exemplary cause" is owed to the influence of Thomas Aquinas for whom God was the exemplary cause of creation. Expanding on Aristotle's four

your heart is touched by this sweet emotion that makes one give up all voluntary impulses other than that of making an account with our sovereign good, and this in the stage where he puts you, for you must follow his inclinations. At least, I asked him to give you this favor since it is one I find to be of great bearing on the pursuit of perfection. It's good to begin doing here below what one desires to do in eternity and to place neither end nor limit on the master of angels, since we know our savior Jesus, who was the first to love us and teach us this lesson. Heed it therefore, in following your saints, who heeded it absolutely in order to become holy and achieve the divine resemblance to this divine spouse, without whose attraction there are no saints.

You ask me how it is possible that one's body can be so close to God and one's spirit so far from him? This is, in fact, a great misery, and the true mark of our infidelities. The true means of extracting us from this misery is this sweet and voluntary servitude of the heart, which is attached to its object without expecting anything in return, and which draws the whole spirit after itself by means of a sweet and loving violence that doesn't kill the body but, to the contrary, nourishes it with its spiritual goods.[70]

How can it be that the spirit withdraws so unjustly from God, you say? That is only too easy for us, in our wretched self-love. It is said that after a heart is broken, it loves everywhere. But that is true only if it allows the jolts of divine inspiration to live in itself without deadening them by means of wretched remedies, that is to say, by reasoning and self-love, which change the movement of the heart such that it lives and breathes only for itself.[71] And this wretched life of ours carries off the

---

causes (formal, material, efficient, and final), Aquinas defined the exemplary cause as the pattern or model which exerts influence on the operating agent, as an idea in the mind of an artist; see Thomas Aquinas, *Summa Theologiae*, I, 15, i, and 44, iii.

70. The ideal of servitude, modeled on the relationship of Christ the Son to God the Father, plays a leading role in the Bérulle's Christocentric theology. See Pierre de Bérulle, *Discours de l'estat et des grandeurs de Jésus, in Œuvres complètes*, vol. 3, ed. Michel Depuy (Paris: Cerf, 1996), 95–7. See also Richard Cadoux and Jean Dujardin, *Bérulle et la question de l'homme: servitude et liberté* (Paris: Cerf, 2005); Erik Varden, *Redeeming Freedom: the Principle of Servitude in Bérulle* (Rome: Pontificio Ateneo Anselmo, 2011).

71. Marie's suggestion here of the antagonism between spiritual growth and intellectual reasoning situates her within the larger context of an emerging seventeenth-century mysticism which privileged experience over learning. See also Letters 68, 177, 247, and 274. See Sluhovsky, *Believe Not Every Spirit*, 102–13, and Michel de Certeau, *The Mystic Fable*, trans. Michael B. Smith (Chicago: University of Chicago Press, 1992), 107–55. Bernard McGinn, however, has argued that the criterion of experience assumed an authority equal to that of the biblical text within the context of Western mysticism as early as the twelfth century. See McGinn, "Changing Shape." Nicholas Paige has elegantly argued for the connection between the privileging of "lived contemplative spirituality" (as opposed to "painstaking theological demonstration") and the tendency toward the feminization of mysticism in the seventeenth century; Nicholas D.

whole spirit and withdraws it from its true and unique good and lives only against nature. This accounts for the severe actions we must take when, by the pique of our consciences, we are called to return to the one for whom we were born.⁷²

Since you wish it, I am asking God for the gift of prayer on your behalf and above all for humility and true abnegation of self; without this virtue there is neither true prayer nor true interior spirit, since unless the two go hand-in-hand all our devotions are suspect.⁷³ And this is the lesson that our true exemplary cause teaches us, so that we might entirely possess his spirit, as we were saying before. You have holy masters. They will tell you this, as will this critical spirit who follows us everywhere and tells us more than one thousand times that we are not practicing it.

I read and re-read your letter and what you say about your holy order, my very dear son. I cannot tell you how it edified my soul and what I believe I owe God for having called you there. You ask me how I feel about it. As for me, I tell you that the whole essence of perfection is enclosed there and that there is no order in the Church that has not borrowed what was holiest from holy Benedict and from his holy children. And this holy reform of yours has, as it were, recovered and swallowed up into itself the sap of this primitive spirit. My son, you will have no excuse, after all the favors your divine savior has given you, if you have affection for others rather than for him. Give yourself entirely to him, and by your submission render yourself open to receiving his principle spirit, which is that

---

Paige, *Being Interior: Autobiography and the Contradiction of Modernity in Seventeenth-Century France* (Philadelphia: University of Pennsylvania Press, 2000), 75. See also Grace Jantzen, *Power, Gender, and Christian Mysticism* (Cambridge: Cambridge University Press, 1995), 157–92, who suggests that the emphasis on experience as a source of spiritual authority distinguishes female mystics from their male counterparts throughout the history of Christian mysticism. For a discussion of experience as a source of knowing in Marie's spiritual writings, see Maria-Paul del Rosario Adriazola, *La connaissance spirituelle chez Marie de l'Incarnation, la Thérèse de France et du nouveau monde* (Paris: Cerf, 2001); and Guy-Marie Oury, "Mystique de l'immanence et mystique nuptiale," in *Femme, mystique et missionnaire: Marie Guyart de l'Incarnation*, ed. Raymond Brodeur, 157–68 (Quebec: Presses de l'Université Laval, 2001).

72. Marie appeals specifically to the notion of synderesis here, understood within the context of scholastic philosophy as the habitual grasp of the basic rules of morality.

73. Marie's emphasis on self-abnegation as a necessary prelude to spiritual progress is symptomatic of the neo-Augustinianism of seventeenth-century France. For the likes of Olier and a young Bérulle, union with God meant destroying, rather than perfecting (à la Thomas Aquinas), human nature. See Bérulle, *Brief discours de l'abnégation intérieur* (Paris, 1597) and Olier, *Introduction à la vie*, 131–5. Under the influence of Jean Eudes, the ideal of abnegation would implicate detachment not only from self and *saeculo*, but also from the pleasures of a familiar intimacy with God. Jean Eudes, *La vie et le royaume de Jésus dans les âmes chrétiennes* (New York: P. J. Kenedy, 1946), 120. Interestingly, the same pessimistic anthropology that fueled the emphasis on self-abnegation among those associated with the French School proved a key feature of a Jansenist theology that trod dangerously close to a Calvinist emphasis on divine

of your holy order.⁷⁴ If your heart has passed and is still passing through the crucible of afflictions and persecutions, it will only be more dazzling. Always give me the consolation (if obedience permits) of telling me about what is new in your heart—progresses as well as struggles. I am so very interested that it seems to me as if I am incorporated there. So, don't be astonished if I make these requests of you. I have a singular obligation to the Reverend Father Prior for having allowed you to speak with me about it so particularly. It seems to me that I am with you, seeing your holy observances. At present, my spiritual reading consists of your rules and spiritual exercises. I can easily see that those who wrote our constitutions and rules took much from them. Let's bless God for everything and make use of his treasures, which he disperses to us through his saints.

I also offer to God your sore throat. I think that it must have happened only because of overheated blood. I pity you because of your choir duties and your studying, with regard to which I imagine that your sore throat is a particular inconvenience. I will, I say, pray hard to God that it doesn't impede you in his service, for suffering is a beautiful gift that His Majesty is giving you.⁷⁵ As for me, he is not giving me any physical infirmity except the little headaches I experience from time to time, which are the residual effects of the great diligence with which I used to do embroidery work; but that's insignificant. All my infirmities are spiritual and, consequently, more difficult to cure. Offer them in particular to God, as well as the other tasks with which His Majesty has charged me, and which pertain to my vocation in Canada. These tasks often compel me to pass through thorny situations and quite trying difficulties, but in the end I find my rest among them.

You ask whether our community is large. We have only eight choir sisters and one converse, but this is a lot, for it is a question of uniting members of two congregations in our community, where a multitude of people would only result in a diversity of sentiments. This is why we must try to strengthen this union which has been wrought and, thanks to God, signed by the two congregations and by us, owing to an extraordinary means of grace. The great peace and union in which we live has already touched several people of great piety in France, and gives reason to hope for the general union of all the Ursulines in France, who are separated

---

grace and predestination. For a discussion of the Jansenist elements of Marie's spiritual writings, see Dominique Deslandres, "Augustinisme, quiétisme ou air du temps? Éléments d'une méthode historique pour aborder un texte religieux," in *Marie de l'Incarnation, entre mère et fils: Le dialogue des vocations*, ed. Raymond Brodeur, 29–41 (Quebec: Presses de l'Université Laval, 2000).

74. Psalm 50:14, Vulgate.

75. That is, God. Although throughout her letters, Marie also uses the royal honorific to refer to the French king, context will aid readers in distinguishing between the two.

into various congregations and, consequently, constitutions, but united under the same rule and functions.⁷⁶ This is a little seed that God will fructify in his own time, as people from all over are writing to me here. Thus, in my responses, I try to offer a few words about this great good to those who can, I think, somehow cooperate in this matter. As this thing is very important for the glory of God and the good of many, I beg you to recommend it to him, and I make the same supplication to my Reverend Fathers. All this nevertheless is a confidential matter, my very dear son. We are waiting for the first fleet to bring us our bull from Rome.⁷⁷ We already have those of our two congregations, but we still need one particular to this country, just as we also have particular rules here, given that there are things that can't be accommodated to the way things are done in France. The climate, supplies, and other circumstances are entirely different here. It's not that we can't do things as perfectly, as in France, according to circumstances and this, in the spirit of the order. My son, this has been my principal burden since I have come to Canada—our current establishment and our union. For, with regard to the study of the language and what relates to the instruction of the Indians, and to teaching my sisters what I was able to learn about it with the grace of God, this was so delightful to me that I didn't consider it difficult, but rather sinned in loving it too much. These, then, are our insignificant affairs, my very dear son. I will tell you more about them another time.

My niece N. wrote to me and told me through our two Mothers that she intends to come and find me.⁷⁸ Don't say anything about it to her, lest our Mothers think that I would like to call her to me. Only recommend the matter to

---

76. There were eight congregations of Ursulines in seventeenth-century France—those of Paris, Bordeaux, Dijon, Toulouse, Lyon, Tulle, Arles, and the Association of Avignon. For a history of the Ursurlines, see T. Ledochowska, *Angèle Mérici et la Compagnie de Sainte-Ursule à la lumière des documents*, 2 vols. (Rome and Milan: Ancora, 1968); Marie de Chantal Gueudré, *Histoire de l'Ordre des Ursulines en France* (Paris: Saint-Paul, 1958–63); Marie-Augustine de Pommereu, *Chroniques de l'Ordre des Ursulines recueillies pour l'usage des religieuses du mesme ordre* (Paris, 1673); Marie André Jégou, *Les Ursulines du faubourg St-Jacques à Paris, 1607–1662* (Paris: Presses Universitaires de France, 1981).

77. The first Ursulines in New France came from two different congregations, Paris and Bordeaux, distinguished by differences in habit and practice. Shortly after arriving in the colony, the Ursulines of Quebec drafted articles of union, agreeing to adopt the Bordeaux habit and to take the additional fourth vow of teaching (along with the traditional vows of poverty, chastity, and obedience) observed in Paris; the articles were approved by the congregations in Paris and Bordeaux in 1641. Successive popes, however, refused to issue a bull affirming the union on the grounds that there was not yet a bishop in New France to receive it. See Guy-Marie Oury, *Marie Guyart (1599–1672)*, trans. Miriam Thompson (Sablé-sur-Sarthe, France: Solesmes Abbey, 1978), 284–94.

78. Marie is referring here to Marie Buisson, her older sister's daughter, with whose family she had lived before entering religious life. By the time of the writing of this letter, Marie Buisson

God, and if she writes to you about it, respond to her as God inspires you without mentioning me, except to say that I love her as my own daughter. The Canadian vocation ought not to be considered through the lens of a natural affection, nor undertaken too hastily, but should rather be pursued in a true and solid perseverance. Otherwise, those who come here will never be satisfied and, not finding what they expected, will soon return to France. We have not yet received novices because of this. Other orders have sent back their novices, which is distressing for the girls. This is why I would worry that this child might let herself be overcome by a natural affection, for she loves me as her mother. Someone wrote to me that at the height of her pain she called out to me as if I had been next to her. She would be sorely tried if she was with me, for I would mortify her more than anyone else, even though I do not have the spirit of mortification.

It is time to finish. We are all praying for you. Our Reverend Fathers love you. Father Poncet is writing to you. Mother Marie [de Saint-Joseph] and Madame our foundress, who endlessly obliges me here, greet you. I greet all my Reverend Fathers as their very humble daughter, who begs them to not refuse her participation in their holy sacrifices and prayers. Farewell.

Letter 97: August 29–September 10, 1646

My very dear and beloved son,

I pray that the king of saints be the unique object of your love for all time and eternity. My desire that you pray, and that you excite people to pray hard for this new Church, leads me to give you a short account of the blessings God continues to shower upon our Indians. This, without doubt, will excite you anew to praise their benefactor and to ask him for perseverance for some and the grace of a perfect conversion for others. It appears that this is not very far off, since we see every day, to our great consolation, new nations attracted by the news of peace, which allows them to circulate freely. Their desire to be instructed and saved compels them to ask for Fathers whom they can take to their country, so that they may bring the rich treasures of the faith and the gospel there, and place them among the number of God's children by means of baptism.

Those who appear the most zealous are the Indians from the north coast, served by the mission at Tadoussac. I spoke to you about this last year and told you how the nations of that coast, who live further inland between terrible mountains and inaccessible rocks, come there each spring, and how the Fathers are diligent about meeting them there in order to instruct them during the three or four months when the weather is more temperate; for the rest of the year it is extraordinarily cold there, and there is still snow and ice even in June. Some days ago, I asked the Father who is in charge of this mission for news about it, having a spiritual association with him for the conversion of these people, for even though we embrace all the nations in he who created them, we nevertheless draw straws each year, each selecting one nation so that we can more particularly focus our devotions upon its conversion. Well, as this mission fell to me, I wanted the Father to let me know about the blessings God was showering upon it, so as to thank him for them. Here is the answer he gave me: I cannot ask for anything better from these parts than the amplification of the kingdom of Jesus Christ.[79] In one day, I baptized thirty Betsiamites and heard the confessions of sixty Christians. I am about to perform six weddings in front of the Church. The day before yesterday, I took all the devils from the sorcerers, their stones, their drums, and similar nonsense, which I boiled up, to make them see how insignificant these things are and so that this evil spirit will no longer appear in the country of these poor people. The Indians of Tadoussac make speeches, which are an invaluable means of encouraging their own people as well as those of foreign nations to believe and to embrace the faith. You would understand them better with your ears than with your eyes.[80] Thank the great master for enlightening all the nations of the north, for there are more than ten different ones who live more than twelve days away from Tadoussac. I don't know if the end of the world is near, but the faith is spreading far. My only regret is that I am such a poor instrument in God's hands, but pray to His Goodness, I beg you, to have mercy on me and make me more worthy. The devotions of our parishioners are quite orderly. There are about sixty who have made their confession two or three times, and since they are preparing to take their first communion, they fast on Saturdays with this intention. There are thirty who took communion for the first time, and the rest will in due time. It was a very significant consolation to me to see them receive this holy sacrament with so much devotion and fervor that the French of two small boats that had arrived, having attended the mass, at the blessing of the water and with the

---

had become a postulant with the Ursulines in Tours. Buisson's desire to join her aunt in New France would prove a persistent one despite Marie's consistently tepid response to such proposals. See Letters 143 and 173.

79. The information provided to Marie by the Jesuit Jean de Quen adds to what the *Jesuit Relations* report about his mission at Tadoussac. Thwaites, *Jesuit Relations*, vol. 22, 220–43, and vol. 24, 121–33.

80. On the Amerindian rhetorical tradition, see Carmen Mata Barreiro, "Traduction et représentations de l'Autre: Ré-énonciation et parole des Amérindiens dans les relations de voyage des Français en Nouvelle-France," *Etudes Canadiennes/Canadian Studies* 37 (1994): 9–24; Rebecca M. Wilkin, "Les mots et les choses 'aux Hurons': L'archéologie d'une rencontre," *French Literature Series* 25 (1998): 55–75; and Réal Ouellet and Marie Parent, "Mise en scène et fonctions de la parole amérindienne dans la relation de voyage," in *Transferts culturels et métissages Amérique/Europe, XVI–XXe siècle / Cultural Transfer, America and Europe: 500 Years*

instruction we gave them, admired them.[81] They continue to observe a policy of exact obedience. They have first, second, and third tables. Persons of importance eat at the first, the officers who have served eat at the second, and the women and children at the last.[82] They made a path for walking after meals in order to discuss business and to pray while walking.

They wish passionately for a little house built in the French style where they can live during the summer and in which they can store their belongings during the winter while they hunt. That is what the Father's letter says.

It is a delightful thing to see our good Indians of Sillery and how careful they are to see that God is served as he ought to be in their little village, that the laws of the Church are kept inviolably, and that sins are punished there in order to appease God.[83] One of the main concerns of the chiefs is to remove anything that could be the occasion of sin, whether in general or in particular. One never goes to the chapel without finding some Indian deep in prayer there, and with so much devotion that it is a delightful thing. If someone founders in the faith or in Christian morals, he distances himself and banishes himself voluntarily, knowing full well that whether he wants to or not, he will have to do penance or be driven out of the village in shame. Some days ago, a young man was arguing with his wife. They were taken before the chiefs, who condemned the man to be chained up inside a cellar of the fort and to fast there for three days on bread and water. The woman was condemned to the same punishment, which was carried out in our monastery. These poor people did their penance with so much devotion that I believe their sins were remitted from the moment the sentence was pronounced. The woman refused the comfort of even a handful of straw, for, she said, "I want to repay the God I have angered."

The Attikameks, who are also from the north coast, are converted and live extraordinarily innocent lives. Four years ago, thirty of them came down here, where they were instructed and baptized, after which they returned to their country and proclaimed with an apostolic fervor to those of their nation the good they had encountered. They explained to their people the articles of the faith, as they had been taught. They converted a great number of them, whom they brought to Trois-Rivières to be baptized, which was granted. Since then they are as orderly as if the Fathers were always among them. Also they come from time to

---

of Inculturation, ed. Laurier Turgeon, Denys Delâge, and Réal Ouellet (Quebec: Presses de l'Université Laval, 1996), 281–304.

81. See also Letters 73 and 81; Thwaites, *Jesuit Relations*, vol. 26, 101, and vol. 29, 71–3, 98–101.

82. See also Thwaites, *Jesuit Relations*, vol. 29, 125.

83. See also Thwaites, *Jesuit Relations*, vol. 29, 63–91.

time, although from quite far away, to testify to their faith and receive new lights. Never has such zeal been seen, even among children.

The peace achieved last year has opened the door to distant nations who come without fear to these parts, delighted to have the freedom to trade and to receive instruction.[84] They ask all the Fathers if they can take them to their countries. And already, some of them are leaving to go to the Abenakis, who were previously inaccessible. Others are going to the Iroquois, the dear mission of Reverend Father Jogues. This mission began by the shedding of his blood, with which he watered that ground, but he has sanctified it much more by his heroic virtues, which will not be evident until judgment day, for this great servant of God hides them with his humble silence. The few virtues that are nevertheless apparent have delighted and impressed even those who tyrannized him. Upon his return from France and his journey back to their country, they received him like an angel from heaven and regard him as their own father.

But I must tell you something about these ambassadors, who had promised when they left to return in the spring. As soon as they arrived in their country, they brought their legation to their chiefs, representing Monsieur de Montmagny our Governor, the French, the Hurons, the Algonquins, and the other nations who were joined in this peace treaty. Here is what happened.[85]

Three days after they arrived, people in the first village gathered to listen to the voice of Onontio, who is Monsieur the Governor, speaking through Sieur Coûture. But before they spoke they were given a gift to grease their throats and wipe away the dust they had picked up on the voyage so that their words might flow more freely. After Sieur Coûture and the others had made their speeches and offered their gifts, the Iroquois gave six of their own.

The first was to heal the ambassadors' feet, which had been bloodied by brambles, thorns, and other impediments on the way.

The second was to say that axes raised in the past against the French, Algonquins, Hurons, and their allies had been thrown far away, so that they could do no more harm.

The third testified to how sorry they had felt about the bad girl who had not been obedient to her mother, who had exhorted her to listen to the voice of her Father Onontio and have regard for his goodness. This shameless girl had indeed been bold enough to come near Montreal again this fall, for the purpose of waging war. That is to say, seven warriors from the nation of the Oneida, which is a small

---

84. For an account of the peace reached between the French, Iroquois, and other nations, see Thwaites, *Jesuit Relations*, vol. 28, 245–303.

85. Thwaites, *Jesuit Relations*, vol. 28, 273–87.

nation dependent on the Iroquois, unwilling to consent to the peace, took up arms against their will at the behest of the Iroquois, and killed a few Algonquins.

The fourth was to show how the whole country was rejoicing because Onontio had united all the peoples and made peace throughout the land.

The fifth was in expression of thanksgiving to the common father, the incomparable Onontio, who had given hope to the Algonquins, which no one had been able to do before.

The sixth was to show that they would have a place in their houses and could light the fire there, which is to say, that they would be welcome and able to talk safely with the French there.

The gifts having been presented and everything brought to an end, Sieur Coûture went back with the Hurons ten days after they had arrived. When they had already gone quite a ways, they were constrained to turn back and retrace their steps because they did not find their canoes where they had left them in order to travel by foot—which God permitted in order to assure them of the sincerity of the Iroquois, for sometime after they returned to the village from which they had departed, those who I just said had gone to war near Montreal and had killed some Algonquins, arrived and asked for an audience in the main village, which was granted them. They revealed the purpose of their embassy, which was to break with the Algonquins. One of them took the floor, showing the scalps of those they had killed, "See," he said, "one of those whom you hate. I have heard you say in the past that you had so little desire to reconcile with them, that if your souls met in the other world, you would persecute them still. I feel the same way about them, and in order to encourage you to stand firm, here are their heads and some ropes to join them together" (it was a large bead necklace, fifty hand-widths long).[86] These heads were those of several of our good Christians from Sillery who were housed near Montreal and killed in treason by these wretched people.

To this speech the Iroquois responded that they were astonished that they had been so bold as to bring them these heads and that without a doubt it was to publicly shame them. "So now," they said, "is Onontio a child? What will he say upon hearing this news? Will he not say, that's just like the Iroquois? They didn't strike the blow themselves, but gave the ax to others, to fell upon the heads of our

---

86. The significance of wampum—beads fashioned from shells—among the Amerindians of North America has been well studied. Often used to cement alliances and confirm treatises, strings or belts of wampum were deployed in a variety of circumstances, including the performance of civic rites, as well as for decoration. See Marshall Joseph Becker, "Small Wampum Bands Used by Native Americans in the Northeast: Functions and Recycling," *Material Culture* 40, no. 1 (April 2008): 1–17; Angela M. Haas, "Wampum as Hypertext: An American Indian Intellectual Tradition of Multimedia Theory and Practice," *Studies in American Indian Literatures* 19, no. 4 (December 2007): 77–100.

friends. But this isn't all. It is not just about our honor, but also our lives. Our relatives are living with the Algonquins as if in their own land. Will they not be in danger of losing their lives there? Will they not be accused of being the authors of these murders when the news is heard? Go and take your scalps and your gifts with you. None of us will touch them."

This behavior made us see that the Iroquois, although barbarous, sincerely wanted peace. And what's more, during the whole winter, according to what Sieur Coûture reported, no one talked about war. On the contrary, everyone was relieved to be free and able to hunt safely. They carried out such a slaughter of deer that they killed more than two thousand. They charged Sieur Coûture with the responsibility of telling the Algonquins and the Hurons that they were going to fetch their daughters and their relatives who had been held captive among them for a long time.

When Coûture returned in the spring with the Iroquois ambassadors, he brought a whole host of gifts for a variety of reasons, but which all culminated in a single one which confirmed the peace.[87] Monsieur the Governor, for his part, also gave them some in order to testify that he would accept their propositions and that for his part, he would uphold the peace with all his might: that hereafter, he would love and protect them as his children, that they would be warmly welcomed in the houses of the French, that they would always find a fire there and a kettle ready, to attest to the contentment the French felt at seeing them allied with them, and that in order to give them conclusive proof of all this, as well as of his affection, he wished not only to attest to this truth himself in the present council, but also to send one of the Fathers and one of the most important Frenchman to carry his message to their whole country and to confirm for the Iroquois the goodwill of which he had assured them.[88] To this end, he had chosen Father Jogues, whom he loved as himself and honored as his father, and said that he would consider himself as obliged for all the assurances and hospitality they'd give Father Jogues as if they had done the same to him. The Iroquois were quite content with these offers and assured Monsieur the Governor of their satisfaction and gratitude.

The Reverend Father Jogues therefore left with the Iroquois last May 16, and Monsieur Bourdon, one of our principal settlers, left with him per the promise

---

87. Thwaites, *Jesuit Relations*, vol. 28, 289–301.

88. For an analysis of the cultural significance of the kettle within the context of colonial New France, see Laurier Turgeon, "Le chaudron de cuivre en Amérique: Parcours historique d'un objet interculturel," *Ethnologie Française* 26, no. 1 (January 1996): 58–73; Turgeon, "The Tale of the Kettle: Odyssey of an Intercultural Object," *Ethnohistory* 44, no. 1 (January 1997): 1–29.

of Monsieur the Governor.[89] They suffered considerable fatigues on this journey because of the rapids, which obliged them to unload their canoes and to carry them on their backs with all their baggage, for in these situations, no one is exempt from carrying his belongings. They arrived in a place where many Iroquois were fishing, in the company of whom they found our Huron Thérèse. The Father spoke to her in private, questioned her, instructed her, and exhorted her to take heart. He told her that the time of her deliverance had come because he was bringing her ransom that we sent for this purpose—which was not exactly a price, because they were obligated to give her back to us according to the peace treaty, but a means of paying her expenses to those who had fed her. She assured him that she was not wavering in the faith, that she was praying to God every day and would be delighted to return with us, to resume studying about the things of God and piety. She was only thirteen or fourteen years old when she was kidnapped, but she held firm in the faith in the midst of this barbarity full of diabolical superstitions.

When the Father arrived in the country of the Hurons, he was received as I noted above. He made speeches and offered his gifts on behalf of Monsieur the Governor according to the manners and customs of the country. The Iroquois responded to everything with applause and many particular things happened that it would take me too long to report. The Reverend Father did not have permission to speak about the faith, but only to introduce himself and make them see that he had no ill-will in his heart on account of all the bad things they had done to him, but on the contrary that he loved them as his brothers and nephews, with whom he indeed wanted to stay after telling Onontio that they consented to what he wanted of them, and that hereafter they would be one with him and his allies.

I must now speak to you about the precious deaths of the Reverend Fathers de Noüe and Massé of the Society of Jesus.[90] By all appearances, the former died on the day of the Purification of the Holy Virgin in the midst of the exercise of obedience and charity. He exposed himself to danger in order to go from Trois-Rivières to Richelieu on the great river, which was frozen and icy, for the purpose of hearing the confessions of the soldiers of the garrison, who were living

---

89. Thwaites, *Jesuit Relations*, vol. 29, 43–61.

90. Thwaites, *Jesuit Relations*, vol. 29, 15–27. For a discussion of the motif of martyrdom in New France, see Greer, "Colonial Saints"; Carole Blackburn, *Harvest of Souls: The Jesuit Missions and Colonialism in North America, 1632–1650* (Montreal: McGill-Queen's University Press, 2000), 61–7; Paul Perron, "Narrating and Reading the Body: The Martyrdom of Isaac Jogues," in *Narratology and Text: Subjectivity and Identity in New France and Québécois Literature* (Toronto: University of Toronto Press, 2003), 103–30; and Perron, "Isaac Jogues: From Martyrdom to Sainthood," in *Colonial Saints*, 153–68.

without a priest. He left Trois-Rivières on the 30th of January accompanied by a Huron and two Frenchmen. The first stop was six leagues from Trois-Rivières on Lac Saint-Pierre on the north coast. After he had rested a little, he left two hours after midnight with the intention of going ahead and advising those of the settlement to come and fetch what they were being sent, which the Father's companions had dragged over the ice from Trois-Rivières. The charity of this good Father and the ardor of his courage made him think more about others than himself. He refused what he was offered, namely a little wine and cooked fat. He left his gun for starting fires and his blanket, which the missionaries use as a coat when they go on mission in the winter in the woods and in the snow. For provisions he contented himself with a morsel of bread and five or six prunes, and for his clothing a simple shirt under a simple tunic in the harshness of an extreme cold on a frozen river. He was walking under the light of the moon, following the north coast from cape to cape, when the sky began to grow cloudy and the snow began to fall so heavily that he could no longer see the island. The two soldiers he had left behind departed only three hours after him and continued to travel more than two hours during the night with as much fear as difficulty, because they were new to the country and couldn't walk with snowshoes on the snow. What's more, they didn't see any trace of the Father. One of them, who had already made the trip to Richelieu, thought to use a compass to get to the middle of the lake and go straight to the islands with his companion and the Huron. That night, overcome with exhaustion, they slept in the snow at the tip of the island of Saint-Ignace, which is opposite the settlement of Richelieu. The Huron, who was stronger and more accustomed to fatigue, went up to the fort and asked for the Father. Because he hadn't arrived, the captain and all his people were grieved for the rest of the night. The next day, they went looking for the two soldiers, who were found to have spent the night without fire and to be half-dead. They were led to the fort, where they were quite surprised not to find the Father. They thought he had crossed the lake in order to be safer on the south side. With this in mind, they dispatched several people who spent all day and a good part of the night looking for him. They cried out, they called for him, they fired off shots to make themselves heard, but in vain. The day after the Feast of Purification, one soldier resolved to go to the place where the Father had first slept and to follow his footprints from there. He took two Hurons with him who accompanied him courageously and happily, for they recognized the traces of the Huron snowshoes the Father had used and followed this trail northwards always staying on the lake and among the islands. Between an island and solid land, they came upon several paths the Father had made, as if lost and trying to find his way. After having walked the same paths, they found the place where he had slept—a little fir tree on the ground from which he had removed the snow. They continued and passed by in sight of Fort

Richelieu, following the Father's trail up to the place called Cap Massacre one league above Richelieu. Presumably the snow and dusk had obscured his view of the settlement, or perhaps he was so enervated by the travails of the journey he had made on his snowshoes, that he didn't recognize where he was. Whatever the case, near Cap Massacre they found another place where he had rested, and three leagues upstream his dead body was found kneeling on the ground in a pit surrounded by snow, upon which he was leaning. Probably, having knelt before giving up his spirit, the weight of his dead body had placed him in this position. His snowshoes and his hat were next to him, and in his pocket he still had the bread that he had taken for his sustenance. The good soldier, after having prayed to God and made a cross at the tree next to the body, wrapped it in a blanket and placed it on a stretcher in the same position in which he had found it. He brought it to Trois-Rivières, where everyone was overcome with sadness and consolation at once—sadness, at seeing this good Father, who, day and night had no greater care than to serve the whole world, thus dead and bereft of all human assistance, and consolation, at seeing his body in the position in which Saint Francis Xavier is ordinarily depicted, his arms crossed at his chest, his eyes opened and fixed toward heaven, which alone had witnessed his agony and was waiting to crown him for his works. His face resembled that of a man in contemplation more than a dead person. Everyone dissolved into tears upon seeing such a devout spectacle. We heard it said by the Fathers who were then at Trois-Rivières that when they tried to warm his body to thaw it out, so that it could be put into the coffin, he became as rosy as if he had been alive, and so beautiful that they could not stop embracing him. The good Father was more than sixty-five years old. He had been in this country since his youth, where he suffered great travails in laying the first foundations of this Church with the good Father Massé, who also died this year at the age of more than seventy. In addition to the famines they had to endure, the storms they suffered at sea, their capture by the English who ransomed them, they laid the foundations of a Church where one encounters an unfathomable number of crosses. And nevertheless neither troubles nor travails nor persecutions could ever undermine or weaken their courage. A nobleman in France wanted to bring Father Noüe to him and insisted on as much to his superiors, having written to him about it last year in such an urgent manner that he assumed he would win him over straight away. Father Noüe responded to him quite curtly in order to deter him from his pursuits, and he asked God daily to take him out of the world rather than permit him to be removed from his dear mission. And in order to win God's heart and persuade him to grant him this grace, he constantly performed heroic deeds which elicited the admiration of everyone. It is believed that God granted his wishes by this precious death. To die alone and neglected in the exercise of charity and obedience—is this not to be like Jesus Christ? As for Father

Massé, he died a natural death but while praying to God. His life was entirely holy and even accompanied by miracles. As I knew quite personally these great servants of God, their deaths occupied my mind much, but the occupation was so sweet that it seemed to me as if I was sensing something of their glory, just as I sensed the odor of their virtues when they were among us in this life.

I just bid farewell to one of our Reverend Fathers who is going to begin the mission of Saint Ignace among the Abenakis, accompanied only by the Indians of that nation, who came to ask that he be sent to their country to teach them the way to heaven.[91] It is a big country into which no one had yet been able to enter. These Abenakis came to us by means of a very particular action of God. Over the past few years, one or two of our good Christians have gone to see them, to talk to them about God, but the Abenakis didn't listen to them. Nevertheless, this seed was blessed for a time ordained by God, for we hope that it will bear fruit. Nearby the Abenakis are a number of Englishmen whose various settlements occupy more than two hundred leagues of land on the sea coast, and the Englishmen trade in furs there like the French do here. When the Englishmen learned that the Indians came here to ask that some Fathers come to them, they encouraged them, saying that the Indians could do no better. This is because among them (so it is said) are a large number of clandestine Catholics, which gives us hope of harvesting a double fruit there.[92]

The letters we have received from the Hurons informed us that a new country has been discovered and an entrance to it has been found. This is the nation of the people of the sea, called Ouinpegoueck Ikimiouek in the Indian tongue.[93] It will be a great mission, which we hope will spread advantageously because these people are numerous and sedentary, by means of whom we will discover still more to give to Jesus Christ, for the Fathers will work hard there.[94] And they will even

---

91. Thwaites, *Jesuit Relations*, vol. 29, 65–9.

92. Thwaites, *Jesuit Relations*, vol. 31, 203. Although the terms of the 1627 charter of the Compagnie des Cents Associés formally excluded Protestants from settling in New France, Marie's allusion to the "clandestine Catholics" of the British settlements of colonial North America reminds us of the ways in which the work of French Catholic missionaries abroad was, in some sense, an extension of the religious wars waged some hundred years earlier back home. For a discussion of the relationship between the Canadian missions and "contemporary religious consciousness and controversy" in Europe, see Peter A. Goddard, "Canada in Seventeenth-Century Jesuit Thought: Backwater or Opportunity?" in *Decentring the Renaissance*, ed. Germaine Warkentin and Caroline Podruchny, 186–99 (Toronto: University of Toronto Press, 2001); see also, Mary Dunn, "The Miracles at Saint-Anne-du-Petit-Cap and Colonial Community Identity," *Canadian Historical Review* 91, no. 4 (December 2010): 611–35.

93. Oury suspects a mistake of typography here and suggests that Marie intended to refer to the Ouinipeg.

94. I have substituted the noun "Fathers" for the impersonal French pronoun "on" here. Worth considering, however, is the possibility that Marie's use of the impersonal pronoun was

venture to go out on the great sea, which is beyond the Hurons and by which they intend to find the way to China. By way of this same sea, which is gentle, they also hope to discover several countries along the coast as well as inland. If God allows this enterprise to succeed this year, and if God preserves my life, I will share my joy with you, for my sole wish is the progress and consummation of the kingdom of Jesus Christ and then to tell you what I know about it, so that you may join yourself to me in what concerns the plan for the greatest glory of God, which lies in the salvation of souls ransomed by the blood of his only Son. I beg you to pursue relentlessly the conversion of these people. Ah! How content I would be if I were told that you had given your life for such a good cause! As for me, how happy I would be if I were found worthy to be chopped into bits for this reason! Pray for your very unworthy mother, that she not present any obstacles to God's plans.

But I must get down to particulars and tell you something about our duties in our parlors as well as in the seminary. The Hurons who come down here are almost continually in our parlor, which is the designated place for their instruction. The mission of Mother Marie de Saint-Joseph, who knows the language, is there. These good neophytes and catechumens regard her as their mother.[95] Last year a chief named Jean Baptiste came down with his whole family to help in the peace treaty with the Iroquois. All winter long, he gave us an opportunity to practice corporeal as well as spiritual works of mercy, for although he was chief and a man of importance among the Indians, since he was outside of his own country he was in need of everything, for these people laden themselves with nothing but goods for trading because of the great difficulty of the roads. I wouldn't know how to describe the zeal they have for the faith and for the practice of pious actions. But what we have admired the most in them is the tenderness of their consciences and the care they take to avoid the littlest sins, or to confess to the utmost when they have committed them. One time the simplicity of the good Jean Baptiste gave us some consolation, and entertained us all a bit. When he was about to go

---

deliberate, intended to suggest an understanding of mission as a project for which the broader colonial community (including both lay and religious, male and female) claimed responsibility. See also Letters 80 and 97.

95. Marie's recourse to familial language here to articulate the relationship between Mother de Saint-Joseph and the indigenous converts recalls the motif of spiritual motherhood so typical to the lives of medieval women saints. For a critique of the model of spiritual motherhood, see Mary Dunn, "'The Cruelest of All Mothers': Marie de l'Incarnation, Motherhood, and Christian Discipleship," *Journal of Feminist Studies in Religion* 28, no. 1 (2012): 43–62. See also Jeannette Nieuwland, "Motherhood and Sanctity in the Life of Saint Birgitta of Sweden: An Insoluble Conflict?" in *Sanctity and Motherhood: Essays on Holy Mothers in the*

Letter 97: August 29–September 10, 1646

on the hunt, some people who had promised to give him what he would need for his journey, which was to take several days, went back on their word just when he was supposed to leave. This upset him so much that he chided them in frustration. Once he pulled himself together, he was so sorry about it that he wanted to make his confession right away. But his confessor was gone and since there was no one else to listen to him, he went to find she who customarily instructed him, in order to tell her his sin and to beg her to tell it to his confessor when he returned, assuring her that he was extremely sad about having sinned, that he had asked repeatedly for God's forgiveness, and that he would try to be more careful in the future. Mother Saint-Joseph consoled him and made him do acts of contrition again. Then he left in peace. When he had gone two leagues down the road, he learned that his confessor had returned. He left his company and hurried back to make his confession, saying that he would not have traveled in ease if, knowing that his confessor was at the house, he had not confessed his impatience.

Another Huron, who had not yet been instructed but had a keen desire to be, was given to Mother Saint-Joseph, whom he regarded from then on as his own mother and to whom he rendered such a punctual obedience that he did everything she ordered him to do. No one had enough influence over him to make him undertake something that would interrupt the time and the hour of her instructions unless she agreed to it. One day, he was obligated for some particular reasons to go on the hunt with some Algonquins, but he didn't want to go without the approval of his mother, "Wait," he told them, "Marie has not given me leave. I will go and ask her for it." She gave him permission, and he left straight away. During his absence, not a day went by that he did not say his rosary and pray. He constantly reviewed in his head what he had been taught about the mysteries of our holy faith lest, he forget them and delay his baptism. Upon his return he had hardly stepped out of his canoe than he came to our grill with unparalleled joy to ask for those women who desired that he become the child of God. "Ah! My mother," he said to his mistress, "I have sinned much since I saw you last, for because I desired to see you and to be instructed for baptism, I often asked to return, and when that was refused me, I was sad and I did not suffer enough in peace, as a result of seeing the effect of my desire delayed." On another occasion, some other Hurons wanted to take him to hunt for beavers, begging him to do so insistently and promising him that he would reap a great profit on this journey. He came as usual to ask for leave from his mother, who told him that if he did not want to be baptized immediately, she didn't think this a great inconvenience, but that if his desires for baptism were such as he had told her, she didn't think it was good preparation for this great grace to thus go gallivanting on the pretext of temporal gain. Thereupon he responded to her with a firm and resolute courage, "I've decided that I will not go. I have no business more urgent than that of my salvation and my baptism. I do not desire to take to my country any riches other than those of the faith and the honor of being numbered among the children of God. From that time on, he did not miss a day of instruction and our Lord blessed his good will, giving him a memory so well suited to remembering all our mysteries that he rarely had to be told anything twice, since he retained it the first time. Finally, the day of his baptism arrived, which he had so desired and which was the day after Pentecost. I cannot describe the joy with which he received this signal favor—his words, his actions, his whole exterior testified to the contentment of his heart. Since then he has made his confession twice a week, and today he is being instructed for communion, which he will solemnly receive for the first time in his country, when it is fitting.

Our little seminary had as much work this year as in the preceding ones. Our greatest harvest is in winter, when the Indians go on the hunt for six months and leave us their daughters to instruct. This time is precious for us, for in the summer children can't leave their mothers, nor mothers their children, and because they use them in their corn fields and to prepare their beaver pelts, we do not have so many of them. Nevertheless, we always have enough of them to keep us busy.

The girl who was the leader and like the chief of this tribe of young neophytes, was a granddaughter of the first Christian of this new Church, to which her father and mother promised her as a child.[96] She was given to us at the age of two, because her mother had died, and we raised her for about three years with the intention of making her a religious in accordance with her parents' vow, in case she had the will for it.[97] Hers was the best and loveliest mind that we had seen since coming to Canada. She had barely learned to speak when, all by herself, she said the Indian prayers by heart and even those we make the French girls say. What she heard us sing in choir, she knew it almost instantaneously, and she sang it with us without hesitation. People on the outside asked for her, to hear her sing, and they were delighted to hear her sing entire psalms. She responded perfectly

---

Middle Ages, ed. Anneke B. Mulder-Bakker, 297–330 (New York: Garland Publishing, 1995); Anja Petrakopolous, "Sanctity and Motherhood: Elizabeth of Thuringia," in *Sanctity and Motherhood*, ed. Mulder-Bakker, 259–96; and Anneke Mulder-Bakker, "Ivetta of Huy: *Mater et Magistra*," in *Sanctity and Motherhood*, ed. Mulder-Bakker, 225–58.

96. Thwaites, *Jesuit Relations*, vol. 29, 79–87.

97. For the history of Amerindian professions among the Ursulines of Quebec, see *Les Ursulines de Québec depuis leur établissement jusqu'à nos jours*, vol. 1 (Quebec: Darveau, 1863), 354–8. For a discussion of the early modern debate over the spiritual capacity of native convert, see Allan Greer, "Iroquois Virgin: the Story of Kateri Tekakwitha in New France and New Spain," in *Colonial Saints*, 235–50; Elisa Sampson Vera Tudela, "Fashioning a *Cacique Nun*: From Saints' Lives to Indian Lives in the Spanish Americas," *Gender & History* 9, no. 2 (August 1997): 171–200.

to the catechism, in which she was the mistress of her companions, and although she was only five and a half years old, her mistress had given her the responsibility of leading the prayers and beginning them aloud all by herself. She did this with a marvelous grace and with so much fervor that it was a consolation to hear her. But our joy was indeed short-lived, for a swelling of the lung soon caused her to lose her voice and her life. This innocent girl was sick for six or seven months, during which time she was so patient, so obedient and reasonable, that one would have had to see it to believe it. Having asked for a Father to hear her confession, she was sent one who was totally surprised to see the attention, devotion, and maturity with which she did this deed. However oppressed and embattled she was by pain, she never refused to pray to God except for one or two hours before her death, when she felt a quite disturbing oppression. But when she was told that it was the devil who was tempting her so that she wouldn't obey, she immediately joined her hands together and did all that she was asked to do. When we visited her, as a testimony of the love she had for us, she told us that she would appeal to God for us when she was in heaven, where she was glad to go. Just as she was about to die, she was asked if she loved God and she responded with as great a presence of mind as an aged person, "Yes, I love him with all my heart," and these were her last words. Her father, having been betrayed and wounded by some stranger, died shortly before her and with great indications of sanctity. After the death of her father, when she was asked about her parents she would say, "I have no other parents than the virgin daughters dressed in black. These are my mothers. My father told me this before he died and commanded me to obey them, and he told me he was giving me to them so that they would be my mothers."[98] She benefited so much from her belief that her father was in heaven, that when she had some minor dispute with her companions, she told them by way of reproach, "My father is in heaven, but yours isn't." These were her childish vengeances. I must confess to you that although we believe she is in heaven, the death of this innocent girl touched us, as well as all our friends, for she was known and loved by the French and the Indians alike, who regarded her as nothing other than a little Ursuline, since she was already doing our duties in the body of a child.

Finally, our Lord is giving us the grace that our seminary is the refuge of the afflicted and oppressed, for if there is some girl who is in danger of losing her life or honor, or the good graces of her parents, or, in brief, who is in any sort of trouble, the chiefs, who keep an eye on whether their people are living as good Christians, bring them to us so that we can protect and instruct them. Bless this good sovereign for all his blessings, and concern yourself with the cause of Jesus

---

98. See also Matthew 12:46–50, Mark 3:31–5, and Luke 8:19–21.

Christ and the amplification of his kingdom, together with me. Let us live and die for this purpose.

Letter 109: Summer, 1647

My very dear and beloved son,

The peace of our very lovable and very adorable Jesus.[99] I received your letter and everything that was in your packet when I was no longer expecting it. Nevertheless, I still held out hope that you would have taken the way of our Reverend Mothers of Paris as the most reliable, and I was not mistaken, for I received everything you sent me when I received their letters. But I have to talk about other things with you, my very dear son. What! You reproach me for a lack of affection, which I can't endure without an appropriate reply, for I am still living since God wills it.[100] You do, in fact, have some reason to complain because I left you. I, too, would willingly complain if I could about he who came to bring a sword to earth, making such strange divisions.[101] It is true that even though you were the only thing left in the world to which my heart was attached, he nevertheless wanted to separate us when you were still at the breast. I struggled to keep you for nearly twelve years, but I still had to share almost half of those years.[102] Finally I had to yield to the force of divine love and suffer this blow of division which was more painful than I can tell you, but which didn't prevent me from considering myself an infinity of times the cruelest of all mothers. I ask you to forgive me, my

---

99. Although jarring to the modern reader, the terms of endearment with which Marie expresses her intimacy with Jesus find their roots in the medieval tradition of affective piety. For a discussion of affective piety, see Clarissa Atkinson, *Mystic and Pilgrim: The Book and the World of Margery Kempe* (Ithaca: Cornell University Press, 1983), 125–56.

100. Claude accused his mother of a "lack of affection" repeatedly over the course of their thirty-one-year correspondence and almost exclusively as a means of persuading Marie to allow him access to her spiritual writings. See also Letters 143 and 155.

101. See Matthew 10:34–7, which reads, "Do not suppose that I have come to bring peace to the earth. I did not come to bring peace, but a sword. For I have come to turn 'a man against his father, a daughter against her mother, a daughter-in-law against her mother-in-law, a man's enemies will be the members of his own household.' Anyone who loves his father or mother more than me is not worthy of me; anyone who loves his son or daughter more than me is not worthy of me." For a contemporary feminist analysis of this and similar troubling verses elsewhere in the canonical gospels, see Julie Hanlon Rubio, *A Christian Theology of Marriage and Family* (New York: Paulist Press, 2003), 48–60. See also Carolyn Oziek, "The Family in Early Christianity: 'family values' revisited,'" *Catholic Biblical Quarterly* 58 (January 1996): 1–24.

102. *Relation de 1633*, 268–77; *Relation de 1654*, 272–5.

very dear son, for I am the cause of your having suffered much affliction. But let us console ourselves that life is short and that, by the mercy of he who thus separated us in this world, we will have an entire eternity to see each other and to celebrate each other in him.[103]

As for my papers, what are they? I have but few, my very dear son, for I do not stop to write about the matters that you think I do. It is true that when I was *in extremis*, I had given the few I had to Mother Marie de Saint-Joseph to burn, but she told me that she would send them to you. Thus, they would have fallen into your hands anyway, even if you had not indicated that you wanted them. But since my writings console you and since you want them, even if I have only one notebook I will write on it that it should be sent to you if I die without speaking, and unexpectedly.

You want to know how God has guided me. I would take satisfaction in telling you, in order to give you reason to bless this ineffable Goodness who has so lovingly called us to his service. But you know that there is such a great risk that the letters will fall into other hands that my fear that this would happen restrains me.[104] Nevertheless, I assure you that from now on I will conceal nothing of my present state from you. Or at least, I will speak of it so clearly that you will be able to know it. In truth, it seems to me that I owe this to a son who has consecrated himself to the service of my divine master and with whom I feel I share the same spirit. Here is a paper that will show you how I was disposed when I was relieved of illness almost two years ago. It's not that I stop to write about my dispositions if I don't need to, but on this occasion a sentence from holy scripture so strongly attracted me that in my infirmity I was unable to bear it, and I was constrained to comfort myself by taking up my pen to write these few words, which will reveal to you the way in which this infinite Goodness guides me.[105] This way is none other

---

103. See Matthew 19:29, which reads, "And everyone who has left houses or brothers or sisters or father or mother or wife or children or fields for my sake will receive a hundred times as much and will inherit eternal life."

104. Marie's keen desire to keep her writings secret corresponds with what Nicholas Paige argues about the emerging autobiographical subject of the seventeenth century, who "stubbornly hid herself from view, rejected publicity, resisted above all writing and then, when forced nonetheless to record her experience, tried to burn her papers lest they become known." This resistance to publicity, Paige continues, at once served to underscore the status of the autobiographical text as a proxy for authoritative personal experience and was at the same time "an easy way around charges of affronts both to good Christian humility and, perhaps more importantly still, to the general invisibility demanded of women religious." Paige, *Being Interior*, 105.

105. For a study of Marie's "experiential" approach to scripture, see Jean Comby, "Dieu donne les mots: Marie de l'Incarnation et l'Écriture sainte," in *L'Itinéraire mystique d'une femme: Rencontre avec Marie de l'Incarnation, ursuline*, ed. Jean Comby et le Laboratoire de

than his loving familiarity and close intimacy, together with an intellectual light, which transports me into this intimacy without my being able to apply myself to any interior occupation other than that to which this light brings me.[106] The most common subjects of this intimacy are the divine attributes, the truths of holy scripture—Old as well as New Testaments, particularly those concerning the maxims of the Son of God, his sovereign domain, and the expansion of his kingdom by the conversion of souls, such that this attraction thoroughly transports me, affecting both my interior actions and my exterior ones. When I say that I can't apply myself to another occupation, I mean I can't focus on anything else, for apart from the occupations that constrain my whole spirit, that is to say, where my liberty is denied me, bound by this most adorable goodness of my divine spouse, I tell him everything I want according to the circumstances, even in the midst of my corporeal exercises and the nuisance of temporal affairs, for he honors me with his continual and familiar presence.[107] It seems to me that you were only a year old when he began to attract me to this way of prayer which, however, consisted of various states where different and particular things happened to me, according to the love-filled and merciful plans that His Goodness had for me, in view of my tremendous vileness, baseness, rusticities, and infidelities—unbearable to anything other than an infinite goodness, the course of which I interrupted countless times.[108] This greatly impeded my progress in sanctity, of which, truth be told, I have not even a vestige. This is what I beg you to recommend to our Lord, for without this I will be like the clanging cymbal that makes but a fleeting sound.[109] And I am quite afraid of ruining God's plans for me and frittering away the graces he is giving me to accomplish them.

Since my illness, my interior disposition has been quite particularly disengaged from everything, such that all exterior things are like crosses for me. Nonetheless, these things cause me no concern and I endure them by submitting to the orders of God, who has placed me in a state of obedience in which nothing can happen

---

recherche de la Faculté de théologie de Lyon, 85–100 (Paris: Cerf, 1993); Guy-Marie Oury, "Quelques sources scripturaires de la lettre LXVIII," in *Marie de l'Incarnation, entre mère et fils: Le dialogue des vocations*, ed. Raymond Brodeur, 45–52 (Quebec: Presses de l'Université Laval, 2000).

106. *Relation de 1654*, 236–41.

107. *Relation de 1633*, 234–6; *Relation de 1654*, 205–8. See also Letters 128, 155, and 177.

108. *Relation de 1654*, 424–8. For a study of Marie de l'Incarnation's approach to prayer and her understanding of the stages thereof, see Dominique Bertrand, "Dieu agit le premier. L'orasion de Marie de l'Incarnation," in *L'Itinéraire mystique*, ed. Comby et al., 101–31.

109. 1 Corinthians 13:1.

to me except by his initiative. I sense something in myself that gives me a continual inclination to follow and embrace what I know is the most conducive to the glory of God, and what seems to me most perfect, according to the maxims of the gospel that are in keeping with my state—and all of this under the direction of my superior.[110] I make countless mistakes, which humiliates me more than I can say.

For nearly three years I have been thinking continually of death, although I do not want and cannot want either life or death, but only he who is the master of life and death, to whose adorable judgment I submit myself in order to do everything he has commanded of me for all eternity. These sentiments give my soul and heart a substantial peace and spiritual nourishment, which allows me to subsist and bear with equanimity events, both general and particular, that happen either to others or to me, at this end of the world where one finds plenty of opportunities to practice patience and other virtues with which I am not familiar.

Do not rejoice, as you say, to have a mother who serves God with purity and fidelity, but after having given thanks to this ineffable Goodness for the favors he has bestowed upon me, ask him pardon for my infidelities and spiritual impurities. And I beg you neither to forget to do this nor to ask him on my behalf for the opposite virtues. Here, therefore, is the paper of which I spoke. I am copying it because it is but a rough draft written without order and only to comfort a feeble mind. On these words of the prophet, *Speciosus forma prae filiis hominum*, a light filled my spirit with the double beauty of the Son of God, and my heart had to comfort itself with my pen, but without reflection, for the spirit did not allow it.[111]

---

110. Marie made a vow of greater perfection towards the end of 1645 under the direction of the Jesuit Jérôme Lalemant, who served as her spiritual director in Quebec from 1645 until her death in 1672; *Relation de 1654*, 408–9. Curiously, Marie was not alone among early modern religious women in binding herself to such a vow. Teresa of Ávila made a similar vow, toward the end of the sixteenth century, as did Luisa de Carvajal, a seventeenth-century Catholic evangelist from Spain. Speculating on the origins of such a vow (so novel in the history of Christianity that Teresa's biographer Francisco de Ribera, admits to never having encountered the like before), Glyn Redworth suggests that it might have been Ignatius of Loyola's *Spiritual Exercises* that had provided the inspiration; see Glyn Redworth, *The She-Apostle: The Extraordinary Life and Death of Luisa de Carvajal* (New York: Oxford University Press, 2008), 52–4. Some decades later, Claude would indicate to his mother the desire to bind himself to the same vow of perfection. See Letters 267 and 274.

111. Psalm 44:3, Vulgate; *Relation de 1633*, 208–12. Whether Marie's insistence on her lack of authorial agency here and elsewhere is a function of her gender or simply an expression of "Christian humility," as Carla Zecher puts it, is difficult to determine; see Carla Zecher, "A New World Model of Female Epistolarity: The Correspondence of Marie de l'Incarnation," *Studies in Canadian Literature* 21, no. 2 (1996): 89–102. See, for example, Letters 155 and 183 and *Relation de 1654*, 241–2, 268–9, 424–5. Although such an abnegation of self in favor of direction by the Holy Spirit figures prominently in the spirituality of the French School, the denial of personal agency also emerges as a conspicuous theme in the writings of holy women.

As it was to the second person of the Holy Trinity that my soul had access, likewise was it to him that my aspirations were addressed following the insights of the spirit. The whole is ineffable in its depth, but here is what can be expressed: You are the most beautiful of all the children of men, O my beloved! You are beautiful, my dear love, in your double beauty, divine and human.[112]

You are beautiful, my dear love, and you transport my spirit to an inexplicable vision of what you are in your Father and what your Father is in you. But how can I bear you in your splendors unless you ravish my heart and my spirit, and if in this ravishing you do not bring it into yourself, transforming it so that it becomes the same as you? Therefore, even though I see you as God from God, light from light, true God from true God, I embrace you as my love and my whole good.[113]

O my divine spouse! What is this? I see that you are everything to your Father and you are everything to me. Your Father and you are everything to me.[114] Your Father is also mine and I don't know how that happens.

I see myself in the one by whom I do what I want, through the control that this one gives me, who is my love and my life.[115]

O my dear beloved! In this intimacy that charms my soul, it seems to me that my nothingness loses itself in a bottomless abyss.[116] This great abyss is you, who

---

See Anya Mali, *Mystic in the New World*, 56–7. For a gendered analysis of a similar rhetorical style in the works of Teresa of Ávila, see Alison Weber, *Teresa of Avila and the Rhetoric of Femininity* (Princeton: Princeton University Press, 1990), and Gillian Ahlgren, *Teresa of Avila and the Politics of Sanctity* (Ithaca: Cornell University Press, 1996). See also Elizabeth Petroff, *Body and Soul: Essays on Medieval Women and Mysticism* (New York: Oxford University Press, 1994), 204–24.

112. The "ineffability" to which Marie refers in this passage corresponds to the *indicible* that Michel de Certeau identifies as integral to the mystical experience. See Certeau, *The Mystic Fable*. Grace Jantzen cautions that we ought not to read ineffability, however, as a frustrated speechlessness but rather as "inexhaustible fecundity" suggestive of divine transcendence; see Jantzen, *Power, Gender*, 284–304. For an analysis of the problem of language in Marie de l'Incarnation's *Relation de 1654*, see Sylvie Robert, "La relation indicible," in *L'Itinéraire mystique*, ed. Comby et al., 195–221. For a treatment of Bérulle's attention to the double features of Christ's humanity and divinity, see Edward Howells, "Relationality and Difference in the Mysticism of Pierre de Bérulle," *Harvard Theological Review* 102, no. 2 (April 2009): 225–43.

113. Nicene Creed.

114. John 14:20, 17:21.

115. Not the imperial implications of the original "empire," which I have rendered here as "control."

116. For an analysis of the way in which Marie's claim to "nothingness" impacts the subjectivity of the *Relations* of 1633 and 1654, see Hélène Trépanier, "Être rien," in *Femme, mystique et missionnaire: Marie Guyart de l'Incarnation*, ed. Raymond Brodeur, 189–98 (Quebec: Presses de l'Université Laval, 2001). Marie's attention to her "nothingness" resonates, again, with the

hold me under your control. And then—or rather at the same time—you inspire me to speak to you as if I had control over you.

Excuse my liberty, of which you yourself are the cause, for you consume me in this state.[117]

This opening that you have made in my heart, which continually breathes in and out, sighing, is a mouth that speaks to you in a language that would kill the body if it had to pass through the senses, since it all ends up in saying that I see what you are in your essence. Ah love! Ah love! Having made me sing this canticle for a long time, which makes me find myself in you, you render me mute.

I am powerless, having been consumed in you by a love I can't express. I see clearly the things of your grandeurs and your amorous outpourings, O Incarnate Word, but they annihilate my thoughts in a profound abyss where they lose themselves.[118]

You know, my dear spouse, how the words my spiritual father spoke, after having heard my confession, affected my heart—that when I was dying alone and in his absence, in light of the access you allow my soul to you, I had no fear, and that otherwise, I wouldn't treat you like a spouse in whom I should trust. My spirit is still touched by this. To not treat you like a spouse—this is unbearable.[119] This is why, after this, I no longer worried about anything.

My beloved, I said to you, you know everything about me. Take care of everything for me. You know the great number of souls that I have the responsibility to present daily to your Father on your divine heart. Today, I am so ill and so

---

theology of the French School. The theme of "nothingness," for example, occupies a central place in the theology of Olier. See Olier, *Introduction à la vie*, 233–42. The language of "abyss," too, courses through the writings of Bérulle. See, for example, Pierre de Bérulle, *Discours de l'estat et des grandeurs de Jésus*, 90, 92.

117. Marie's recourse to language of "consuming" here recalls not only Condren's theology of sacrifice, but also Eudes's description of the obligation of the priest to "offer yourself also with [Christ] as a victim…you should pray that Jesus Christ…unite himself to you and that he unite and incorporate you with him as host, in order to sacrifice you with him…Pray that he will consume you in the sacred fire of his divine love" (Jean Eudes, *La vie et le royaume de Jésus*, reprinted and translated in Thompson, *Bérulle and the French School*, 324). See also Brémond, *Histoire litteraire*, vol. 1, Tome III, 1131–47.

118. *Relation de 1633*, 200–03; *Relation de 1654*, 243–6.

119. The tradition of bridal mysticism (which Marie invokes here) owes much to the theology of the twelfth-century Cistercian monk Bernard of Clairvaux, who develops the notion of mystical union as a passionate and affective marriage between the soul (gendered female) and God (gendered male); see Bernard McGinn, *The Growth of Mysticism* (New York: Crossroad, 1994), 193–223. For a feminist critique of the tradition of bridal mysticism, see Rosemary Radford

powerless that I wouldn't know how to do it anymore. Thus I am abandoned to your disposition.[120]

After that, I found myself relieved of all my cares, and, my heart sighing toward you, I spoke to you from time to time as if abandoned in you: My beloved, you are managing my affairs, my dear love. You have taken the responsibility.

I found myself struggling when my Father ordered me to ask you where you would put me if you called me to you, for, my dear love, I am so abandoned to your dispositions that I hardly thought about what you would do with me.

Nevertheless, I asked you what obedience demanded of me. But in asking you this, I felt myself carried away in this abandon. Put me wherever you want—you will be my love no matter where.[121] I hope I will see you, in your double divine and human beauty, amid the splendor of the saints on the day of your power, you, my beloved, who became man for the love of men and made yourself accessible to make men into gods by participation.[122]

I would gladly hope for your ultimate coming, so that seeing you triumph over your enemies, my soul might sing about your victories with you.

What I think here is ineffable to me in view of the insight your beloved ones will have into you.

If my heart follows its inclination, you alone know the access it has to your divine heart.

Ah! I must stop here, my dear love, my pledge, my security, and my life. You are everything to me and it seems to me that I am everything to you notwithstanding my simplicity and my weaknesses.

Ruether, *Goddesses and the Divine Feminine: a Western Religious History* (Berkeley: University of California Press, 2005), 179; and Carolyn Walker Bynum, "Christian Women in the Later Middle Ages," in *Christian Spirituality: High Middle Ages and Reformation*, ed. Jill Raitt, Bernard McGinn, and John Meyendorff, 243–4 (New York: Crossroad, 1987).

120. *Relation de 1654*, 371–4.

121. See also Francis de Sales, who, elaborating on the ideal of self-abnegation, compares the soul at repose in the presence of the divine beloved to a statue in a niche. If the statue, explains de Sales, "were endowed with understanding, and could reason and talk; and if it were asked: O fair statue, tell me now, why art thou in that niche? It would answer, Because my master placed me there. And if one should reply, But why stayest thou there without doing anything? Because, would it say, my master did not place me here to do anything, but simply that I should be here motionless. But if one should urge it further, saying: But, poor statue, what art thou the better for remaining there in that sort? Well! would it say, I am not there for my own interest and service, but to obey and accomplish the will of my master and maker; and this suffices me...and [it] would protest that it desired to do nothing but what its master wished. Francis de Sales, *Treatise on the Love of God*, trans. Henry Benedict Mackey, OSB (London: Burn and Oates, 1884), Book VI, Chap. xi.

122. Psalm 109:3, Vulgate.

Enough on these matters, my very dear son, for this year. I am so constrained by the nuisance of exterior affairs that I write you only when I steal a brief moment. Meanwhile I must answer, I believe, more than one hundred twenty letters, in addition to sending off the community's writings to France. See how one must pass this life in waiting for eternity, which does not pass. You consoled me in letting me know the state of your holy congregation and the happy success of its affairs. For you, all in due time, be known only by God. Steer clear of all conversation, except from those in which you see that God will be glorified. Beyond that, remain hidden in our very adorable Jesus, our unique good, our life and our all.

Letter 128: August 30, 1650

My very dear and beloved son,[123]

May the life and love of Jesus be your life and your love for eternity. It is a great testimony of your affection for me to wish me the same lot as that of our Reverend Fathers. But alas! I am unworthy of such an honor and such an exalted grace, although it seems quite close to us. For since I wrote you something about the great and extraordinary persecution of the Iroquois, there has been again a big clash between the French and these barbarians in an encounter that took place close to Trois-Rivières when some people went to search for the nine French and others who had been captured and taken away.[124] Today, they are planning to capture Trois-Rivières and you will note that they have with them several Dutch who are helping them. Someone recognized one of them in a skirmish and a Huron who escaped confirmed as much. Once they have taken Trois-Rivières they have resolved, so we're told, to come and attack us. Now although by all appearances, we have little to fear in our houses, which are sturdy, what has happened in the Huron villages that have been destroyed by fire or arms (for certainly they are powerful) should make the French dread a like calamity if prompt aid doesn't come our way. This is the feeling of the wisest and most experienced, like the Reverend Fathers who have come down from the Hurons and who have borne the weight of the tyranny of these barbarians. This aid can only come to us from France because there isn't enough force in the whole country to resist them. Therefore, if France fails us, in short, we'll have to leave or die. But because not all of the more than two thousand French here will be able to find means of leaving, they will be

---

123. Following the conclusion of his studies at Jumièges in 1648, Claude spent a year in retreat at the abbey of Saint-Martin of Sées. He received sacerdotal orders in November 1649 and by 1650 was serving as prior of Notre-Dame de Bonne-Nouvelle near Rouen.

124. See Thwaites, *Jesuit Relations*, vol. 35, 181–203.

forced to perish either from misery or the cruelty of their enemies. And what's more, the prospect of leaving behind the belongings they have acquired in this country and seeing themselves deprived of all comforts in France, would make them rather chose death in this country than misery in another. As for the rest of us, we have other motives by the mercy of our Lord. It is not material goods that retain us here, but rather what's left of our good Christians, with whom we would consider ourselves fortunate to die a million times if that were possible. These are our treasure, our brothers, our spiritual children, whom we cherish more than our lives and more than everything under heaven. So, rejoice if we die and someone brings you the news that our blood and ashes are mixed with theirs. It seems that this will come to pass if the thousand Iroquois who have broken off to go to the Neutral nation come to rejoin those who are at our doors. Reverend Father Daran to whom I have entrusted this present letter is one of those who came from the Hurons. He suffered all that can be suffered without dying, so he will be able to converse with you at leisure about all that has happened these last years in this new church. I promise that you will be extremely edified in listening to him. He is going to travel around France while waiting to be called back, in the event that the circumstances of the country so permit, for he is sorely missed here. I miss him like the others, but ask that you relieve my sorrow by receiving him as he deserves. Others like Reverend Fathers Ragueneau and Pijart are also going to France to ask for aid from His Majesty. The former will garner more interest there because he is the superior of the mission to the Hurons. He's one of the greats and one of the most zealous missionaries in New France, but I esteem him more for his great holiness than for all his great natural talents and for all his free graces. We hope to see him again next year.

When I was finishing talking to you about Reverend Father Ragueneau, someone came to tell me that he was asking for me, to bid me *adieu*. He promised me that he would see you and to this end, he wrote down your name. He's one of the best friends of our seminary and has a great knowledge of the graces that the Divine Goodness is spreading there. He again assured me based on his experience with the furor and strength of the Iroquois that unless we have prompt aid on the part of France, or unless it pleases God to help our country in an extraordinary way, all is lost. This is not an exaggeration. I am telling you the same based on what little I know.

You see by the above that in waiting for aid we are in the pure providence of God. As for me, my very dear son, I find myself well here and my spirit and heart could not be more content. If it comes to pass that someone brings you the news of my death next year, bless God for it and offer him the holy sacrifice of the mass on my behalf. Procure for me again the petitions of your holy congregation, which has always been very dear to me. If God calls me to him and it pleases him to have mercy on me, your congregation will be all the more dear to me, and I myself will be better situated to beg the Divine Majesty to increase his holy blessings upon it.

I am extremely consoled that God has detached you from creatures and from the love or the pretension of love that you could expect from them. Ah! My son, the kingdom of peace is in a heart thus stripped of all things, and which, by a holy hatred of self, enjoys destroying the remains of corrupted nature. The holiest of these hearts suffer attacks even unto death, which constitute the true grounds of their humiliation. From the time a soul enters into this truth, convinced of it by its own experience, it humiliates itself not only before God in its interior and exterior operations where it constantly discovers new sins, but also before creatures, taking pleasure in publicly accusing itself of its defects, in subjecting itself to penitence, and in miring itself in confusion. It doesn't blame third or fourth parties for the sin, although someone else might have had a hand in it. It attributes all sins to itself and afterwards is convinced that it is still full of more malice than it ever admitted or knew, and more than others had discovered, whence it persuades itself that it is only worthy of punishment by God, who deprives it of his greatest favors, as well as by his creatures, who share the creator's interests, correcting us each in his own way. There are many other means of practicing humility that follow from their opposites.[125] The glorious Father Saint Benedict spoke highly of this humility just as, I believe, he practiced it. He is your patron and your father, who will attract to you the influence of this spirit which is better tasted interiorly rather than expressed exteriorly. Ask him to obtain this exalted virtue for me, for this is what makes saints, as we have again observed in the five servants of God who were martyred here, for they were so humble before their martyrdom that they astonished those who had the pleasure of living in their company.[126] I would have to write an overly long letter if I wanted to give all the particulars, but time doesn't permit me to dwell on it.

I responded by another letter to how you propose for me to instruct some Indians so that they can win their companions to the faith. In addition to what I'm writing you, talk with Reverend Father Daran about it. He will tell you that

---

125. *Relation de 1654*, 374–86, 397–400.

126. The five martyrs to whom Marie alludes are Jean de Brébeuf, Antoine Daniel, Gabriel Lalemant, Noël Chabanel, and Charles Garnier. Marie's abbreviated discussion of the virtue of humility here betrays the competing discourses of specularity (humility is something that can be observed) and interiority (humility is "tasted interiorly rather than expressed exteriorly"), suggesting the endurance of a more medieval conviction in the visibility of virtue within the context of an emerging privileging of the interior. See also Letters 68 and 81. For an elaboration of the virtue of humility (which he proposes as the foundation of all Christian virtues), see Olier, *Introduction à la vie*, 27–50.

even though the country is returning to normal, we will always have to depend on Europe for gospel workers. The nature of American Indians, even the most holy and spiritual, renders them unsuitable to perform the functions of clerics and disposes them only to be instructed and directed gently in the way of heaven, which makes one suspect in this reversal of affairs that maybe God wants only a temporary church here.

It is true that the Reverend Father Brébeuf received the sacred gift I mentioned. The Reverend Father Garnier, one of those who won the crown this year, had it especially.[127] Never, my very dear son, will you know this gift by study or by force of speculation, but in humble prayer and the submission of the soul at the foot of the crucifix. This adorable Word incarnate and crucified is the living source of this spirit. It's he who portions it out to chosen souls who are dearest to him, so that they may follow and teach his divine maxims and by this practice consume themselves to the end in imitating him. This holy spirit—this union, I say—of which I am speaking to you, isn't the one of glory, but only a foretaste of it. And don't think that this holy spirit always makes one's labors easy, since it doesn't always affect the senses.[128] But it provides an invincible strength in the depths of the soul to support whatever burdens and troubles there are. It would take a hefty book to describe the life of this Reverend Father animated by this holy spirit. He was eminently humble, mild, obedient, and full of virtue acquired by much travail. We had the pleasure of seeing the outcome of his virtues in practice. He was in a continual colloquy and familiar exchange with God. Even riddled by blows, he was still seen in the exercise of charity, trying to drag himself to a poor woman who, having received many blows of the hatchet, was desperate and in need of help to die well.

Reverend Father Chabanel, one of those who were massacred this year, had the greatest possible natural aversion to living in the cabins of the Indians.[129] For this reason, his superiors often wanted to spare him and send him on other missions where he would not have had to be engaged in that sort of life. But by an extraordinary generosity and borne by the spirit I mentioned, he made a vow to persevere and die there if it pleased God to grant him this mercy. Nevertheless, his superior, knowing that he was extremely fatigued by the work of his mission, called him back. It was on this journey that he was captured and massacred, though we can't determine which enemy killed him or what they did with his body. In any event, he died in the act of obedience.

---

127. Thwaites, *Jesuit Relations*, vol. 35, 105–43.

128. *Relation de 1654*, 378–81.

129. Thwaites, *Jesuit Relations*, vol. 35, 145–59.

The other Reverend Fathers who withdrew here from distant missions suffered so appallingly that no human words can express it. I exaggerate not a bit, and if the great humility of Reverend Father Daran doesn't conceal it, ask him some particularities of his sufferings, for his experience has made him knowledgeable. I give you these examples to convince you that our union is never more eminent than in trials suffered in the imitation and for the love of Jesus Christ, who was in the time of his sufferings and above all at the point of death, in the highest degree of union and love for humanity with God his Father. Sweet and loving union is already the beatitude initiated in a mortal flesh, and its merit is in acts of charity toward God and one's neighbor and in other theological virtues. But the union of which I speak, which is however an outcome of that one, consists in giving one's life in a consummation of works which come to resemble Jesus Christ. Ah! Certainly we must esteem this one most highly and wait until the next life to understand its merit and excellence, for at present our speech is too base to be able to talk about it as we ought.

I bless God for the desire he gives you to suffer martyrdom. You are still young, my dear son, and if you want to be faithful to the grace, you will suffer for it a good long time yet while you remain enclosed in your solitude. This desire must be a powerful incentive for you to lead a penitent, mortified, and regular life. This is the martyrdom that you must suffer and that God is demanding of you, while waiting, perhaps, for some opportunity that the Divine Majesty is keeping hidden from you and which you neither expect nor foresee. Nevertheless, you must clothe yourself with the virtues necessary to such an exalted grace. And still, after all your fine preparations, you must consider yourself unworthy.

I agree with you that a lack of money could indeed impede the dispatch of our bull to Rome.[130] I see besides that the affairs of the country will keep things in suspense, for there are three things that we must seriously consider, given the gravity of the situation. The first is that neither we nor Canada as a whole will be able to subsist for two more years without help. The second is that if we don't get this help, we must either die or return to France, according to the opinion of the most sensible. I nevertheless believe that if the enemy goes to war against the Neutral nation and the Andaste, this will cause a division of forces that will allow us to subsist a while longer. But if their conquests and victories continue, there is nothing more to do here for the French. Commerce will no longer be able to continue here. And if commerce no longer continues, no more ships will come. And if no more ships come, we will be without all the essentials for living, like fabric, linen, and the majority of supplies like fat and flour, which the garrison

---

130. See also Letter 81.

and the religious houses can't do without. It's not that people don't work very hard and that they don't produce food, but the country doesn't yet yield what it needs to sustain itself. The third thing that delays our affairs is that if commerce fails because of the continuing war, Indians who only stop here to trade will scatter in the woods. Thus, we will no longer have need of the bull, since we, who are here only to attract them to the faith and win them for God, will have nothing more to do. You can imagine from the above that a bishop will not come here in such calamitous times, in addition to which, the church here being only temporary, there is no need for priests.[131] I am speaking under the assumption that God permits the disaster we dread to come about.

Given that this new church is in so manifest a danger, do me the charity of making some devotion before the image of the very Holy Virgin so that it pleases her to take it under her wing. Pray also for me and for our election, which we are going to hold the week of Pentecost. This danger and these fears, though, do not take away from the worship that Christians—French as well as Indian—are accustomed to rendering to God. You would have been deeply moved had you seen the procession that took place in Quebec on the day of the Assumption of this Mother of goodness. Two fathers of the Company of Jesus carried her image in relief on a highly ornamented sled to three religious houses, which were designated as stations. As these places are fairly far from each other, two other fathers prepared to follow them and relieve them of this holy responsibility. In addition to the crowds of French, there were about six hundred Indians who walked in order. The devotion of these good neophytes was so great that it brought tears to the eyes of those who watched. Out of curiosity, I watched them from a place where I couldn't be seen, and I assure you that I have never seen in France a procession of such order and apparent devotion. As for what pertains to the Indians, that is still new to me, for the thought of what they were before knowing God, and what they are now that they know him, touches me more profoundly than I can say. You can imagine, then, how I suffer to see the tyranny that the Iroquois barbarians are exercising against them. Ah! My very dear son, how happy I would be, how content, if all this persecution would end in me! Present this desire of mine to the Holy Virgin again, to whom I present yours with a good heart.

I have already written this letter in fits and starts, and in the intervals some news always comes. The captive who escaped the Iroquois reports that the warriors of the Andouesteronons and those of the Neutral nation took two hundred Iroquois prisoners. If that's true, they will be treated in a terrible manner and this will be a great burden for us. It will be still a good fifteen days before this captive

---

131. See Letter 183.

tells everything he knows, for it's the custom of the Indians to say what they know only little by little and on various days. This custom makes our French, who are curious and want to know things right away, impatient, especially when it involves important matters reported by a single messenger.

Since the above, two more Hurons have escaped from the captivity of the Iroquois. They are both good Christians in their hearts and catechumens in fact. The desire for holy baptism led them to make very intense efforts, coming here by means of arduous journeys through the woods and without any provisions. They reported that our ten Algonquins of Sillery who were captured last June were burned alive, with very great sentiments of faith and religion. One of them, for the love of whom I am writing you this piece, was particularly distinguished by his zeal and fervor.[132] He was about twenty-two or so and was my spiritual son, loving me as much or more than his own mother. He spent three days and nights in very horrible torments carried out in contempt of the faith that he boldly made his confession to his last breath. These barbarians said to him, mocking him, "Where is your God? He's not helping you at all." Then they began tormenting him again and also mocking him, saying, "Pray to your God to see if he'll help you." Nevertheless, this courageous servant of God renewed his prayers and his praises to the one for the love of whom he was suffering, for by nature he sang quite well and this enraged these barbarians. His name was Joseph and he had been raised in the faith by the Reverend Father Le Jeune, almost since childhood. In your opinion, have I not in him a good son? He is, rather, my father and my advocate before God. Because of the love I bore for him, I am delighted by the lofty grace he received in persevering so selflessly. He was a perfectly well-formed young man and extremely modest, but I praise him only for his faithfulness. If someone came to tell me as much about you, my very dear son, ah! Who would be able to describe the joy this would give me? But these signal favors are not ours to select. They are among the treasures of God who communicates them to chosen souls. I must close this letter with this last wish, which is that of the greatest testimonies of my affection for the person in the world who is dearest to me.

Letter 135: September 13, 1651

My very dear son,[133]

May Jesus be our all for eternity. A small ship that arrived here has brought us letters from our Mothers of Tours, by means of which I have learned about your

---

132. Thwaites, *Jesuit Relations*, vol. 35, 221–31.

133. In the spring of 1651, Claude was appointed under-prior at Vendôme.

news. It is returning without any other having appeared, and yet it is already the thirteenth of September. I don't want to let it leave without giving you testimonies of my sincere affection and telling you what you could learn about us, preferring that you come to know it from me than from anyone else.

We have not died at the hands of the Iroquois but we have passed through the fire in an unexpected calamity that happened at our monastery last December thirtieth, and which reduced it to ashes, together with all our temporal goods, our people alone having been saved from this horrible fire by a totally particular providence of God.[134] I was the last to get out, with fires both above and below me and another following me. I escaped through the grills that one or two of our sisters had broken because they were made only of wood, and if I had not found this way out I would have had to go out through a window that was still open but was on the third floor, as did a poor Huron woman, who threw herself onto the frozen snow, which caused her serious injury. I then found my poor sisters on the snow where they were nearly naked. I am not reporting to you all the details of this calamity here, but am writing only briefly about it. Our friends assisted us with habits, provisions, and other necessities. They even loaned us money to rebuild our monastery, which had to be constructed again from the foundations. It is 108 feet long and twenty-eight feet wide. The parlors are thirty feet long and twenty-four feet wide. I'll leave you to judge whether we have not experienced a harsh blow. Our loss is close to sixty thousand *livres*, which the providence of God had given us. It has also taken them away from us.[135] It is from God's providence that we wait for it again, for the debts we have incurred for this building exceed our foundation. You will perhaps say, as have several of our friends, that we would have done better to return to France than to incur such considerable and risky expenses, given how uncertain everything is here due to the incursions of the Iroquois. We discussed this affair with the most important men of the country, who showed us the goodness of their hearts and the care with which they protect us. The conclusion was that we would not leave, but we would put ourselves in a position to render to God the services appropriate to our vocation, which by his mercy is stronger than ever. For I must tell you, my very dear son, to the glory of His Majesty, we have received such a great reinforcement of graces and encouragement, that the more we were deprived of our temporal goods, the more grace abounded in us.[136] This here is only a little word in passing. I will tell you by another way the secret dispositions of my heart.

---

134. See also Letter 136; Thwaites, *Jesuit Relations*, vol. 36, 167–71.

135. Job 1:21.

136. *Relation de 1654*, 437–40.

Once the resolution to lift ourselves up had been made, I was charged with the direction and organization of this building. This caused me a great deal of pain and fatigue because of the difficulties one encounters in this country, which is covered with snow until May, and because of the need to gather materials and other necessities for a structure like ours. Our elections were then held.[137] See how many burdens fall upon such weak shoulders in such a poor country and among the inconveniences of a calamity like ours. Do not think, however, my very dear son, that all this demoralizes my heart. No, I began our establishment here with the support of the divine providence. Our foundation provided us only with things to live on. The rest, which we needed for building and for helping our poor Indians, this lovable providence had given us. The reach of His hand has not been shortened and if he has withdrawn it for a time, he can extend it again to fill us with his blessings.[138] I hope that he will strengthen me in the work he wants me to undertake for his glory. As for me, I assure you that I am a very idiotic creature, and it is in my idiocy that the magnificence of his glory will shine all the more.

Our building is already as high as the palisade. They are erecting the chimneys and in eight days they will raise the frame. If the ships had arrived from France we would have tried to borrow the workers of our friends who are bringing them from France, which would have allowed us to live there within four to six months. But lacking this help we won't be able to live there until around this time next year. It is astonishing how expensive artisans and laborers are here. We pay them between forty-five and fifty-five *sols* per day. The laborers cost thirty *sols* per day plus food. Since our calamity happened unexpectedly, we were deprived of all those people and this is why they are expensive for us. Accordingly, we had no choice but to have them come from France at a more reasonable price. We engage them for three years and thus they get something out of it and so do we. Now there are some days when we get a day's worth of labor for thirty *livres*, not to mention those who work by the measure or by the task. We have four oxen that do our plowing, lugging materials of wood and sand. We extract stone on the spot. This is how things are handled in this country.

In the meantime, we are staying in a small house which is at the end of our enclosure, measuring thirty feet long and twenty wide. It serves for us as a church, parlor, lodging, refectory, offices and every other purpose, except that we hold our classes in a cabin made of bark. Before our fire we rented it out, but today we are

---

137. Marie was elected superior of her community June 12, 1651, a position she would retain until 1657. Between her arrival in Canada in 1639 and her death in 1672, Marie would serve as superior of the Ursulines in Quebec for a total of three six-year terms.

138. Isaiah 50:2 and 59:1.

only too happy to live there. It is convenient for us in that we can watch over our buildings without leaving our enclosure. Pray to God for me, my very dear son, that he strengthens me and renders me worthy to serve him at the expense of my life and my honor. It is from there that I derive my glory, from which I likewise make him a new sacrifice with all my heart. I am.

After having finished my letter, I must tell you again that it seems that our good God wants to triumph over us in reducing us to desperation. Would you believe that for the forty to fifty people we have here, including our workers, we only have enough for three batches of bread and we have no news of the ships that are bringing fresh provisions to this country. I can do nothing else but rejoice in everything it will please His paternal Goodness to do. Blessed be he eternally.

Letter 136: October–November, 1651

My very dear son,

May the love and life of Jesus be our life and our love for all eternity. You have infinitely obliged me with the good advice you give me and the wishes you make for me. You have seen by my other letters that I was not been fortunate enough to die by the fire of the Iroquois, but that my sisters and I were almost consumed by that of providence.[139] I did not want to tell you openly in my other letter about what happened in my interior in the moments of that affliction. I reserved such information for this letter. You must know therefore that after I had done everything humanly possible to avoid the total loss of our monastery, on the one hand calling for help and on the other hand working with the others, I returned to our room to save what was most important for the affairs of our community seeing that there was no remedy for the rest. In all the trips I made, I had such presence of mind and was so attuned to everything I was doing that it was as if nothing had happened to us.[140] It seemed to me that an interior voice was telling me what I should throw out of the window and what I should let perish in the fire. I saw in a single moment the nothingness of all earthly things, and God gave me a grace of destitution so great that I can express its effect neither in speech nor in writing. I wanted to throw out our crucifix which was on our table, but I felt myself restrained as if someone had suggested to me that this was disrespectful and that it mattered little if it burned. It was the same with all the rest, for I left my papers and everything that pertained to my personal usage. These papers were those you

---

139. See Letter 135.

140. *Relation de 1654*, 434–7.

had asked me for and which I had recently written out of obedience. Before this calamity, my intention was to send them to you because I had agreed to give you this satisfaction, but on the condition that you burn them after having read them. The thought occurred to me to throw them out the window, but my fear that they would fall into someone's hands made me abandon them voluntarily to the fire. And, in fact, that came about by a particular providence of God, because the few I had thrown out were safeguarded by a respectable young lady whose children certainly glanced over them. After all these reflections, I again put my hand on the papers as if by chance and I felt myself compelled interiorly to leave them. I therefore left them to obey the spirit of God who guided me, for I assure you that I would not want that anyone had seen them for anything, for they revealed how God has guided me since I have known myself. I had put off carrying out this act of obedience for more than five years. I felt so much repugnance toward it that it had been necessary to command me to do so three times over. I finally obeyed, but at present it is done, my very dear son, and we must forget about it.[141]

When I settled down with my sisters whom I found on the snow, my interior peace and acquiescence to God's plans for us worked great operations in my heart. It was a sum of pleasures corresponding to God's good pleasure in an excess that I can't express. I saw that all the nuisances and consequences of this calamity were going to fall on my shoulders and that I would have to dispose myself to work more than ever. My whole being consented to all the travails that could befall me, and God gave me such a strong vocation for this that the difficulties I have continually encountered since have been sweet and light to me. It seemed to me that I was flying when the work was hardest, helped by the grace that possessed me.[142] I was put in the position of superior on June twelfth of last year, which added even more to my cares. So much for the weight of my interior dispositions. If time

---

141. Marie's insistence here that obedience alone compelled her to record and share her spiritual experiences resonates with what Gillian T. W. Ahlgren has called the "rhetoric of obedience" in Teresa of Ávila's writings. Ahlgren persuasively demonstrates the ways in which Teresa appeals to the virtues of both humility and obedience as a means of authorizing her writings both as a woman and within the context of the Spanish Inquisition; see Ahlgren, *Teresa of Avila and the Politics of Sanctity*, 72, 67–84. See also, Weber, *Teresa of Avila and the Rhetoric of Femininity*, 42–76. But see Nicholas Paige, who argues that the role of the spiritual director in compelling these autobiographical texts from women religious had changed by the time of Marie de l'Incarnation, such that "what was normally the role of the examiner…[was] emptied of its censoring content" (Paige, *Being Interior*, 100).

142. This passage offers telling testimony to the ways in which the difficulties of life in Canada enhanced Marie's practice of the abnegation idealized by the French School. At the same time, Marie's insistence here (as elsewhere) on her interior equanimity in the midst of exterior commotion draws attention to what Paige identifies as a "neo-stoic motif" in the lives of religious women in the seventeenth century. Paige, *Being Interior*, 163–4. See also Letters 177 and 267.

permitted, I would talk to you about it in more detail and would respond point by point to your letter, but the ships are leaving almost as soon as they arrived.

Our fire was no harder for me to bear than I just told you. But I must admit to you that I have received word from France about some things which have displeased me. God was not displeased by the burning of our monastery, but rather his will was done and assented to, I believe, by us. But I fear that he has been by the news I have received, since such news is contrary to the truth and could undermine the practice of charity. Our Mothers of Tours were told that when we passed through Dieppe to come to Canada, we made a new contract with the Mothers of the congregation of Paris, which contained clauses prejudicial to our congregation of Tours. This rumor spread throughout the whole community such that all those who wrote me did not forget to mention it, and some with resentment. They are even writing me the terms of this supposed contract and are saying that I allowed myself to be deceived and that my easy-going nature was abused. I can well imagine who gave them this report, which is neither true nor well-founded, for neither Madame our foundress nor I have ever even thought of such a thing, and we have never made a treaty in France other than the one our Mothers saw and approved.[143] You cannot imagine, however, the bad effect this has wrought in the minds of some. I just mentioned that they consented to the treaty and all its clauses, although there was one clause that greatly displeased me. But as one is not always able to bend the spirit of the founders to one's wishes, I consented to it like the others and saw clearly that we must wait for the opportunity to remedy it, for had we wanted to do it prematurely, as well as provoking anger, we would have spoiled everything. It could only be done last year, when Madame our foundress, having seen with her own eyes by the defeat of the Hurons that her plan could be ruined if she didn't make a new contract, determined that one be made, which provided that we could use her foundation to establish a house in France in the event that affairs in Canada became entirely desperate; or, better put, that the funds she gave us would follow us wherever we establish ourselves, whether in New or Old France. Finally, this was done as resolutely as possible. When the Reverend Father Lalement passed through Tours, he assured our Mothers of all of this, but their impression of this false report is so strong that they can't let it go. However, that doesn't prevent them from maintaining hearts full of charity for us and from urging us as strongly as they can to go back to France and return to our house, assuring us that we will be received there with open arms. They are

---

143. Marie discusses these events more extensively in a letter written in 1656 to the Superior of the Ursulines of Tours. See Lettre CLXXI, *Correspondance*, 574–81. See also Letter 142.

unbelievably afraid for us, and they beg us not to wait until something extreme happens, but instead, to anticipate our ultimate demise.

What has displeased me most about these reports is that they do damage to the reputations of the Reverend Fathers of the Society, who are said to have acted in their own interests with regard to this matter, which is, with all due respect, a very big lie. You have seen by my other letter how much they help us.[144] All who are in need receive the same from them. Young and old, and everyone generally, have recourse to them in their times of distress. Someone reported to Reverend Father Lalemant how our Mothers felt when he passed through Tours. Someone even told him who caused the trouble, but in his modesty, he didn't reveal it to me. He told me only that he visited them and that he corrected some ill-founded belief that they had. Finally, he told me that he is completely satisfied with this community and this was not insincere, for you will know he is a man who tenderly cherishes those who wrong him.

You see my weakness, my very dear son. For to see those who practice an excess of spiritual as well as temporal charity toward us offended for no reason and on our account, displeases me, and in these situations I must practice virtue. God nevertheless gives me the grace that nothing stays in my heart when I have been wronged or when someone else has been wronged on my account or on ours. Above all, I feel that we should all live with more integrity and simplicity. If we were closer to each other, we would communicate more about these matters of virtue which I love more than I actually practice. But since he is keeping us apart, let us see each other and speak to each other in him, since it is in him that I am.

Letter 142: September 1, 1652

My very dear and beloved son,[145]

May Jesus be our all for eternity. I don't doubt that the tenderness of your affection for us has given rise to the sentiments of compassion you expressed to me. But I can easily see by your letters that you did not receive all those I wrote you last year. There were many that were lost, as those were, because of the capture and wreckage of two of our ships.[146] But what can we do about that? These are the sorts of calamity we can deal with only by means of our acquiescence to the divine

---

144. See Lettre CXXXIII, *Correspondance*, 414–16.

145. Claude became prior of Saint-Nicaire de Meulan in the spring of 1652; see Oury, *Dom Claude Martin*, 93.

146. Thwaites, *Jesuit Relations*, vol. 37, 79–85.

will. Therein lies the remedy to all our troubles and I have experienced it again more than ever in the aftermath of our fire. But let me begin to respond to you.

I assure you, in general, that everything you wrote me last year so pleased and consoled me that I reread your letter from time to time to refresh my memory. Nevertheless, I easily see by your short letter that I did not explain myself enough with regard to certain reports that had been made to our Mothers of Tours to the prejudice of our Jesuit Reverend Fathers.[147] I did not tell you the name of the person who had made them because the respect I have for her didn't permit me to reveal her identity. But, my very dear son, you thought that it was you about whom I meant to speak, and whom I suspected to have been the author of this little mess. Just as the thing itself is not true, so also the thought never came to me. If I had something against you I would tell you frankly and candidly. What obliged me to speak to you about it was that I had been told that you had to go to Tours, and I believed that if you knew the truth you could disabuse our Mothers of their false beliefs. That is how things came to pass, and I beg you to believe that I opened my heart to you about this, as the person in the world whom I trust the most. I see that this has caused you pain and this upsets me, my very dear son, and I repeat that you have told me nothing that was not well taken and that does not give me consolation and many reasons to bless God. But let me respond to the particular points of your letter.

It's true that given the extent and multitude of problems in this country, and that we've lost everything, we ought to return to France, according to all human reason.[148] And what ought to lead us still further to this conclusion is that according to a new contract, which we have concluded with Madame our foundress, our foundation must follow us in the event that we are obliged to leave the country, whether on account of the failure of the French colony or other events that are thought to oblige us to pull out.[149] All that is certain. But you must know that the religious houses here constitute one of the most considerable parts of the colony, and that the departure of even one would be capable of discouraging the bulk of

---

147. See Letter 136.

148. Despite the best efforts of the various trading companies to grow the Canadian colony, its population was sparse and its economy underdeveloped in the middle of the seventeenth century. See Eccles, *The Canadian Frontier*, 38, who argues that the religious orders "were responsible for what little development there was in the colony." For a synthesis of the social and economic development of New France, see *Historical Atlas of Canada*, vol. 1 (Toronto: University of Toronto Press, 1987). The already precarious situation of the colony was made worse by the escalation of conflicts with the Iroquois and, for the Marie and her sisters, by the destruction of the Ursuline monastery by the fire of 1650. See Letters 128, 135, and 143.

149. See also Letter 136.

the French population, which has been supported only by the religious houses and their resources. What's more, the French girls would be true brutes without the education they receive from us and which they need more than the Indians, for the Reverend Fathers can provide the Indians with education, but they cannot do so for the others for reasons you can imagine.[150] In the third place, since the country is not so desperate as to preclude our reestablishment, our retreat would not have been legitimate. That being the case, we could not stay there without rebuilding our monastery, a point on which all the most important people agreed, and we have made an effort to put our monastery in the state in which it is at present.

You will say that since we are here for the benefit of the public, the public should have rebuilt for us at its expense. I respond that the country was not in a position to do this. We had to come up with more than twenty-five thousand *livres* for our building as well as for our other needs, for having lost everything we had nothing. Of this sum we owe sixteen thousand, which we will pay off when the divine providence gives us the means. We have borrowed eight of it, on which we will begin to pay interest only in 1656. The country has helped us with the rest, which is no small effort. I will tell you that God helped us last year in a totally extraordinary way. Since people in France were not aware of the calamity that had happened to us, they didn't send any help. But our confessor saw that we were in need and responsible for a great number of workers, so he took it upon himself to farm some land that we had cleared but had abandoned to do more urgent work. He put people there and worked there himself more than anyone else. And God so blessed his charity and labor that we harvested thirty *poinçons* of wheat and sixteen *poinçons* of peas and barley.[151] Peas are mixed with wheat to make bread, and they fetch an equal price. The barley is for our livestock. We also make tea out of it, to drink. With this help and that which has come to us from France, we have gotten through the year—all forty of us including our workers.[152]

We were in our new building on the eve of Pentecost. The parish and all the clergy and a great crowd of people came there to transport the very holy sacrament from where we had been staying. The forty hours' prayer was then begun, which lasted until the Tuesday of Pentecost. Everyone was overjoyed to see us

---

150. The *Jesuit Relations* second this assessment of the importance of the Ursulines. Thwaites, *Jesuit Relations*, vol. 36, 171.

151. A *poinçon* is a liquid measurement equal to approximately 53 gallons.

152. Records preserved by the monastery for the year 1651 indicate that the Ursulines received donations totaling 1064 *livres* (compared to 1905 *livres* in 1650 and 2434 *livres* in 1652), as well as gifts of 130–40 yards of cloth, three bushels of green pea seeds, and a *poinçon* of flour and a barrel of lard. See Lettre XCLII, *Correspondance*, 481, n. 16.

living where we were before, and freed from the great inconveniences we had suffered since our fire. Over the course of these three days the parish came here in a procession with the people singing music, for all was done here as in a cathedral, in terms of both the song and the ceremonies, which the most well-informed say were observed with as much majesty as in the best-run choirs of France.

I will confess to you anyway that your reasons seem very good to me, and I have often thought the same myself, although with peace of mind. But the way in which God governs this country is quite contrary to such reasoning. One sees absolutely nothing and one gropes one's way in the dark. And although very enlightened and well-advised people are consulted, ordinarily things don't happen as they had been anticipated or planned for. However, one goes on, and when one thinks one has fallen into a deep abyss, one finds oneself upright. This pattern is universal, both in the majority of public affairs as well as in each private family. When people get wind of some misfortune that has come to pass because of the Iroquois, like the great one that happened a month ago, everyone wants to go back to France. And yet at the same time people are marrying, people are building, the country is multiplying, the lands are cultivated, and everyone thinks about establishing himself. Three-quarters of the settlers earn their subsistence from working the land. We, too, are going to cultivate as much land as we can, in order to help feed both ourselves and our livestock. We have four oxen, which we use for cartage and labor, and six cows, which provide us with butter and most of our food during the summer when the girls practically do without dairy. By a providence of God these livestock were on our grounds at St. Joseph when the monastery was burned and thus they were saved. Thus are households managed in this country, and without this, neither we nor the others could subsist, regardless of the help we receive from France. But that is not what keeps us here. On the contrary, these domestic tasks are distracting. Rather, it is the fidelity that we want to render to God in the vocations by which he has so lovingly called us here. Until we receive a sign that his holy will is content with our insignificant services in this country and that we must render them to him elsewhere, we will remain constant and unwavering in our resolutions. And that, my very dear son, is the only thing that keeps me here. And yet, it seems to me that my soul is ready to leave at any moment if His Divine Majesty wants it. Therein I find my peace and repose. Last year someone from France who had not yet heard about our fire counseled me to arrange for our return to France, telling me that people would only be edified by it, that I would be excused for having had a little mix-up, and that people would laugh a little about it, but that it would soon be forgotten. I confess to you that this proposition appeared so base to me and these grounds so facile that I didn't respond to it. I nevertheless do not doubt that many suspect that things will thus come to pass. But if God had permitted that we return to France, I would go back with the same tranquility and spiritual contentment with which I came here. If the obedience that brought me here also took me away, it seems to me that I would be very well supported by having relied on God's orders. In this case I would hardly worry about the judgments of men, which are often quite far from the judgments of the one to whom we owe the glory of obedience.[153]

I say to you, therefore, that just as nothing is certain in this country, so also there is nothing new that ought to make us more afraid than before. Nevertheless, many were frightened by the event I told you about, in which Monsieur the Governor of Trois-Rivières, a very brave and respectable gentleman, was killed by the Iroquois, along with twenty-two Frenchmen, in a battle where he went out into the woods contrary to the advice of those who were accompanying him and were experienced in the ways of these barbarians.[154] This is a significant defeat, not only in itself, but also because of what happened after. For on top of that, several notable Frenchmen have been seized and made captives, and several women have been left widows. Until this point, the Iroquois believed that they hadn't done anything, because they had had no advantage over the persons of the sword, but now that they have killed the Governor of Trois-Rivières, they think they are the masters of all of New France, for these people do not respect authority and are becoming completely insolent.[155] They are not feared in the settlements, but in remote places and houses near the woods. Because experience teaches that there is nothing to gain in pursuing them, we are merely keeping ourselves on the defensive, and this is indeed best. If Monsieur du Plessis had acted thus, this misfortune would never have befallen him or his people. But his courage brought him down. The Iroquois are extremely afraid of canons, so they don't dare come near to the forts. In order to chase them off and terrorize them, the settlers have redoubts in their houses, for the purpose of defending themselves with small arms. As for us, our weapons are the protection of the Holy Virgin and our good angels. Our people do, however, have several firearms

---

153. 1 Corinthians 4:3. The antagonism Marie supposes here between the judgment of God and the judgments of men extends not only the familiar Pauline opposition between the (sacred) spirit and the (secular) flesh, but also suggests an emerging seventeenth-century sense of an interior experience—forever elusive and necessarily opaque—subject to misapprehension by an uncomprehending public; see Paige, *Being Interior*, 119–78. See also Letters 135 and 142.

154. Thwaites, *Jesuit Relations*, vol. 38, 55–7.

155. Seventeenth-century French society consisted of three estates. The various grades of French clergy comprised the first estate, the sword-bearing nobility the second estate, and the non-noble laity the third estate. Here, Marie refers to the members of the second estate. For a discussion of the three estates in early modern France, see William Beik, *Absolutisim and Society in Seventeenth-Century France: State Power and Provincial Aristocracy in Languedoc* (Cambridge, UK: Cambridge University Press, 1985), 117–47.

which they have not yet used against the Iroquois, but only to hunt pigeons and ducks in the summer and autumn when we have sick people staying with us, for beyond that we don't trouble ourselves about guns since we need them for more useful tasks. There are ten of them and if there was reason to fear the Iroquois, we would put them in the position to defend us. But after all, if God were to open the eyes of this enemy, who is strong enough to destroy everything, the whole country would be in great danger. But we ceaselessly experience the protections of a strong and powerful God.

The Reverend Father Buteux was massacred by these barbarians while on his mission among the Attikameks, and he received the crown of martyrdom with a French soldier who accompanied him and several of his neophytes.[156] This is an unbelievable loss for the mission, but one must bless God who takes his time to crown his martyrs and compensate his workers. They also struck a French woman from Montreal seven times with an axe, who put up a good fight. She threw one of them to the ground and escaped by crying out so loudly that she was heard by the fort. Someone went to help her, and she was rescued. It's not as if the Iroquois always have such an advantage that they don't sometimes suffer setbacks. Two victories were won over them in which two of their greatest chiefs were captured and burned alive. This is what angered them and made them come two hundred strong, divided into two bands, to attack and burn Trois-Rivières. They attacked hastily and immediately withdrew, taking with them the prisoners of whom I spoke, together with fifty horned cattle belonging to the settlers of the place.

As far as commerce goes, trading along the southern coast is almost ruined, but there is more going on in the north than ever. If the merchants were careful to bring goods from France in a timely manner, such that the beaver pelts were not diverted elsewhere because of the delay, they would be rich. But fundamentally, while the settlers dither with this trade, they do not get ahead as much as if they worked to cultivate the land and committed themselves to dealing in fish, seal, and porpoise oils, and other similar staples, which are beginning to be introduced into commerce.

I will tell you by another way about the death of Mother Marie de Saint-Joseph. Pray for us all, and particularly for me, so that I can be a perfect holocaust to the Divine Majesty in the manner he deems most suitable for his greatest glory.[157]

---

156. Thwaites, *Jesuit Relations*, vol. 37, 97.

157. See Lettres CXXXIX and CXL, *Correspondance*, 434–5 and 436–73. Marie's extensive account of the life and death of Marie de Saint-Joseph is reproduced substantially in Thwaites, *Jesuit Relations*, vol. 38, 67–163.

Letter 143: September 9, 1652

My very dear son,

Here is the response to your letter of April 13, for I have written you plenty about the general affairs of the country and the particular affairs of our community, by three other letters which you have received or will receive from me this year. This fourth is to speak to you in confidence and to tell you in the first place that I was upset that the letter I wrote you last year caused you grief, giving you reason to believe that it was you about whom I meant to speak in the third person.[158] But why did you think it was about you? I wasn't worried about saying it since I never even thought it, and the thought didn't dare to come to me since I know for certain that it isn't true. I was telling you about the reproaches our Mothers of Tours had made to me in error, although innocently, and I referred in the third person to the one who had been the author of the rumors, not wanting to name her because of the respect I have for her and the obligations I owe her. So, believe, my very dear son, that everything you write me is so pleasing to me that I find only truth and soundness there.

I find everything you tell me regarding whether we should stay in this country or go back to France, in accordance with genuinely prudent reasoning. I feel the same way you do. But what happens rarely accords with what we think should happen, as noted by those who are familiar with how God operates in these parts, where it seems that his providence makes light of all human prudence. I am just as certain that His Divine Majesty wanted our reestablishment, and that my vocation to work at it came from him, as I am that I will die one day. Notwithstanding this certitude and the outlays we have made, we don't know what will become of this country. There is, however, more of an indication that it will subsist than otherwise, and I feel my vocation to be as strong as ever, though I am prepared for our retreat to France at all times and whenever it pleases God to signify it to me, by those who hold his place for me on earth.[159] Madame our foundress is likewise disposed with regard to her vocation but not with regard to going back to France, God not yet having given her this grace of destitution. To the contrary, she has such strong impulses to build us a church that the insults of the Iroquois do not stop her from gathering the materials for this purpose. She is strongly advised not to think about it, but she says that her greatest desire is to make a house for the good God. These are her terms, and afterwards she will build him living temples. She means to say that she will gather together some poor French girls living

---

158. See Letter 142.

159. Martin, *Vie*, 592–3.

outside the city so as to raise them in piety and give them a good education, which is unavailable to them where they are. She has not been inspired to help us with our buildings. Her whole heart is dedicated to her church, which she will build little by little with her relatively modest income. This year Monsieur de Bernières sent her five *poinçons* of flour, which are worth five hundred *livres* here. He also sent us a clock together with one hundred *livres* for our poor Hurons. What will you say to all that? As for me, my entire interior inclination is to let myself be led by such a lovable providence and to agree to whatever his guidance will impose upon me from moment to moment.

    I spoke again this morning to two people who are very experienced in the affairs of the country, about two girls we want to bring over from France as converse sisters. They didn't find any problem with it. As for me, I find many: firstly, because of the dangers of the sea; secondly, because of the troubles of the kingdom; and finally, because of the society or conjunction of persons.[160] This is why we have not yet resolved this matter. It is not the hostility of the Iroquois that holds us back. There are some who consider this country lost, but I don't see that we have as much reason to fear the Iroquois as people of our sex and condition have to fear French soldiers, according to what someone from France told me. What I have been told about it makes me shudder. The Iroquois are indeed barbarous, but they certainly do not carry out against persons of our sex the ignominies I hear the French have carried out. Those who have lived among them have assured me that they don't use violence and that they leave alone women who are not willing to acquiesce to them. I would not, however, depend on that, because these people are barbarians and infidels. We would rather be killed than allow ourselves to be taken away, for it is in the context of this sort of rebellion that they kill; but, thanks to our Lord, we are not there yet. If we knew that this enemy was approaching, we would not wait for them, and you would see us again as early as this year. If I saw only seven or eight French families returning to France, I would believe it reckless to stay, and even if I had had a revelation that there was nothing to fear, I would consider my vision suspect, so as to anchor my sisters and myself to something more clear and certain.[161] The

---

160. Marie elaborates on the difficulties arising from the fact that the Ursulines of Quebec consisted of women religious from a diversity of congregations in France in Lettres CLXXI (to Mère Ursuline de Sainte-Catherine) and Lettre CCXXI (to Mère Charlotte des Anges), *Correspondance*, 574–81 and 762–3. See also Letters 81, 143, and 173.

161. *Relation de 1654*, 418–21. For an excellent study of the problem of discernment of spirits in early modern Europe, see Sluhovsky, *Believe Not Every Spirit*, especially 169–229. Marie's allusion here to the weight of reason in the process of discernment contrasts with her subordination of reason to experience elsewhere, raising interesting questions about the place of reason within the mystical tradition more generally. For a discussion of the complexities of the

Hospitaller Mothers have reached the same resolution. But to tell you simply, it is the difficulty we have in getting what we need in the way of food and clothing that will make us leave, if we do leave, rather than the Iroquois, although truthfully, they will always be the root cause of it, since their excursions and the terror they sow everywhere interrupts the commerce of many items. Thus, we cultivate as much as we can. The bread here tastes better than French bread, but it is not as white and nutritious for working people. The vegetables are also better here and plentiful, as well.[162] You see, my very dear son, where we are with regard to the Iroquois.

I agree strongly with your feelings about the need to provide for the observance of our rules in the future. For now, I say to my embarrassment, I see not a single virtue in myself capable of edifying my sisters. I can't answer for the future, but from what I can see, I would be as certain about the majority of those who have come over from France as I am of myself. And regardless of whether they would like to go back to France, which they are quite far from doing, those from this country that we have professed, having been raised in our rules and never having sampled another rule, would be capable of maintaining it. Thus we are not in a hurry to ask for more sisters from France. What's more, the wound that the hand of God has inflicted upon us is still too recent, and we are still too inconvenienced by it. We still fear that we will be sent subjects who are not suitable for us and would have trouble accommodating themselves to living here, to the air, to the people. But what we fear more is that they won't be tractable and won't have a good vocation, for since they bring with them a disposition different from our own, if they are not submissive and tractable they will have trouble accommodating themselves—and perhaps we will have trouble, too, in putting up with them. This clash of dispositions has already compelled two Hospitaller sisters to go back to France, and this example we have before our eyes is the reason for my fear, for what a spectacle to make people of our sex and condition travel one thousand or twelve hundred leagues among the dangers of the sea and enemies, only to send them right back where they came from. I would have trouble resolving myself to that, short of an absolute necessity, such as if a girl was so determined to go back that she could only be kept here by force and perhaps to the prejudice of her salvation. I had a great desire to bring over my Niece de l'Incarnation, whom I have been told several

---

relationship between reason and the pursuit of mystical union, see Bernard McGinn, "Love, Knowledge, and Mystical Union in Western Christianity: Twelfth to Sixteenth Centuries," *Church History* 56 (1987): 7–24.

162. See also Letter 246.

times is wise and virtuous and has a great vocation.¹⁶³ I would have taken pleasure in training her in all our duties and everything that pertains to the country. But I feared that she would not be happy and that I would be exposing her to the risk of returning to France. That is what held me back. What's more, I am old, and my death would leave her in a solitude that would perhaps be onerous for her. And finally, the impediments to Christianity imposed by the Iroquois do not allow us to have as many Indian girls as before, and it would grieve her much to be deprived of the purpose for which she had come, for truthfully this point is extremely disturbing and demoralizing. How will a young girl have the heart to learn very difficult languages, seeing herself deprived of the subjects upon whom she hoped to practice them? If these hostilities were to last but a short time, one would make an effort to overcome this reluctance; but death will perhaps come before peace.

That is what holds me back with regard to my niece, notwithstanding my desire to satisfy her and the consolation I could have hoped for from it. For since I am far away from you and without opportunities to see you, she would have taken your place, since you are the two people for whom my spirit most often journeys to France. Instead, I visit you both in the heart of our lovable Jesus, in the wishes I make for your sanctification and for the perfect consummation of your whole selves. But I am making a sacrifice of this satisfaction to my divine Jesus, abandoning everything to his guidance for all time and eternity. He knows what he wants to do with us, so let us take pleasure in letting him do it, and if we are faithful to him our reunion will be all the more perfect in heaven, for we will have broken our ties in this world to obey the maxims of his gospel.¹⁶⁴ But let's get back to our subject.

We are therefore not in a hurry to ask for choir sisters in France, and we believe that we must delay a bit, so as to take appropriate measures to ensure that neither we nor they have any reason to be dissatisfied. Nevertheless, notwithstanding all the reasons I gave, we will not be able to avoid asking for two converse sisters, and perhaps as early as this year.

I don't remember if I told you elsewhere that since there is no bishop here, the one of Rouen has declared that he is acting as bishop for us. And in order to take possession of this authority, he has ordained as his grand-vicar the Reverend Father Superior of the missions, who is the principal ecclesiastic of the country and also the one upon whose authority we rely for the validity of our professions,

---

163. See also Letters 81 and 173.

164. Matthew 19:29.

according to the consultation on the subject which was produced at the Sorbonne and signed by six doctors.[165]

As far as what pertains to you, do not assume it's for a lack of affection that I haven't sent you the papers you had asked me for. I was only keeping them for that purpose, for otherwise I would have let them burn after having satisfied my superior, who had ordered me to write them and then given them back to me. But as I told you last year, another fire consumed them.[166] Nevertheless, since you want them, if I can steal some moments from my occupations, which are pretty constant, I will write what my memory and my affection supplies me, so as to send it to you next year.

See, my very dear son, how life unfolds. If our good God did not compensate with an infusion of his ongoing grace, who could survive? I confess to you that I have nothing to complain about, but rather I have reason to sing his mercy. I assure you that I need more courage than a man to bear the crosses that pile up in relation to our personal affairs, as well as the general affairs of the country, where everything is full of thorns among which one must walk in darkness, where the most clear-sighted are blind and everything is uncertain. Despite all this my spirit and my heart are at peace, and they await from moment to moment the orders and events of providence, so as to submit to it. In the midst of all this darkness, I see my vocation more clearly than ever and discover in myself lights that were obscure and incomprehensible to me when God gave me them before I came to Canada. I will tell you about it in the writings I am promising you, so you can know and admire how the Divine Goodness has acted upon me, and how he wanted me to obey him without human reason, losing myself in his ways in a manner I cannot express. On her death bed, our dear Mother de Saint-Joseph predicted that I would have many crosses to bear. I am awaiting them, my very dear son, and embracing them as they present themselves. And after all, our dear savior makes me experience that his yoke is easy and his burden light.[167] Blessed be

---

165. That is, doctors of theology. Since the Middle Ages, the theology faculty of the University of Paris had claimed "a particular type of religious authority," according to Jacques M. Gres-Gayer, "The Magisterium of the Faculty of Theology of Paris in the Seventeenth Century," *Theological Studies* 53 (1992): 426. Emboldened by the academic qualifications of its members, the faculty intervened in religious disputes throughout the Middle Ages and early modern period, issuing its "'doctrinal judgment' on disputed matters" in the form of *Censures* (condemning theological errors) and *Declarations* (confirming theological orthodoxy). Gres-Gayer, "Magisterium," 426. Over the course of the seventeenth century, the authority enjoyed by the faculty was challenged and redefined under pressure from both the Church in Rome and the French state.

166. See Letter 136.

167. Matthew 11:30.

he eternally for having such regard for my weaknesses that he wanted to taste all the bitterness of the cross in order to leave me only with its sweetness.[168]

When I speak to you about our poverty, don't think that I'm asking you for anything but prayers, which I consider genuine riches. I leave everything else to the guidance of the divine providence, which is extravagantly rich in order to meet our needs. I assure you that amidst all our losses, he has not yet allowed us to lack what we need to live on, nor even what we need for clothing, and he has paternally provided for everything. And even during the long illness of the good Mother de Saint-Joseph, this providence helped us so much that she could not have been better cared for in France among her relatives, save the inconvenience of the lodging. I have already spoken to you about her death, so I am saying nothing more about it here.[169] I have lost in this privation, but I console myself with the fact that she is God's now, for otherwise this loss of so a worthy subject would affect me considerably. But in the end, blessed be God by everyone. He is my all and my life in whatever part I can be.

Letter 153: October 26, 1653

My very dear and beloved son,

May the love and life of Jesus be our life for eternity. I received your letter dated the third of April together with the lovely gift that accompanied it.[170] You indeed have reason to say that it was for my consolation that you sent it to me, for I was, in fact, very consoled by it, and I rendered to God and his Holy Spirit my very humble thanks both for what he is offering you personally for your sanctification and for the talents he is giving you for helping your neighbor, whether by preaching or by managing the responsibility with which he has charged you. I hope that the Divine Majesty will never abandon you as long as you faithfully dispense his spiritual goods, for he says to his faithful servant in the gospel: *Come, my good and faithful servant, because you have been faithful in a few things, I will raise you up and put you in charge of many.*[171]

---

168. For a discussion of the significance of *douceur* (translated here as "sweetness"), see Delphine Denis, "La douceur, une catégorie critique au XVIIe siècle," in *Le doux au XVIe et XVIIe siècle: Écriture, esthétique, politique, spiritualité*, ed. Marie-Helene Prat and Pierre Servet (Lyon: Centre Jean Prévost, 2003), 239–60.

169. Lettre CXLI, *Correspondance*, 474.

170. Oury reports that this was a panegyric of St. Benedict.

171. Matthew 25:21–3.

But you know well, my very dear son, that it has never been possible for me to ask anything for you from him except the virtues of the gospel, and above all that you were one of his true poor in spirit. It seemed to me that if you were filled with this divine virtue, you would possess all the others in abundance, for I think that the totally holy emptiness of the poor in spirit is capable of possessing all the spiritual goods God offers to his creature. Since you want me to speak to you without reserve, twenty-five years ago the Divine Goodness gave me such a strong impression of this truth in your regard that I could have no other impulse than to present you to him, asking him *with inexpressible groans that his divine spirit made come out of my heart*, that you share in this divine poverty of spirit. To me, the spirit of the world was a horrible monster for you, and this made me triumph over all the obstacles that formed against your studies, because based on what God made me feel about you, I saw that I had to use these means to achieve what I was aiming for, and to put you in the state in which you could possess this true poverty of spirit.[172]

I render very humble thanks to His Goodness for the attraction that he is giving you for the mystical life.[173] This is one of the corollaries to this poverty of spirit that will again purify what could be too human in the exercise of preaching, which I am not counseling you to abandon unless it does harm to your perfection or your health or the exercise of your responsibilities. If, therefore, you devote yourself entirely to the interior life, over time your sermons will be more useful to your neighbor and God will be more glorified by them. The one you sent me pleased me much. A good son praises his father and that is quite suitable to him. If

---

172. Romans 8:26. *Relation de 1654*, 220–22 and 449–61; see also Letters 56 and 128. Marie's emphasis here on spiritual poverty echoes a theme elaborated in the mysticism of the thirteenth-century Dominican Meister Eckhart (who connects spiritual poverty with self-purgation and willful ignorance) and further developed by those associated with the French School. See Robert Blakney, *Meister Eckhart: A Modern Translation* (New York: Harper and Row, 1941), 127–32; and Olier, *Introduction à la vie*, 114–35. See also Amy Hollywood, *The Soul as Virgin Wife: Mechthild of Magdeburg, Marguerite Porete, and Meister Eckhart* (Notre Dame: University of Notre Dame Press, 1995), who argues that Eckhart's emphases on spiritual poverty and detachment drew on the resources of a prior *béguine* spirituality.

173. See also Letter 155. In his pursuit of the mystical life, Claude stands apart from his fellow Maurists, most of whom resisted the mystic invasion of the seventeenth century; see Oury, *Dom Claude Martin*, 144–6. Claude's enthusiasm for the mystical experience is all the more surprising given that by the middle of the seventeenth century, France was witness to what Louis Cognet has famously called "le crépuscule des mystiques" brought about by the ultimate defeat of Quietism by its conservative critics ; see Louis Cognet, "Dom Claude Martin (1619–1696) et le mysticisme français," *Revue d'histoire de l'Église de France* 43, no. 140 (1957): 125–49; and Jamet, introduction, *Marie de l'Incarnation: Écrits*, 89–94. Claude would enter into a contract for mystical marriage with Divine Wisdom sometime around 1665–6; see Lettre CCXXII, *Correspondance*, 765.

our very dear Father Poncet had not fallen into the hands of the Iroquois, I would have shared it with him, so as to console him with the work of his student.[174]

But let us get to the point of the promises I made you, the outcome of which you are expecting this year.[175] I have done what was possible in order to give you this satisfaction. I will tell you that no one writes here in winter except next to the fire and in view of all who are present. But as it is inappropriate that anyone knows about this writing, I was obliged, against the inclination of my desires, to delay its execution until the month of May. Since then I have written three notebooks of sixteen leafs each *in quarto*, in the hours I was able to steal away from my usual occupations. I was writing about my vocation in Canada in the month of August when the ships arrived, and I had to put everything aside to do more pressing work. My plan was to send you these writings while you waited for the rest, except that as I was carrying out my spiritual exercises from Ascension to Pentecost and reflecting upon myself, I had quite particular insights into the states of prayer and grace that the Divine Majesty has communicated to me since I had use of reason. Then, without thinking about what purpose it could serve, I took some paper and immediately wrote an index or abridgement which I put in my portfolio. At that time my superior and director, who is the Reverend Father Lalemant, had told me to ask our Lord that it might please him to let me know whether he wanted something from me before my death that could contribute to his glory. After having obediently said my prayer, I had only two thoughts: the first, to offer myself as a holocaust to the Divine Majesty, to be consumed in the way he would like to prescribe for this whole desolate country, and the other, that I should write down the operations he had worked upon me since calling me to the interior life. As regards the first, I discussed it right away with my Reverend Father, telling him about my other current dispositions, but as regards the other, I was embarrassed and didn't dare say anything about it. However, this *Index* was the point of the matter, and it continued to come to me in spirit, together with scruples about having written what I had planned to send you without the blessing of obedience. It's true that my superior had obliged me to rewrite the same things that I had written before, and which had been burned with our monastery, but it was my intention to send them to you that troubled me, because I had not disclosed it to my director. Finally, pressed by an interior spirit, I was constrained to reveal what I had concealed, to show my *Index* and to admit that I had committed to send you some writings for your consolation. I told him about the order

---

174. Claude had studied under Joseph-Antoine Poncet while in Orléans between 1633 and 1634. See *Relation de 1654*, 299.

175. Letter 143.

I was keeping therein, which he approved, and he was not content only to tell me that it was right that I give you this satisfaction—he even commanded me to do it. I am sending you this *Index*, in which you will see more or less the order I'm keeping in the principal work that I will send you next year, if I don't die this year, or if some extraordinary event doesn't happen to me that prevents me from doing it, and I will try to keep a copy of it as a safeguard against the risks of the sea.

In the outline that I have begun for you, therefore, I am discussing all my adventures. That is to say, not only what has happened in my interior, but my exterior history as well—namely, the states through which I passed in the world and in religion, God's providence and operations upon me, my actions, my occupations, and how I raised you. Generally, I am making a summary by which you will be able to know me entirely, for I am speaking of things simply and as they are.[176] The matters you will see treated in this abridgment are included there, each one according to the time when it happened. Pray to our Lord that it pleases him to give me the necessary lights to carry out this act of obedience which I did not expect. Since God wants it, I will obey blindly. I don't know what his plans are, but since I am obliged by my vow to pursue greater perfection, which includes seeking out in all things what I know will bring him or procure for him the most glory, I am neither responding to nor reflecting on the directions given to me by he who holds God's place for me.[177]

Moreover, there are many things, and I can say that almost all are of this nature. It would be impossible for me to write about these in full, all the more so because in the interior operations that the goodness of God carries out in me, these graces are so intimate and the impressions so spiritual by way of union with the Divine Majesty in the depths of my soul, that they cannot be expressed in words. And what's more, there are certain communications between God and the soul that would be unbelievable if communicated on the outside as they happen interiorly. When I presented my *Index* to my superior, he read it and said to me. "Go right away and write me these two chapters, namely the twenty-second and

---

176. See also *Relation de 1654*, 246. In describing her writings as both simple and direct, Marie deploys what Alison Weber and Michèle Farrell have, in different historical contexts, identified as a feminine rhetorical strategy designed to legitimate women writing in a man's world. For an analysis of the "rhetoric of femininity" (characterized by an "affected modesty," informal speech, and deliberate imprecision, inter alia) in the writings of Teresa of Ávila, see Weber, *Teresa of Avila and the Rhetoric of Femininity*. Farrell, similarly, draws attention to the cultivated sense of spontaneity or "looseness" in the letters of Madame de Sévigné's correspondence with her daughter which at once reinscribed and transformed an androcentric scriptorial model; see Michèle Longino Farrell, *Performing Motherhood: The Sévigné Correspondence* (Hanover, NH: University Press of New England, 1991).

177. That is, Jérôme Lalemant, Marie's spiritual director.

the twenty-fifth." I immediately obeyed and wrote down everything I could, but the most intimate details were not in my power. This is, in part, what gives me a distaste for writing about these matters, although I delight in finding no bottom to this great abyss and in being forced to lose all powers of speech in losing myself therein. The older one grows, the more one is incapable of writing about such things because the spiritual life simplifies the soul in a consuming love such that one can no longer find the words to describe it.

Twenty years ago, I would have done it more profitably and more easily, and there would be matters that would give substantial grounds for admiring the great and prodigious generosity of God toward an earthworm like me, for I had left some papers with my Reverend Mother Françoise de Saint-Bernard, which are my prayers for ten-day exercises which I was obliged to write out of obedience.[178] I had also made several other remarks touching on the same matters in a booklet. If I had those writings they would be of great service to me and would refresh my memory about many things which have escaped my mind. I left two copies of all that, for since my director wanted to have my originals, I made a duplicate in a little booklet to help me on certain occasions. When I was about to leave France, I carefully removed the originals, which have since stayed with the copies. I have since asked for both from this Reverend Mother, so that no one sees any of my writings in the world, but she absolutely refused to give them to me, just as she mortified me much before my departure because I had burned a number of other papers of this nature.

These writings to which I refer have only to do with God's operations upon me in France. As for Canada, it would be difficult for me to write about all the dispositions in which I have found myself since God called me here. I have suffered great crosses here because of God, other people, and myself who am the worst of all.[179] I will say a bit about it, but for many reasons I am obliged not to reveal the rest and I believe it is God's will that I act in this way. If I had your ear, there is no secret in my heart that I would not want to confide to you. I would willingly make my general and particular confessions to you, because God has marked you with a holy character. You see thus that I have no reserve toward you, and that only geographic distance impedes our commerce of the things of God, for we need have no other now or in eternity. Therefore, so that this *Index* remains secret, I am enclosing it in this letter which, as you can see by the quality of the things I treat here, must be kept between you and me.

[Abridgement of the life of the M. Marie de l'Incarnation]

---

178. *Retraites de la Vénérable Mère Marie de L'Incarnation* (Paris, 1682).

179. *Relation de 1654*, 376–8.

First state of Prayer

1. By which God makes the soul lose its affection for vain things and creatures who keep it attached [1–2].[180]
2. Great inclination to frequent the sacraments, and the significant effects these sources of sanctity operate in her, particularly hope and confidence in God [3].
3. She feels herself powerfully attracted by the ceremonies of the Church [5].
4. Of the powerful attraction she has to hear preaching and the effects that the word of God worked in her [4].

Second state of Prayer

5. Change of state whereby God illuminates the soul, making it see the deformity of its past life [6].
6. Powerful effects by an operation and extraordinary illumination caused by the blood of Jesus Christ [6].
7. Confession of her sins following the preceding operation [6–7].
8. God gives her the gift of ongoing and continuing prayer by means of a union with Jesus Christ [7].
9. Various illuminations subsequent to this spirit of prayer; several virtues are also given to her, particularly patience, humility, and above all a great love for the poverty of the spirit [8].

Third state of Prayer

10. By which God gives her a spirit of extraordinary interior and exterior penance [9].
11. Of the insights and reasons that bring her to this spirit of penitence [9].
12. Of the opportunities God creates to make her enter into the practice of humility, abnegation, and patience [9].
13. She loves humiliation so much that she fears losing opportunities for it [9].

Fourth state of Prayer

14. By which God, having illuminated the soul, directs it by interior words taken from holy scripture [10].
15. Profound view of her nothingness following these interior words [11].
16. Of a manner of intimacy with God in which the soul feels itself pushed passively without being able to act otherwise [12].

---

180. The numbers in the brackets refer to the relevant chapters of the *Relation* of 1654 as it was edited and published by Claude Martin.

Fifth state of Prayer

17. By which God applies the soul to the practice of the maxims and virtues of the gospel taught by Jesus Christ [13–14].
18. In this state, although the body is in the world, the spirit is in religion where these holy and divine maxims of the Incarnate Word are practiced [13–14–15].
19. The great problems of the world are not capable of distracting the soul from the view of its spiritual object, which leads it to greater acts of virtue [16].
20. She suffers a martyrdom in the world, seeing it so contrary to the life and maxims of Jesus Christ [17].

Sixth state of Prayer

21. By which God calls the soul to a state of extraordinary interior purity which he works in it by means of his mercy [18].
22. Following the preceding operation, the three persons of the holy trinity reveal themselves to her in an extraordinary way and give her various insights into the operations of God in the angels and in pure souls [18–19].
23. Various knowledges are given to her relating to the distinction of the divine attributes [21].
24. Of the dispositions that are passively given to the soul to put it in a state of purity capable of the great operations that God wants to carry out in it, and which make it languish in love and aspire to divine marriage [20].

Seventh state of Prayer

25. By which the very holy trinity reveals itself anew to the soul in a manner more lofty and sublime than the first, and in this operation the second divine person takes it as his spouse [22].
26. The effects that this divine marriage of the soul with the sacred person of the Word operates in her [23].
27. In this state of prayer the spirit is totally abstracted from earthly things, from which follows a continual ecstasy in the love of the second divine person [24].
28. The Holy Spirit by a continual motion makes her sing a hymn comparable to the Song of Songs [25].
29. Amorous listlessness of the soul in which it lives no longer in itself, but in he who has absorbed it in all his love [26].
30. Of a suspension or operation that agonizes the soul, keeping it in a martyrdom of extreme love [27].

31. Of the relief that is given to her in this quite crucifying operation, without which it wouldn't be possible for her to live on the earth [27].
32. New sufferings and agonies of the soul, to see itself still held back in the world since the body does not die; and about the relief God gives it in this matter [28].
33. Of the means God uses to make her leave the world and her relatives, so as to draw her to religion [29].
34. Of the traps that the devil sets out for her in order to stand in her way [30].

Eighth state of Prayer

35. Which includes what God operates in the soul in this new state of life [31–2].
36. Third grace by the operation of the very holy trinity, where the three divine persons communicate to the soul in a more sublime manner than before [33].
37. Of the insight God gives her into several passages from holy scripture on the subject of the sacred Incarnate Word [34].
38. She suffers great interior pains; and how the Divine Majesty uses the Reverend Fathers of the Company of Jesus to help her [35–6].

Ninth state of Prayer

39. Which brings a particular grace for spiritually helping one's neighbor [37].
40. Particular vocation for procuring the salvation of souls [38–9].
41. God manifests his will to her, revealing that he wants to use her in the mission of Canada [40].
42. The means God uses to bring about the execution of this vocation [41].
43. Desires that consume the soul, relating to the salvation of its neighbor; and the execution of God's will pertaining to this plan [41].

Tenth state of Prayer

44. By which God makes the soul die to its desires, wanting, in this zeal that seemed to devour it, to triumph over it in removing its will from it [42].
45. She remains happily captivated by God's will, which makes her see that he wants to be the master in the execution of the plan about Canada [43].
46. Revelation that God gives to a holy man touching on the vocation of serving him through the salvation of souls in the mission of Canada, which accords with the operations that the Divine Majesty carries out in N. on this subject [44].[181]

---

181. Here the unnamed person is Marie de l'Incarnation herself.

Eleventh state of Prayer

47. By which God obliges the soul to pursue the execution of his plan [45].
48. What happens in the soul in this pursuit, God executing this plan after it has been examined and approved by the superiors [46].
49. Disposition and visit from God, who makes the soul see what it will have to suffer in Canada and how he manifests his holy will to her [46].
50. The love with which she abandons herself to the divine dispositions and ordinances, and the inclination she feels to burn for Jesus Christ in return for his favors [47–8].

Twelfth state of Prayer

51. The soul experiences what God had made known to it about the abandonments it would have to suffer in Canada [49–50].
52. Various contradictions: Interior dispositions on this subject [52–3].
53. Her nature suffers much and the spirit still more by the revolt of the passions [54].
54. She experiences very strong and enduring temptations [55].
55. How she behaves in her long crosses with her neighbor and in her duties for the service of God [56].
56. The soul suffers terribly in the thought that it is deprived of the perfection and practice of virtue: How God inspires her on this subject [57].

Thirteenth state of Prayer

57. In which by a special grace that the soul receives through the intercession of the Holy Virgin, she is delivered in a single moment from her crucifying dispositions [58].
58. The great peace she possesses in a new love that the sacred Incarnate Word gives her for his divine maxims [59–60].
59. The great love and union of her will in relation to what God does and permits in her, outside of her, in chance events, etc. [61].
60. The soul having known the will of God, who seems to want to use her, executes it with love, and His Divine Majesty furnishes it with grace for this execution [62–3].
61. Presence and assistance of the Holy Virgin, who accompanies the soul in this execution in an extraordinary manner [64].
62. The soul burns more and more in the love of the sacred Incarnate Word. Various effects of this consuming love [65–6].
63. The differences between this state and preceding ones, although they seem to have some resemblance, in relation to the sacred Incarnate Word [67–8].

Honor, Glory, and Praise to the most adorable Incarnate Word.

It seems to me, my very dear son, that this short but substantial writing will give you a sufficient sense of the interior spirit that guides me, while waiting for me to give you a more complete knowledge of it. Pray to the Holy Spirit that it may please him to give me the light and grace to be able to do this if his holy name should be glorified by it. He has given me considerable and numerous mercies, which I have been infinitely far from deserving. This is why I believe that although His Divine Majesty had prepared a great place in heaven for me had I been faithful to him, he will give it to a more deserving soul and maybe to my dear and faithful companion, Mother Marie de Saint-Joseph. This is a great loss, but it is less than I deserve. I love the justice that avenges the injuries of God, and I will thus glory in this just as he will be glorified in his saints even to my exclusion.[182] My heart is at peace in the knowledge that he takes souls according to his divine pleasure. Blessed be he forever.

I had ordered that someone send you a copy of the account I made for our Mothers about the life and death of our dear departed. I have been told that this has not yet been done, because this writing fell into the hands of the Reverend Father Le Jeune. This good Father took what he wanted from it to put into the *Relation*, without me having asked him to do so. He much obliged me by doing it, but he had given me the singular pleasure of not publishing my name. Knowing nothing of all that, as the reader in the refectory I found myself just about to begin with this story. I was embarrassed about it and put it aside to make someone else read it. The memory of this dear Mother is precious to me, and I think and talk about her only with tenderness. God give us the grace to imitate her so as to share in the spiritual goods she now possesses.

Letter 155: August 9, 1654

My very dear and beloved son,[183]

May the love and the life of Jesus be our life and our love for all time and eternity. Several years ago, you urged me with a holy candor to give you an account of the operations that it pleased the Divine Majesty to carry out on me, and to share with you the graces and favors he has given to me since the time when, by his infinite mercy, he called me to his holy service.[184] If I have made you wait, not

---

182. 2 Thessalonians 1:8–10.

183. In 1654, Claude was elected Prior of the Blancs-Manteaux in Paris; see Oury, *Dom Claude Martin*, 99.

184. Claude had first asked for his mother's writings some eight years earlier; see Letter 109.

giving you the satisfaction you desired nor heeding your pleas, although they proceeded from a true sentiment of piety, it was not for lack of affection. But unable to prevail over myself to communicate about these matters to anyone other than God and he who holds his place for me on earth, I was obliged to keep silent toward you and to mortify myself in thus mortifying you. This delay that you took for a tacit refusal didn't deter you at all. You beseeched me anew by means of the most insistent motives and the most touching reasons that your intellect could supply, accusing me of a lack of affection and testifying to me that I had abandoned you so young, such that you scarcely knew your mother; that not content with this first abandonment, I had departed from France and left you forever; that when you were a child you were not capable of the instructions I gave you, and that since you are of a more enlightened age today, I must not refuse you the lights God had communicated to me; that having embraced a condition similar to mine, we are both in God, and thus our spiritual goods must be shared; that in your present state I could not refuse you, without some sort of injustice and hardness, that which could console you and serve you in the practice of perfection that you had professed; and finally that if I gave you this consolation you would help me bless he who gave me such a substantial share of his graces and celestial favors. I confess to you that this last argument moved me, and that since my heart received it, I have felt compelled to converse with you in my letters about more points of spirituality. But this wasn't what you wanted. You believed, and with reason, that I was keeping something back from you as, indeed, I did, for the reasons I suggested to you. But in the end, urged by your reasons and vanquished by your petitions, I communicated your desire to he who directs my soul, representing to him that I could no longer refuse you of my own accord and that if it was necessary to continue, he would have to order me to do so. Not only did he find it fitting that I should give you this consolation, he even commanded me to do it. This is why I am doing so, after having invoked the help of the Holy Spirit and received the blessing of obedience.[185]

Don't think that the notebooks I am sending you were planned and organized as one observes of well-edited works. That wouldn't have been possible in the state where God is keeping me, and the path by which His Divine Majesty guides me prevents me from adhering to any method in my writing. When I took up my pen to begin, I didn't know a word of what I was going to say, but in the process of writing the spirit of grace that guides me made me produce what it pleased him to, making me consider the matter in its principle and its source, and making me lead it right up to the state in which he keeps me today, and always amid much

---

185. See also Letter 153.

interruption and the great distraction of our domestic affairs. You might think that this amounts to few pages for so many years of spiritual life, during which the Divine Goodness made me go through many states and experiences. But I will tell you that God guides souls in different ways. There are some ways about which one can speak only with difficulty, and others about which one can't speak at all. Among these latter sort are those that bring graces that neither the exterior nor interior senses can perceive, as you will be able to see in several chapters or articles of what I wrote, in which I said what I could say and passed over, in silence, what I couldn't express. If you have trouble with these matters or with the way I have explained myself, send me your thoughts and questions, indicating to me the place in my writings, and I will try with the assistance of the Holy Spirit to satisfy you. You have sometimes testified to me that there is nothing that would profit you more for advancing in the spiritual life than this little bit of light that God gives me and makes me put down on paper when I am obliged to write you each year. This thought never came to my mind, but if it is so, blessed be God forever for such a happy success, for if there is something good in these writings, it comes from him and not from me, who am but a miserable sinner.[186]

If in reading the writings I'm sending you, you wonder what could have persuaded the Divine Goodness to grant me such great mercy and to apprise me of the blessings of his clemency, I will tell you that I have often reflected on this myself, and after having thought hard about it, I saw nothing in myself but misery and indignity. If any creature played a part in it, I can only suppose it was you, whom I abandoned out of love for him at a time when, according to all human reason, you needed me most, and above all, which I had planned and resolved to do even before you were born. If there are other grounds that could have drawn his mercy upon me, I am not aware of them. And anyway, it's not for us to enter into the domain of his providence or to penetrate the profound secrets of his operations upon us, but only to conclude that he wanted it thus, without having regard for his creature, and that if his mercy toward us was so magnificent

---

186. Marie's account of Claude's persistence in compelling her to share her spiritual writings, on the one hand, and her deflection of authorial agency to the Holy Spirit, on the other, gestures toward a generational fissure in the perception of religious women's writings. While Claude's dogged determination to secure his mother's own account of her spiritual life points forward to a seventeenth-century privileging of the autobiographical text consistent with the rise of a culture of interiority, Marie's appeal to the Holy Spirit recalls an older model in which writing women cast themselves as vessels of a divine author. Although Paige argues that the rising status of the autobiography "depended on the rejection of the concept of the 'human vessel,'" Goldsmith proposes that it was precisely Marie's claim to have been inspired by the Holy Spirit that prompted her son to preserve—with, allegedly, only minor edits—her original writings; see Paige, *Being Interior*, 105; Goldsmith, *Publishing Women's Life Stories*, 33–4.

in so many respects, it's an effect of his pure generosity. For if I abandoned you in your childhood, moved by his grace, without leaving you with any support other than his totally pure providence, he took you into his paternal protection and richly provided for you, giving you the honor of calling you to his service at a time preordained by his eternal counsel, as he had given me the honor and the grace of promising to me.[187] You have therefore won much in losing me, and my abandonment has been useful to you. And similarly with me, having left in you what was dearest and most precious to me in all the world and, in a word, having voluntarily lost you, I found myself together with you in the bosom of this totally lovable God, by means of the holy vocation that you and I have followed, and for which, according to the promises of our Lord, we are rewarded one hundred-fold in this life—not to mention the eternal reward for which we hope in heaven.[188]

So, let us go solely to the source, my very dear son, and together give glory and magnificence to our benefactor for the excesses of his mercy upon us. And for those, in particular, that His very lovable Goodness has conferred upon me, help me in singing praises to him which will cease only with life itself in order to continue afterwards in eternity. Let us confess together that he has given us everything freely by his holy choice, without us having been able to anticipate his will to enrich us with so many spiritual goods and confer upon us such magnificent gifts. And as for me, I confess that when this God of goodness called me, I deserved all rejection and contempt. Even now as he fills me with his riches, I don't see that I live up to his graces or further his plans, which means that I will never stop saying that it is freely and by his pure goodness that he gave me and continues to give me his favors. *Let us therefore confess and praise the Lord, because he is good and his mercy is eternal.*[189]

So, accept, my very dear son, the gift I am giving you insofar as the hazards of the sea permit it to reach you. If you find something there that can serve for your edification and your spiritual advancement, I will bless the Holy Spirit who helped me produce my sentiments for your benefit. Ah! My very dear son, render yourself worthy to be the true temple of the living God, empty yourself of

---

187. The confidence Marie claims here in Claude's eventual spiritual success contrasts markedly with the uncertainties and anxieties surrounding the abandonment to which she admits elsewhere; see, for example, Letters 56, 68, and 267.

188. Matthew 19:29.

189. Psalm 135:1, Vulgate. Her insistence upon the freely given nature of divine grace situates Marie within the neo-Augustinian current of seventeenth-century French spirituality (which tended, at the extremes of orthodoxy, toward Jansenism and even toward Calvinism). For a discussion of the revival of an emphasis on grace—and the controversies to which it gave rise—in early modern Catholic Spain, Italy, and France, see Sluhovsky, *Believe Not Every Spirit*, 98–136.

everything to make room for the divine spirit. I believe that this is God's plan for you, for I have learned that he is calling you to the mystical life, which greatly consoles me.[190] But that is a major thing, and few people understand the importance of this hidden life which, to conform to its name, cannot tolerate mixing. When I speak of mixing, I don't mean to speak of the tasks, however distracting, with which one is engaged in the midst of temporal and exterior affairs, particularly when they correspond to the glory of God and the salvation of one's neighbor. When God calls a soul there, he gives it his double spirit in order to attend to it both within and without, in him and for the love of him, whether we must command, when he has elevated us to a position of superiority, or whether we must obey, when he keeps us in a state of dependence and submission. This is what our divine master, the extremely lovable Incarnate Word, wanted to teach us when he said: *That he is the gate and whoever enters by him into the sheepfold will come in and go out and will find pasture*, which must be understood by this double spirit.[191] But the mixing I want to discuss is that of our own selves, with which we are ordinarily filled up, and which makes us pursue the appetites of our own excellence or our own self-love under the shadow of zeal for the glory of God or under the pretext of some other pious reason. This happens with such subtlety that sometimes the most enlightened are trapped and deceived thereby, such that they lose themselves or at least suffer a significant weakening of virtue and of the spiritual life, unless they are supported by the Holy Spirit, who, in order to save them, renders itself merciless toward them and takes vengeance upon them, making them pass through quite crucifying purgations, which purify and polish their interiors, such that being cleansed of their stains, they are worthy to be his temple and will be more circumspect in the future about themselves and their conduct.[192] Without this lovable severity of the divine spirit, it would happen to them according to God's plan, because having sought nothing but their own interests in the past, they would ultimately have produced only gusts of wind, such that thinking they would find themselves in God, they would find themselves in emptiness and nothingness.

It is therefore a question of great purity in everything and everywhere—and of purity, as I said, without mixing—to progress in the mystical life and achieve the perfection to which God is calling you and me.

When you read what the Divine Majesty has done to my soul, tremble for me because he has placed his treasures in the most fragile earthly vessel in the world,

---

190. See also Letter 153.

191. John 10:9.

192. *Relation de 1654*, 449–52. See also Letter 68.

because this vessel can fall and in falling, break and lose all the riches it contains, and finally because nothing is certain in this life where, however saintly we seem, we can't say *whether we deserve love or hate*.[193] I am certain of only one thing, that God, for his part, will never neglect me, but that I myself can go astray in a thousand ways by means of my faults and infidelities. This is why I beg you, my very dear son, to take great care for my salvation, remembering me when you are at the holy altar and praying to the Divine Majesty to send me tortures crueler than those of a thousand martyrdoms, rather than permit me to ever be unfaithful to him by spoiling the noble thoughts and generous intentions that his children ought to have, and above all that it may please him to make me worthy of bearing the burden of humility.[194] I pray to him for the same on your behalf, prostrated at the feet of Jesus our sovereign master and Lord, obliged to procure for you in his grace and in his love the same spiritual goods as for myself, who am,
My very dear and beloved son,
Your very humble and very affectionate mother,
Sister Marie de l'Incarnation Reverend U.I.

Letter 162: September 27, 1654

My very dear and beloved son,

The love and affection I have for you, and the consolation I feel for the fact that you belong to God, have made me overcome myself to send you the writings that you have desired from me. I wrote them with repugnance and send them with difficulty. But since grace and nature have overcome all my inclinations, I have to tell you my intentions, namely that I desire that these writings not be shared with or made known to anyone but you. I trust that you will keep the fidelity for which I am asking, and that after I granted you what you asked of me, you will not refuse me what I desire of you. And because religious houses are subject to visits, I beg you to write on the cover, *Papers of conscience*, so that no one touches them and glances at them without scruple.[195] With this precaution people of your condition can easily keep papers of this nature where no one can see them. If you happened

---

193. Ecclesiastes 9:1.

194. See also Letter 234.

195. In addition to the mandate of the Rule of Saint Benedict, which subjected Benedictine houses to canonical visitation three to four times a year, the Council of Trent directed ecclesiastic superiors to visit their dioceses annually in order to ensure "sound and orthodox doctrine,...to maintain good morals, and to correct such as are evil"; see "Decree on Reformation," sess. XXIV, in *The Council of Trent*, ed. and trans. J. Waterworth (London: Dolman, 1848), 208–10.

to fall ill and were in danger of death, have them thrown into the fire, or rather, so that I am more assured, send them to my niece who will take care to keep them for me if I survive you. Such are my conditions. But, my very dear son, I am sensitive on this point, and you are enlightened enough to see that I have reason to be. This letter is short, so that it will make more of an impression on you, and so that you will more easily reflect on the necessity of what I am asking and hoping for from you, my very dear and beloved son.

Your very humble and very affectionate mother,
Sister Marie de l'Incarnation, Reverend U.I.

Letter 163: October 18, 1654

My very dear and beloved son,

May the life and love of Jesus be your life and your love for all time and eternity. I have written you by all the ships that have departed. This letter is only a little abridgment of the others, so that if they are lost you can have our news by this last ship. I am sending you the papers I had promised you and have entrusted them to Reverend Father de Lionne to put them into your own hands. I am asking you for the secret that you have promised me, for I do not want anyone to see them except you.[196] If you see a risk that this might happen, burn them instead, or even, to put my mind at rest, send them back to me. You will find there clarifications of certain matters for which you asked me, if these writings reach you.

As for what you have proposed to me and what regards you personally, don't afflict yourself and don't stop practicing charity toward this good lady.[197] It is the novelty of this task that causes you this difficulty. When experience has hardened you, it will not be the same. However, even if it were like this your whole life, you should not stop practicing charity. The devil, who is afraid of charity, usually does these sorts of things in order to intimidate souls.[198] I know a holy man who is a

---

196. See also Letter 153 and 162.

197. While prior at Meulan, Claude served as the spiritual director to a young seventeen- or eighteen-year-old woman to whom, Martène reports, he developed a sexual attraction. Powerfully inclined to terminate his relationship with the woman, Claude was dissuaded from doing so by his mother who interpreted the situation as the devil's way of trying to frustrate Claude's work with regard to the salvation of souls. Claude's attraction to the young woman would last some eight or nine years, during the course of which he engaged in a variety of mortifications in an attempt to rid himself of this corporeal temptation; see Oury, *Dom Claude Martin*, 94–7.

198. Just as Marie cast Claude's spiritual struggles as demonic temptations intended to impede his spiritual progress, so she understood her own anxiety about abandoning the young Claude for religious life as the devil's attempt to distract her from religious life. See, for example, *Relation de 1633*, 192.

martyr for it, but who doesn't neglect to courageously pursue his objective. Do likewise for the love of God and the salvation of this soul.

As for your other affairs, which give you so much work, this is also a temptation in one sense, and in another a drill that God is giving you. You will find something similar in my writings, and you will also see the outcomes and successes that result from them. One must, my very dear son, go through various temptations and afflictions to achieve the purity of body and spirit that God demands of us, and for this it is necessary to have considerable courage and to be unforgiving toward oneself, or else one will not advance in this way of the spirit. All the saints have gone through this in order to be saints. I don't count myself among them, for I am a great sinner, but see, I beg you, what I have passed through over the course of more than seven years, and even before in various situations. It is impossible to abide in the spiritual life for long without going through these tests.[199] I therefore refer you to the cited passage, and you can believe that as far as I am concerned your interests are so dear to me that I am recommending them to our good Jesus.

As for my physical health, it is pretty good, and I am not yet feeling many of the inconveniences of age, although my vision is weakening. To relieve it, I use glasses with which I see as clearly as I did at age twenty-five. They relieve me, as well, of a habitual headache, which is much less acute because of them. I have also become a bit plump. People of my temperament become so in this country, where it is more humid than in France, although the air is very fine here.[200] But let us leave the body for the things of this world and give our spirit to God.

My very dear son, I have already written you a letter with the news of the country. Since then two of the Iroquois nations have come into conflict.[201] The subject of their differences is that both had asked for the Fathers. The one, which is the nation of the Mohawks, asked for Father Chaumonot and for the Hurons to unite with them to live together and become one people, but these people did not want to hear about the faith. The Onondagas also asked for the Hurons along with the Fathers, and wanted to receive the faith. The Hurons, who are free, didn't want to get involved and promised to both in turn that with time they would go and visit them, and that meanwhile they had to be patient. They responded thus in order to adroitly rid themselves of these people whom they

---

199. 2 Timothy 3:12.

200. For a discussion of early modern physiology, including the notion of temperament and the effect of climate on physical health, see Mary Lindemann, *Medicine and Society in Early Modern Europe* (Cambridge, UK: Cambridge University Press, 1999), 12–21.

201. Thwaites, *Jesuit Relations*, vol. 41, 41–63.

can't trust after so many experiences of their infidelity. Therefore, a Father was sent to the Onondagas with an order to visit the Mohawks as well.[202] But since time was short, he couldn't visit the latter, but stayed with the former where the Iroquois nations had come and gathered to receive the faith. The Father brought this good news here which gave great joy to everyone, and it was found fitting that he himself return to execute such a good plan. When he was on his way the Mohawks, piqued by jealousy, met up with him pretending to be friends, but when the Father and his companions were in range of their guns, they opened fire, in an act of deception fitting for a barbarous Nation. A chief who was accompanying him out of respect was killed, several Hurons were wounded, and the others were taken prisoners. Another chief who was spared said to them, "My brothers, what have you done? I am declaring war on you." They were not troubled by this declaration, but addressed themselves to the Father and told him that he was stupid to have preferred the others to them. Having thus reproached him they left, saying they did not want to do any harm to the Frenchmen, but to the Hurons and Algonquins and that they wanted to kill them all. In fact, they did everything they could to execute their plan. We have learned however that it is not the elders of the nation who pulled this fast one, and that they don't even know about it, but that it is a bastard son of a Dutchman and an Iroquois woman who lives in Iroquois territory, for these Indians are neighbors of New Holland. He is a quite well-formed man, skillful and brave, who looks like a European except that he has no beard. Now, close to one hundred fifty men, Hurons as well as Algonquins, are pursuing him. If they can capture him, he's done for, for he is a miserable man who is opposed to the faith and the peace. But I return to the Father. He continued on his way to Montreal, where he had no sooner arrived than the other Iroquois nations sent deputies to compliment him and give him gifts. They protested anew to him that they wanted to believe in God and begged him to prepare with his brothers to come and instruct them. Above all, they gave him a gift, to invite him to open his eyes to consider what they were going to do to the Mohawks to avenge the injury they had done to him. Here is where things stand. But as you have quite rightly noted, nothing is certain with the Indians, especially when they are infidels. Although we live well with them, we are always on guard. The Fathers come and go among these peoples, and they in turn come and go here, but always warily. Let us pray to the God of peace that he gives it to you and to me and to all these peoples. It is from him alone that we must wait for it. The world cannot give it to us.

---

202. Thwaites, *Jesuit Relations*, vol. 41, 89–127.

Letter 173: September 2, 1656

My very dear son,

In one of my previous letters, I told you that the Reverend Father Lalemant is going to make a trip to France, but I don't remember if I told you that we have begged him to bring us three professed religious, two choir sisters and one converse. We are asking for one choir sister from our Mothers of Tours, where my niece could present herself if her eye has healed well. I would be delighted to see her here, supposing that she had a good vocation, for if this were not the case, she would have a great deal of difficulty and I would be grieved still more to see her suffer. The one who returned last year never had the vocation for Canada, but only a certain fleeting passion which lasted only part of the way, and thus she did not succeed. It was the same with the other, who accompanied her on her way back. My niece has a sober mind and an excellent nature and it is said that she is virtuous, but regardless of whatever advantage she might have, I would not counsel her to venture here without a vocation. If she has a good one, and if her eye is entirely healed, and if she does not fear the hazards of the sea, this will be a great good for her perfection. I have learned that she is held quite dear by seculars and even by noblepersons who visit her often. These sorts of visits are a mortal poison for a religious soul, especially for a young girl who is attractive, as she is. I have been told that she is good and well-behaved, but certainly unless it is quite particularly protected by God, virtue suffers great breaches amidst the opportunities of the parlor. Thus there is reason to believe that distance would be best for her, as it was for our dear departed Mother Marie de Saint-Joseph. I say all this, my very dear son, so that you pay close attention and inform yourself, lest she make a decision lightly. I preferred to write to you about it rather than anyone else, because I trust you. I think that you must write about it with an open heart to my Reverend Mother Françoise de Saint-Bernard, begging her to tell you her thoughts in confidence.[203] Therefore do this for the love of God, my very dear son, and you will much oblige me, as you will as well in seeing often the Reverend Father Jérôme Lalemant, my good and true Father in our Lord. We have put all the affairs of our community in his hands, as our truest friend. Now the ships are about to depart. Farewell for this year.

Letter 176: October 15, 1657

My very dear and beloved son,

Here is the last letter you will receive from me this year because there is only one ship here, which is lifting its anchor to leave. This here is but a reiteration

---

203. See also Letters 81 and 143.

of those I have already written you as far as my affection for you is concerned, since I have not told you anything except on account of the love I bear toward your soul. We—you and I—have only one thing to do, which is to serve God in the state and in the way in which he wants us. That is clear to us. Perhaps you were mortified by some points of my letters and believed that I was worried about the affair in question.[204] I admit, and I have already told you as much, that my spirit was afflicted but not worried. But you have shed light on my hesitations in the letter that you wrote me through Monsieur d'Argençon, our new Governor, such that I am satisfied. So, let's not talk about it anymore. Let's talk only about growing in virtue and in the way of the interior spirit where one enjoys God and all the divine truths. It seems to me that I am still quite far from the purity that this interior depth demands. I discover something about it, but I don't hold onto it, because I am still attached to a weak nature, fragile and susceptible to the impurities of the earth. Ah, my God! When will I be delivered from this self which is hardly faithful to the spirit of grace? Although in my depths, I want neither life nor death, nevertheless when I think about death or when I hear talk about it, my heart blossoms and dilates, because death will deliver me from this self, which does more harm to me than all the things of the world.[205] Pray to the Divine Goodness that he delivers me from it by the ways that please him most, and which he knows are the most suitable for me.

Letter 177: August 24, 1658

My very dear son,[206]

May Jesus be our life and our love. Here is the reply to your letter of the 28th of August which I received with two others from you, to which I hope to reply likewise with time.

If God has placed you in solitude and gives you the love for it, this is a sign that he wants to give you a new grace, and that he intends to strengthen you and to set you up so that you can serve as he asks you to, for this is how His Majesty usually directs those he wants to use to direct the souls of others. I was quite consoled to

---

204. The "affair in question" likely alludes to the problem of Claude's sexual attraction to the young woman who had been under his spiritual direction in Meulan; see Letter 163. Claude had been sent back to Meulan earlier in the year 1657, which no doubt renewed the scruples of his conscience.

205. Romans 7:24.

206. In 1658, Claude was again reassigned, this time as prior at Saint-Corneille de Compiègne; see Oury, *Dom Claude Martin*, 103–4.

learn that your studies are presenting no impediment to the service of God. The fact that he is asking this of you in your solitude is a sign. I praise and esteem the plan you have adopted in your solitude, which tends only to holiness, but I will say a word to you about the issue you raise, which is troubling you. The little experience I have has made me understand this truth, that one must banish all superfluous reasoning and excessive reflections on these sorts of matters, which in most cases are temptations rather than real things. I believe that what plagues you from time to time is of this nature, and I come to this conclusion on the basis of the consolation you feel when, in the midst of your troubles, you abandon yourself to God and to his holy operations upon you.

I am delighted about the inclination that God is giving you for perfection, calling you by stages to a holy union with him.[207] You are obliged to deal in a variety of business, spiritual as well as temporal, which cannot help but get you a bit dusty, given the reality of human weakness. These sorts of faults are not infidelities, but weaknesses which heal themselves by means of this depth of union with God in the heart and spirit.[208] Yes, acts repeated in this union marvelously sanctify a soul. And don't figure that the distractions caused by your studies or your affairs are infidelities, unless you are amusing yourself overmuch by reasoning about matters which are curious, controversial, subjects of vanity, or, in a word, contrary to the spirit of Jesus Christ. Once God has given a soul the gifts of wisdom and understanding, which he ordinarily does in this holy union, distractions are not harmful. I beg that His Goodness wishes to dispense both to you for his greatest glory, for your sanctification, and for the good of the souls he has submitted to your direction. I don't know if you so little enjoy the pleasures of this union that you take activity for a distraction. The activity that comes from the sources I just mentioned is a kind of prayer, because it comes from God and ends in God.[209] Therefore, don't afflict yourself in the midst of your occupations and don't distinguish what is the most perfect, except in the state where you are and in which you did not put yourself.

When one belongs to God one must follow him where he wills, and one must always come back to this point, to lose oneself in his holy will. I reckon that this is what the spirit of God means to say in scripture: *She will have a name, my will is in her.* In order to achieve this loss of self, one must live by faith, for again scripture says: *my just will live by faith.*[210] So, let the troubles that agitate your spirit go

---

207. See also Letters 153 and 155.

208. *Relation de 1633*, 305–7.

209. *Relation de 1633*, 234–5.

210. Isaiah 62:4; Hebrews 10:38.

or else you would stumble into the problem that your friend pointed out to you, after which your perfection would suffer a considerable change for the worse, and interior trouble would impede the holy enterprises that you have conceived for the glory of God and the service of the Church.

Monsieur de Bernières tells me, and the Reverend Father Lalemant confirms, that they want to send us Monsieur l'Abbé de Montigny, who is said to be a great servant of God, for our bishop.[211] It would be a great good for this country to have a permanent superior, and the time is ripe, provided that he is united with the Reverend Fathers Jesuit in the zeal of religion, otherwise the whole thing would be to the disadvantage of the glory of God and the salvation of souls. Those people who say that the Jesuits constrain consciences in this country are wrong, I assure you, for one lives here in a holy liberty of spirit.[212] It is true that they alone are engaged in the direction of souls, but they constrain no one, and those who seek God and want to live according to his maxims have peace in their hearts. Nevertheless, certain cases could arise in which one could need to have recourse to others, and it is partly for that reason that a bishop is wanted here. God in his mercy is giving us a holy one.

The Iroquois have gone back on their word and broken the peace. They had even conspired to kill all the Fathers and all the French who were with them, but our Lord protected them and took them by their hands without anyone having been harmed. I will speak to you about this at greater length in another letter. This breach, in addition to the dangers of the sea, which are significant, compels us not to ask for any religious from France this year. There is still another reason I spoke to you about last year, namely the losses that our Lord has permitted to befall us. Two days before our harvests a great whirlwind accompanied by a crack of thunder flattened the barn of our little farm, killed our oxen, and crushed our plowman in an instant, causing us a loss of more than four thousand *livres*. Two days ago, yet another calamity befell us. In that place only one little house remained, where our workmen were in the habit of retiring, for we had to have the barn

---

211. That is, François de Laval, born at Montigny-sur-Avre in 1623.

212. During the second half of the seventeenth century, the Jesuits were accused of exercising what Marie-Aimée Cliche has called "une véritable tyrannie morale" over the colonial population; see Marie-Aimée Cliche, *Les Pratiques de dévotion en Nouvelle-France: Comportements populaires et encadrement ecclésial dans le gouvernement de Québec* (Quebec: Presses de l'Université Laval, 1988), 219. See also Dominique Deslandres, "French Catholicism in the era of exploration and early colonization," in *Cambridge History of Religions in America (CHRA)*, vol. 1, ed. Stephen J. Stein (Cambridge: Cambridge University Press, 2012), 200–18; and Jaenen, *Role of the Church in New France*, 120–57, for a discussion of the moral rigorism of the Canadian clergy, generally.

rebuilt in the court of our monastery, which is only about an eighth of a league away from our land. At eight o'clock in the evening, the Iroquois called from afar to a young man who was staying there alone in order to graze our oxen, intending (it was believed) to take him alive, as they had done to a cowherd several days earlier. This young man remained so frightened that he left the house to go hide in the brush of the countryside. Once he composed himself, he came to tell us what he had heard, and immediately ten of our people left to go defend the place. But they arrived too late, because they found the house in flames and our five oxen gone. The next day these oxen were found in a quite distant place to which, terrified by the fire, they had retreated, having dragged with them a long piece of wood to which they had been attached. God kept them for us, except a single one which was found stabbed all over by a knife. The house was of little value, but the loss of furniture, arms, tools, and all the equipment causes us major inconvenience. It is thus that His Goodness visits us from time to time. He giveth to us and he taketh from us. Blessed be he in all the events of his providence.[213]

This here is only my first reply. I hope to write you by all the ships, but I am so tied up, my very dear son, with managing our trivial temporal affairs that I can write only by stops and starts. It is I who would have good reason to say that I am distracted to no end, and that I commit an innumerable number of infidelities vis-à-vis God who, out of his goodness, does not reject me, but rather continues to give me his grace and mercy. As for you, continue to serve him generously, using the talents he is giving you according to his will and in the manner by which he will be most glorified. I beg him to give his blessing for this and to place the works of his spirit on your tongue and in your heart, so that his word is not bound or smothered in you by overly human considerations, and so that by a holy audacity accompanied by a divine prudence, you can give your neighbor the help of which his grace renders you capable. I am in his holy love what you know and in what, in truth, I am. Yours.

Letter 179: October 4, 1658

My very dear son,

May the love and the life of Jesus be our life and our love for all time and eternity. In the letters I wrote you about what has happened, I did not speak to you about this new Church. I don't want to let this ship leave without saying a word about it, as you await the *Relation* which will discuss it at greater length. Last year's *Relation* informed you about the hope for a great progress of our holy

---

213. Job 1:21.

faith, but eventually you received a letter which gave you reason to fear what has happened. Just when the affairs of God were most beautifully disposed, a group of Iroquois conspired to massacre all the Reverend Fathers and all the French people of their house and their garrison.[214] This was the work of demons, who were enraged that so many souls were being snatched away from them. This barbarous plan would without doubt have succeeded, had an Iroquois Christian not secretly warned the Fathers about it and advised them to put their affairs in order immediately. Knowing the nature of the Indians, they saw clearly that there was more to the plan, and that the Iroquois had resolved, after having taken down the French there, to come here in the guise of friendship in order to wreak havoc everywhere. This is why the Fathers immediately informed people here about what was happening, while they looked for ways to get out. This was rather difficult for them since they didn't have canoes, but because they had none and couldn't get any without the help of the Indians, they resolved to make little boats like those of our Loire. They worked on these boats ceaselessly in the granary and meanwhile, the Fathers who were dispersed on mission were advised to meet them on the designated day. It should be noted that from morning to evening the Fathers' house was continually full of people, because of the large crowd from the Iroquois nations. It was there that the council of elders was held, and on the day designated for the departure there was to be a special general assembly of Indians. So as to surprise them, the Fathers were advised to hold a feast for them. To this end, a young Frenchman who had been adopted by a famous Iroquois and had learned their language, said to his father that he had dreamed he must hold a gluttonous feast for everyone, and that if there was a single morsel left, he would surely die.[215] "Ah," responded this man, "you are my son. I do not want you to

---

214. Thwaites, *Jesuit Relations*, vol. 44, 67–77 and 191–233.

215. The *Jesuit Relations* make mention of the significance of dreams to various North American peoples. See, for example, Thwaites, *Jesuit Relations*, vol. 33, 187–95 and vol. 39, 17–19 (discussing the importance of dreams among the Huron), vol. 42, 143–59 and vol. 57, 151–61 and 273–95 (the Onondaga), vol. 54, 63–71 (the Cayuga), and vol. 54, 95–101 (the Seneca). For a study of the experience and significance of dreams across the early modern Americas, see Anne Marie Plane and Leslie Tuttle, eds., *Dreams, Dreamers, and Visions in the Early Modern Atlantic World* (Philadelphia: University of Pennsylvania Press, 2013). See also, Dominique Deslandres, "Dreams Clash: The War over Authorized Interpretation in Seventeenth-Century French Missions," in *Empires of God. Religious Encounter in the Early Modern Atlantic*, ed. Linda Gregerson and Susan Juster (Philadelphia: University of Pennsylvania Press, 2010), 241–61. For an analysis of the centrality of dreams in Huron culture, see Bruce Trigger, *The Children of Aataentsic* (Montreal: McGill-Queens University Press, 1976), 81–4; and Denys Dêlage, *Bitter Feast: Amerindians and Europeans in Northeastern North America, 1600–64*, trans. Jane Brierley (Vancouver: University of British Columbia Press, 1993), 71–7. For a discussion of the Jesuit perspective on the Amerindian "all-eating" feasts, see Catherine Briand,

die. Hold this feast for us and we will eat everything." The Fathers gave pigs that they were feeding in order to save the species in this country and to live partly in the French style. In addition, they provided what they had of bustards, fish, and more, and all that, together with what the young Frenchman had been able to procure besides, was put into the big cauldrons in order to prepare the banquet in the style of the Indians. Once everything was ready they began to eat during the night. They so stuffed themselves that they could eat no more. They said to the young man who was holding the feast, "Have pity on us, send us away to rest." The other replied, "But then I will die." Upon this word "die" they gorged themselves so as to oblige him. At the same time, he ordered that flutes, trumpets, and drums be played so as to make them dance and relieve the boredom of such a long meal. Meanwhile the French were preparing to leave. They had the boats brought down and loaded them with everything they planned to take with them, and all that was done so secretly that no Indian noticed. When everything was ready, the young Frenchman was told that he must skillfully bring the feast to an end. So he said to his father, "It is done. I pity you, stop eating, I will not die. I will have someone play a sweet instrument to put you to sleep, but do not get up until late tomorrow. Sleep until someone comes to wake you to say prayers." Upon these words, someone played a guitar and immediately they fell into the most profound sleep. Then the French who were present went their separate ways and went to set sail with the others who were waiting for them. Please note that never had anyone taken a boat on this big lake or river because of the waterfalls and rapids encountered there—and even to cross it one had to go to great trouble to carry the canoes and baggage. There was yet another hitch, namely, that the lake was beginning to ice over. However, the boats of our fugitives sailed with unparalleled speed amidst all these perils and between the bands of ice that were on both sides. They all traveled in a single file, because since the river was beginning to set, they had to follow the first boat, which opened the way. Finally, thanks to what is considered the miraculous assistance of God, they arrived in Montreal in ten days time, which is quite prompt, without suffering a single accident, whether on account of the Iroquois or the ice or the other dangers of navigation.

When the barbarians awoke and noticed that the day was unfolding unusually, without the sound of prayer or any noise coming from the Fathers' house, they were quite surprised. They were still more so when they entered the house and found neither people nor furniture nor baggage. They understood then that the French had left, which greatly surprised them, for they had hidden their

---

"The Performance of the Meal in 17th-Century French Travel Accounts to New France: From Hospitality to Hybridity," *Food, Culture, and Society* 11, no. 2 (June 2008): 219–41.

conspiracy so well, they didn't think anyone in all the world knew about it. But what astonished them more than anything else was how the French had gone, for knowing that the French didn't have canoes and that the river was frozen besides, they didn't know what to think. Then another event occurred which astonished them more than anything, for it had snowed all night long, and, not seeing any human tracks in the snow, they couldn't imagine anything other than that the Fathers and the French had flown away.

Seeing that their conspiracy had been exposed, and suspecting that the French would go wage war on them with a mighty hand, the Indians immediately sent gifts to the neighboring nations who were allied with them, so as to get help from them in this time of need. The French, for their part, were here, and feared that the five Iroquois nations would unite together to come ravage us, and even before the Fathers had arrived they kept a constant watch for fear of a surprise attack, especially after having learned that three Frenchmen had been killed near Montreal by the Iroquois Onondagas. Thus, war has been declared on both sides. Everyone is frightened, yet everyone nevertheless is attacking and defending themselves. Several of these barbarians were captured and several killed. They, in turn, killed an Algonquin woman and captured two others along with their children. One of the two was so courageous that she stabbed her Iroquois attacker in the stomach with her knife.[216] His companions were so frightened by this that they dropped the weapons, baggage, women, and children that they were holding and fled. Thus freed, these captives brought their booty to the feet of Monsieur the Governor, who has imprisoned twenty-one of the most famous men of all the Iroquois nations, who were quite astonished to see themselves in such dire straits, although care was taken to treat them well. They begged Monsieur the Governor to send one of them back to their country to renew the peace and to see to it that the Fathers return there. That was granted them, and one hopes great success will come of it.

A few days ago, the leader of these prisoners complained to Reverend Father Chaumonot, saying that it was stupid to have left them and that he was the cause of all the evil, that he was regarded as the foremost man in the world and that thus they had him preside in all their councils—that they were blamed but that it was on him that all the blame should fall, that as for the act of hostility that had been carried out, it had not come from him or the elders but from some young

---

216. Elsewhere, Marie recounts similar stories of virile Amerindian woman who maim, murder, and perform spectacular feats of endurance. See, for example, Letter 183. For a discussion of the treatment of Amerindian women in Marie's writings, see Marie-Florine Bruneau, *Women Mystics*, 101–34. For a more general discussion of the place of gender in New World narratives, see Montrose, "Work of Gender."

and stupid fools. Then he added, speaking of Monsieur the Governor, Onontio despises us, and we are now his tethered dogs. Still, we could tolerate this if we were his domestic dogs and could go indoors. But whatever complaints this Indian makes, they must remained tethered, because they would soon run off if they were made domestic dogs, as they say. Articles of peace were drawn up, borne by the ambassadors. The most essential one of all is that they will not be granted the return of the Fathers unless they give us hostages, namely girls to be kept in our seminary, for men and boys cannot be trusted.[217]

You learned last year about what had happened to the poor Hurons that the Reverend Father Ragueneau led to Onontagué on the good faith of the Iroquois, and how they were massacred.[218] In this group there were good Huron women who had been our seminarians and who were still very excellent Christians. There was, in particular, a young widow who was brought along expressly to give a good example to the Iroquois women. She was taken captive by a barbarian who wanted to ravish her honor in a trench that had been dug in the ground. This woman, although weak and delicate, tore herself out of his hands and ran away into the woods such that, unable to follow her, he was constrained to let her go. He set off again with his companions, while she remained lost in this immense forest where no man has ever lived, but only all sorts of savage beasts. She went a good thirty days without eating anything other than the roots of wild grasses. Finally, realizing that she was a hair's breadth from death, she dragged herself as best she could onto a rock at the water's edge, abandoning herself to the providence of God. Because she is a person of prayer and virtue, she conversed on the rock with God while awaiting the disposition of his will. But this divine Father of the abandoned, who did not want to lose her, permitted that someone from a fleet of canoes piloted by Reverend Father du Peron, which was on its way to the Iroquois, noticed something moving on the rock. He wanted to go over there but was prevented by an Iroquois who put her in his canoe, saying she was his captive. She was not, however, in his power for long, because the Reverend Father bought her back and after fortifying her, set her free. When she was captured, her sisters and her niece were massacred, and since they were excellent Christians I believe they are high up in heaven. She alone was brought back from Iroquois territory, where the Reverend Fathers had no choice but to leave around five hundred Christians. This is the reason for their sorrow, for these good neophytes are in an extreme danger of losing either their faith or their lives.[219] Thus the Fathers long to return so as

---

217. Thwaites, *Jesuit Relations*, vol. 44, 83–233.

218. Thwaites, *Jesuit Relations*, vol. 44, 67–77.

219. The captivity narrative, of which the above account is a variety, has been well studied, particularly within the context of Puritan North America. See, for example, Gary Ebersole, *Captured*

to help them and risk their lives with those of their children in Jesus Christ. The Fathers never would have abandoned them if they had not been compelled to come and guarantee the safety of the French of our settlements, for these barbarians had resolved, after having taken down those who were in their country, to come in the guise of friendship and raid all the settlements and then, in treason, to pillage and burn everything there. You see, my very dear son, from what a calamity our Lord has delivered us, and how it hardly does any good to trust the barbarians when demons possess their hearts, for without doubt this conspiracy is the work of these princes of darkness, who, envious of the great progress that had been made in such a short time, will smother this new Church in its crib. The Mohawk Iroquois have not carried out any act of hostility against the French in four years. Their neighbors, the Dutch of New Holland, are likewise asking for Fathers to assist them, because in certain districts there are more Catholics than heretics. Moreover, in a newly discovered land there is a colony of English Catholics who are fugitives from their country for the faith and have come there to establish themselves. From New Holland to their settlement, it is only a two-day journey. In general the Dutch have received the Reverend Father Le Moyne very well, although he was in his Jesuit habit, which will greatly facilitate communication with the Mohawks. Because commerce is substantial between the French and the Dutch, there is a boat currently at our port from that country which is going back there. As for our French colony, it is growing such that the country is no longer recognizable on account of the number of settlers. God has so blessed the plowing that the ground yields very good wheat and in sufficient quantity to feed its settlers. The air here is warmer now that the land has been cleared and is less shadowed by these great forests which used to make it so cold. Nevertheless winter was long this year and since the planting was delayed, there is still wheat to cut at present. Here you have, my very dear son, an abridgement of what you will see at greater length in the *Relation*, if you don't mind reading it. Continue, I beg you, to recommend me to our Lord, and above all do not forget our poor Christians who are

---

by *Texts: Puritan to Postmodern Images of Indian Captivity* (Charlottesville: University of Virginia Press, 1995); John Demos, *The Unredeemed Captive: A Family Story from Early America* (New York: Alfred Knopf, 1994); William Henry Foster, *The Captor's Narrative: Catholic Women and Their Puritan Men on the Early American Frontier* (Ithaca: Cornell University Press, 2003); and Pauline Turner, *Captive Selves, Captivating Others: The Politics and Poetics of Colonial American Captivity Narratives* (Boulder: Westview, 1999). Much of the recent research on captivity narratives draws attention to the implications of these stories for the construction of colonial identities in which issues of race, gender, religion, and culture take center-stage. The extent to which Marie's own variation on the theme of the captivity narrative functions to draw the boundaries of a specifically Christian identity deserves further study. See also Letters 128, 142, and 183. For an analysis of Marie's own autobiography as a captivity narrative, see Caroline M. Woidat, "Captivity, Freedom, and the New World Convent: The Spiritual Autobiography of Marie de l'Incarnation Guyart," *Legacy* 25, no. 1 (2008): 1–22.

among the Iroquois, nor the Reverend Fathers' intention to go help them at the risk of their lives. I don't have time to reread my letter. Excuse my mistakes and my haste.

Letter 183: September–October 1659

My very dear and beloved son,

It was a great privation for me to see a ship arrive and not to receive any letters from you. I was, however, convinced that you had written me, but I believed—and I was not wrong—that your letters were in the first ship, which was bringing us the news that we would have a bishop this year, but which showed up long after the others. Because of this delay we received a bishop before we received the news that promised us one.[220] But that was a pleasant surprise in all respects, for in addition to the happiness it brings the whole country to have an ecclesiastic superior, it consoles everyone that the bishop is a man of rare and extraordinary personal qualities. Without mentioning his birth, which is quite illustrious, for he is of the house of Laval, he is a man of high merit and singular virtue. I have indeed understood what you wanted to tell me about his election, but although people will say what they want, it was not men who chose him.[221] I am not saying that he is a saint—this would be saying too much—but I will say truthfully that he lives righteously and as an apostle. He doesn't know what it is to care about the opinions of others.[222] He prefers to speak the truth to everyone and he speaks it freely on all occasions. We needed a man of this sort of strength here in order to extirpate the gossip that was proliferating and putting down deep roots. In a word, his life is so exemplary that the whole country admires him. He is an intimate friend of Monsieur de Bernières with whom he lived for four years out of devotion, and we should not be surprised to see that, having attended this school, he has achieved a sublime level of prayer. A nephew of Monsieur de Bernières wanted to come with him. He is a young gentleman who delights everyone with

---

220. François de Laval arrived in Quebec on June 16, 1659.

221. *The Dictionary of Canadian Biography* gives a succinct account of the complications—and interests—involved in Laval's appointment as vicar apostolic; see André Vachon, "Laval, François de," *Dictionary of Canadian Biography Online*, accessed August 16, 2011, http://www.biographi.ca/en/bio/laval_francois_de_2E.html.

222. A popular subject of moralizing treatises and sermons in seventeenth-century France, the notion of *respect humain* was one of social conformity suggestive of a prioritization of the things of this world over and above the things of God. Along with self-love, *respect humain* presented a great impediment to spiritual progress and the exercise of Christian liberty; see "Sur le Respect Humain," *Choix de sermons de Bourdaloue* (Paris, 1881), 29–52; and Hyacinthe de Montargon, *Dictionnaire apostolique, à l'usage de MM les curés des villes et de la campagne*, vol. 5 (Paris: A.M. Lottin l'aîné, 1776).

his modesty. He wanted to give everything to God in imitation of his uncle and to consecrate himself to the service of this new Church. And so as to succeed more brilliantly, he is preparing himself to receive priestly orders from the hands of our new prelate. I told you that we did not expect a bishop this year. Consequently, he found nothing ready to receive him when he arrived. We have loaned him our seminary, which is located at one of the corners of our enclosure and quite close to the parish. There he will have the comfort and pleasure of a beautiful garden, and so that we are both living according to the canons, he had a fence of separation made. We will be inconvenienced by it, because we have to lodge our seminarians in our own quarters, but the subject merits it, and we will bear this inconvenience with pleasure until his episcopal residence is built.

As soon as he was consecrated bishop in Paris, he asked Father Lalemant, the Reverend Father General of the Jesuits, who has been the Rector of la Flèche for three months, to accompany him. This is a boon for the whole country and for us in particular, and for me more than anyone else, for I will tell you in confidence that I was suffering in the privation of someone with whom I could talk about what was going on in my interior.[223] All year long I had an interior impulse that our Lord would send me help. He did so when the time was right. Blessed be his holy name for it forever.

You are aware of what has happened over the past years with regard to Monsieur l'Abbé de Queylus.[224] He is currently the director of a seminary of priests from

---

223. Jérôme Lalemant, Marie's spiritual director, had returned to France in 1656; see Letter 173.

224. From the time of his arrival in New France in 1657 until his departure in 1661, Thubières de Levy de Queylus found himself embroiled in a series of conflicts with the Jesuits over questions of ecclesiastical jurisdiction. In 1657, the Sulpician was named vicar general of New France in 1657 by the archbishop of Rouen who had long claimed ecclesiastical jurisdiction over the colony. De Queylus's appointment as vicar general, however, clashed with the archbishop's appointment some eight years earlier of the superior of the Jesuits in Quebec to the same position—an appointment which had not been explicitly revoked. The conflict between the two camps would only intensify with the appointment in 1658 of the Jesuit Laval as vicar apostolic of New France under the title of Bishop of Petrea. Questions about who had ecclesiastical jurisdiction in the colony—de Queylus, the vicar general, or Laval, the vicar apostolic—were still unresolved when Laval arrived in Quebec in June 1659. Eventually, with the support of King Louis XIV, Laval's claims to authority over the Church in New France were recognized in fact and de Queylus returned, for the time being, to France in October of the same year. Finally, in 1668, an order from the court in Rome confirming Laval's rights as vicar apostolic brought the jurisdictional conflict between de Queylus and Laval to a close. For a concise summary of the conflict between de Queylus and Laval, see *Les Prêtres de Saint-Sulpice au Canada, grandes figures de leur histoire* (Québec: Presses de l'Université Laval, 1992), 81–9. See also Olivier Maurault, "Saint-Sulpice et le Canada: L'imbroglio Queylus-Laval," *SCHEC Rapport* (1955–6): 73–81. For a study of the Sulpicians in Canada, see Dominique Deslandres, John Dickinson, and Ollivier Hubert, eds., *The Sulpicians of Montreal: a History of Power and Discretion, 1657–2007* (Montreal: Librarie Wilson and Lafleur Limitée, 2013).

Saint Sulpice of Paris that Monsieur de Bretonvilliers has undertaken to build in Montreal along with a very beautiful church. This abbot, I say, who came down from Montreal to greet our prelate, was made Grand Vicar there by Monsignor the Archbishop of Rouen, but today all that is irrelevant and his authority ceases. Nevertheless, the mission there is making significant progress. The Hospitallers came from la Flèche and thirty families will be established there right away, the last ship having brought a number of girls for this purpose. We are being urged to establish ourselves there too, but we are not in a position to do it.[225] Monsignor our prelate will have the authority to examine all that, although he is here only under the title of Bishop of Petrea and not of Quebec or Canada. Indeed, this title was the talk of the town. But it came about because of a dispute between the Court of Rome and that of France. The king wants the bishop of Canada to be under his authority and take an oath of fidelity to him, like the other bishops in France. And the Holy Father claims to have some particular right in foreign nations. Thus he sent us a bishop, not as a bishop of the country, but as Apostolic Commissar under the foreign title of Bishop of Petrea.[226]

You are troubled by the affairs of this country. They are as they were before the Iroquois had made peace, for they broke it and already have captured and killed nine Frenchmen in an unexpected confrontation, and at a time when no one thought they were badly disposed toward the French.[227] They have already burned one of their prisoners alive, and it will be a marvel if the others are treated any better. Since then, eleven of their people have been killed and the others are being guarded against, for it has been discovered from a Huron captive who left them that they are assembling a powerful army to come and carry off our new Christians and, as I understand it, as many Frenchmen as they can. This Huron escaped in the following manner. He was in a canoe full of Iroquois, who,

---

225. The Hospitallers of Saint Joseph arrived in Montreal in October, 1659. For a study of the development of Montreal, see Dechêne, *Habitants and Merchants*. Patricia Simpson's study of Montreal in its early years focuses on the contributions of Marguerite Bourgeoys, whose role in colonial development offers a constructive comparison to that of Marie de l'Incarnation; see Patricia Simpson, *Marguerite Bourgeoys, 1640–1665* (Montreal: McGill-Queen's University Press, 1997).

226. Laval would not be appointed bishop of Quebec until 1674. Until then his official title in the colony was Bishop of Petrea *in partibus infidelum*, which rendered him beyond the ecclesiastical jurisdiction of the archbishop of Rouen—and the Gallican church at large—and under the authority of the pope alone. For a discussion of the ways in which the conflict between Laval and de Queylus was one, in an important sense, between the competing theologies of Gallicanism and ultramontanism, see Sister M. Theodosia O'Callaghan, "Echoes of Gallicanism in New France," *Catholic Historical Review* 12, no. 1 (April 1926): 16–58.

227. Thwaites, *Jesuit Relations*, vol. 45, 31–3; *Jesuit Journal*, trans. William Lonc (Midland, ON: Steve Catlin, 2005), 283.

seeing a canoe of Hurons on their way to harpoon eels, let it pass by in order to ambush it when the Hurons would no longer be together and able to defend themselves. This captive, touched by tenderness for those of his nation, drew back from these masters who had gone ashore and retraced his steps to warn his compatriots about the Iroquois's plans and the danger they were in. They set off right away—he was with them—and they all came promptly to Quebec where they warned others about what the Iroquois were doing. Without that, quite a few heads would have been broken, for in addition to the Hurons who could not have avoided their rage, they would have crept in among the harvesters, who, in good faith of the peace, were working without fear and without suspicion. That happened, in fact, in Trois-Rivières where they captured the nine Frenchmen of whom I just spoke. As I write, Monsieur our Governor is in the countryside to hunt them down or capture one of them. He went because the Iroquois he had imprisoned between strong walls enclosed by iron doors, upon learning that their nation had broken the peace, and believing that they would all certainly be burned alive, broke out of their fortress on that night and scaled the walls of the fort. When the sentinel saw them, he gave a warning signal, and they were immediately given chase. I don't know yet if they have been captured, for these people run like deer.

You astonish me when you say that our Mothers wanted to call us back. God save us from this calamity. If we did not leave after our fire and on account of all our other losses, we will not leave on account of the Iroquois, unless the whole country leaves or a superior obliges us to do so, for we are daughters of obedience and we must prefer it to everything. Nevertheless, I will be surprised if that ever happens. There is talk that an army of our enemies is preparing to come here, but now that their plan is exposed that will not be easy for them.[228] Nevertheless, if our Lord was letting them do it, they would have brought us down long ago, but His Goodness is subverting their plans in warning us about them, so that we are on our guard against them. If our affairs were in danger, I would be the first to warn you, so as to enable you to provide for our safety, since our Mothers are confiding their feelings in you. But, thank God, we don't see or believe that this is happening. If however it did happen contrary to our expectations, wouldn't we be fortunate to end our lives in the service of our master and to give them back to he who gave them to us? These are my sentiments, which you will make known to our Mothers if you think it appropriate.[229]

---

228. Thwaites, *Jesuit Relations*, vol. 45, 33.

229. Letters 142 and 143.

My personal feeling is that if we are suffering corporally in Canada, it is because of poverty rather than the sword of the Iroquois. And as for the country in general, its downfall in my opinion will not come about by means of these barbarians as much as by certain people, who, because of envy or otherwise, write a lot of lies to the Messieurs of the Company about the holiest and most virtuous people, and whose calumny is dividing even those who maintain justice here and sustain the country by their prudence. Since these nasty attacks are carried out in secret they can't be averted, and since corrupted nature leads one to believe evil things more readily than good ones, these lies are easily believed. Whence it happens that when we least expect it, we receive very unwelcome orders and decrees here. God is quite grievously offended by all this, and he would give us a great grace if he purged the country of these captious and contradictory minds.[230]

Upon its arrival, the last ship was found infected with scarlet fever and pestilence. It was carrying two hundred people, nearly all of whom were sick. Eight of them died at sea and others on land. Practically the whole country was infected and the hospital filled with sick people. Monsignor our prelate is there continually to serve the sick and make their beds. One does what one can to stop him from it and preserve his body, but no eloquence can dissuade him from these acts of humility. The Reverend Father de Quen by his great charity contracted this disease and died from it. This is a considerable loss for the mission, for he was the former missionary to the Algonquins among whom he had worked for twenty-five years with unbelievable toil. Finally, quitting his post as the superior of the missions, he lost his life in the exercise of charity. Two Hospitaller nuns were quite ill from this disease. Thank God, our community was not attacked by it. We are in a quite healthy place here, which is exposed to strong winds that purify the air. As for me personally, my health is very good. I continue to long achingly for eternity, although I am prepared to live as long as it pleases our Lord.

---

230. Marie's diplomatic refusal to name names—or, for that matter, concrete historical events—makes it difficult to determine the nature and dimensions of the colonial conflict to which she refers. It is reasonable to suppose, however, that she is alluding to the tensions between the new governor (Pierre Voyer d'Argenson, who had arrived in New France in 1658) and the Jesuits, on the one hand, and the Compagnie des Cents Associés, on the other. Although the debts accumulated by the Compagnie des Cents Associés as a consequence, in part, of the disruptions in trade caused by the English invasions and the hostilities of the Iroquois finally compelled the company to cede its trading monopoly to the Communauté des Habitants in 1645, it retained title to the seigneury of New France and preserved its right to appoint governors and ministers of justice in the colony until it was dissolved by Louis XIV in 1663; see Eccles, *The Canadian Frontier*, 43–4. For a brief discussion of the difficulties of d'Argenson's term as governor of New France, see Jacques Mathieu, "Voyer d'Argenson, Pierre de," *Dictionary of Canadian Biography Online*, accessed September 2, 2011, http://www.biographi.ca/en/bio/voyer_d_argenson_pierre_de_2E.html.

Letter 188: October 13, 1660

My very dear son,[231]

I finally received your three letters, with a joy all the more profound since I had almost lost hope of receiving them. The cause of this delay is that our parcels and those of our friends were interfered with, but in the end we both received everything. I am quite concerned that the great infirmity that's plaguing you is growing more and more acute. Nothing weakens the body as much as the circumstances you describe, and what makes your infirmity worse is the type of life your rule obliges you to live. I keenly felt your infirmity, but blessed be God, you are more his than mine, and your life and my own are in his hands.[232] This is what I have to tell you for your consolation, and to give you reason to be patient and acquiesce to the orders of God.

It is not for a lack of good will if I don't converse with you about spiritual things according to your inclination and my own, but, like you, I am so overwhelmed by external affairs that all I can do after having satisfied these obligations is to acquit myself of regular observances. I long for retreat and solitude, but it is not in my disposition to choose this state. It's not that, as regards God, my spirit isn't attached to him by means of his attraction, and that my heart doesn't have the benefit of being united to His Divine Majesty with his intimacy and his ordinary grace. The Monsieur of Geneva says that there are birds that eat while flying.[233] I am the same way in terms of the life of the spirit, for in the midst of the troubles to which I am bound by necessity, I take in hearty and continual food like I just told you. Thus I assure you that I can't write anything about spiritual things and if I could, nothing would give me more satisfaction than giving you this contentment. Let's stop talking about it, if you please, until it pleases God to dispose otherwise. In the meantime, let us think of sanctifying ourselves in the midst of these troubles, you and me, since what is most perfect and agreeable in

---

231. By the spring of 1660, Claude had been ordered to leave Compiègne to assume the position of Prior of the monastery of Saint-Serge d'Angers; see Oury, *Dom Claude Martin*, 109.

232. Claude had become gravely ill the previous winter. See also Letters 195 and 216.

233. That is, Francis de Sales. Although Oury points out that the published works of Francis de Sales contain no such image, the sense of the sentiment is surely that of de Sales, whose emphasis on active service (as well as the spiritual potential of the laity) proved enormously influential on the development of a distinctive brand of seventeenth-century French spirituality; see Barbara Diefendorf, *From Penitence to Charity: Pious Women and the Catholic Reformation in Paris* (New York: Oxford University Press, 2004), 240. Marie herself attests to having read de Sales's *Introduction à la vie dévote*; see *Relation de 1654*, 192. See also Oury, *Marie Guyart*, 30–33, for a further discussion of the written texts to which Marie might have been exposed and which might have influenced her spirituality.

his eyes is that we follow his orders. As for me, I have a strong inclination to offer myself at every moment in a spirit of sacrifice, and to forget myself and let myself be consumed by he who is glorified by annihilated souls.[234]

You have much obliged me by not having shared our writings to be inserted in the work of this good Father who is composing the history of Canada.[235] More than ten years ago, he urged me to give him something similar, but I always excused myself from it. I don't know if the Reverend Father Lalemant has given him any of his own recollections of it. He could if he wanted to, for he knows me better than anyone else in the world. If he did, he did so without discussing it with me. Let us die entirely to the world and let us say together with a saint: we will be truly servants of Jesus Christ if the world sees nothing of us.[236] As I am united to you in all the good works that the Divine Goodness does through you, so also what I do in him, for without him I can do nothing, is likewise yours.[237] Let us remain in this union and communication of spiritual goods for the love, honor, and glory of Jesus. My other letters tell you the news of the country.

Letter 195: September 16, 1661

My very dear son,

I received with a very particular consolation your three letters which all informed me that our Lord returned your health to you. I admit that I feared this illness would carry you off and I had already made my sacrifice in stripping my heart of what it loves most on earth to obey His Divine Majesty. Well, here you are again. Therefore, be a worthy worker of his glory and consume yourself in his service. To this end, I am quite content that you are no longer in Compiègne where temporal cares claimed a share of your spirit.[238] Use this rest like a refreshment offered to you by heaven, in order to amass new stores of virtue and good works and to direct all your energies to the glory of the one for whom we live. You are off to a good start, and I took pleasure in the skill with which you righteously

---

234. See Letters 56, 68, and 216.

235. François du Creux, *Historia canadensis* (Paris, 1664).

236. That is, Saint Ignatius of Antioch, who writes in his *Letter to the Romans*, "Then shall I truly be a disciple of Christ, when the world shall not see so much as my body" (Ignatius of Antioch, *Letter to the Romans*, IV).

237. John 15:5.

238. In 1656, while Claude was at Compiègne, the abbey of Saint-Corneille de Compiègne came under the control of the abbey of Val-de-Grâce.

fooled Monsignor d'Angers concerning the reform of Saint Aubin.[239] Sometimes, it's necessary to pull tricks like this to advance the interests of God, who then takes care to fix the problems that can arise because of the humans involved. You have proof of it, since this great prelate likes you and is no longer set against you. I am hearing again that you are serving God and neighbor by your preaching. You much obliged me by sending me the one you wrote on the grandeurs of Jesus, and you have reason to say that it treats a subject of which I am fond. I am, in fact, fond of it because everything having to do with the grandeurs of our very lovable Jesus pleases me more than I can express to you. I leave you to imagine how content my spirit is when I receive something similar from my son, for whom I always wished a life rooted in the gospel, practicing its maxims and proclaiming the praises and grandeurs of the sacred Incarnate Word.[240] You had not yet been born when my ambition for you was that you be a servant of Jesus Christ and totally devoted to his divine counsels, at the expense of your life and mine. The piece is beautiful and well conceived in all aspects, but I fear that these major productions pain you too much and that this is, in part, the cause of your exhaustion. I note therein a great labor, but a gentleness of spirit is found there, too. If I were like those saints who heard preaching from far away, I would take pleasure in listening to you; but I am not worthy of this grace. We must believe that we will see each other in the next world rather than this one. Nevertheless, God has his ways, although they are unknown to us, especially in a drifting and uncertain country like this one where, naturally speaking, we have no more assurance than do the leaves of the trees when they blow in the wind.

You ask me about some of my personal devotional practices. If I could wish for one thing in this world, it would be to be close enough to you to pour my heart into yours, but our good God has appointed us each to our own station, to which we must hold. You know well that exterior devotions are difficult for me. Nevertheless, I will tell you simply that God inspired me to adopt one, which I think I spoke to you about in my writings. This devotion is to the most adorable

---

239. The bishop of Angers to whom Marie refers was Henri Arnauld, the brother of the controversial Jansenist Antoine Arnauld. For a contemporary study of Arnauld, see Isabelle Bonnot, *Hérétique ou Saint? Henri Arnauld, évêque janséniste d'Angers au XVIIe siècle* (Paris: Nouvelles Éditions latines, 1984). As Oury notes, there is no historical record of the reform of Saint-Aubin in Angers and Bishop Arnauld does not seem to have opposed the comparable reform of Saint-Serge; Lettre CXCV, *Correspondance*, 663, n. 3.

240. This shared exchange over the grandeurs of Jesus locates Claude (together with his mother) within the Bérullian current of the seventeenth century; see Bérulle, *Les Grandeurs de Jésus*, in *Œuvres completes*, vols. 7 and 8 (Paris: Cerf, 1995). For an analysis of the place of the Incarnate Word within the context of seventeenth-century French spirituality, see Brémond, *Histoire littéraire*, vol. III, 935–46.

heart of the Incarnate Word.²⁴¹ I have practiced it for more than thirty years, and here is how I came to adopt it.

One evening when I was in our cell conversing with the eternal Father about the conversion of souls and wishing with an ardent desire that the kingdom of Jesus Christ was realized, it seemed to me that the eternal Father wasn't listening to me and that he wasn't regarding me as favorably as usual. This afflicted me; but at that moment, I heard an interior voice say to me, "Ask me by the heart of my son. It is through him that I will grant your prayers." This divine touch was effective, for my whole interior found itself in a very intimate communication with that adorable heart, such that I wasn't able to speak with the eternal Father except through it. This happened to me from about eight to nine o'clock in the evening, and since then, at about that hour, I have completed my daily devotions with this practice. As far as I can remember, I have never neglected to do it, unless I was weak from illness or constrained in my interior action. Here is something akin to what I do when I am free to talk to the eternal Father.

*It is by the heart of my Jesus, my way, my truth, and my life that I approach you, O eternal Father.*²⁴² *By this divine heart, I adore you for all who do not adore you; I love you for all who do not love you; I adore you for all the willfully blind who do not know you on account of contempt. I want by this divine heart to satisfy the obligation of all mortals. I go around the world to seek all the souls redeemed by the very precious blood of my divine spouse. I want to satisfy you for all of them through this divine heart. I embrace them all in order to present them to you through him. I ask you for their conversion. Are you willing to tolerate that they not know my Jesus? Will you permit that they not live in he who died for everyone? You see, O divine Father, that they do not yet live. Ah! Make it so that they live through this divine heart.* It is here that I talk about this new Church and present to God all its needs. Then I add: *On this adorable heart, I present to you all the workers of the gospel. Fill them with your Holy Spirit by the merits of this divine heart.* From the workers of the gospel, my heart turns to our enemies, the Iroquois, for whose conversion I ask as insistently as possible. Then I talk about two souls whom you know and I say: *On this sacred heart as on a divine altar, I present to you N. and N., your little servants.*²⁴³ *I ask you in the name of my divine spouse that you*

---

241. *Relation de 1654*, 315. Devotion to the heart of Jesus, though typical to the seventeenth-century French school generally, is richly developed in the theology of Jean Eudes; see, Paul Milcent, *Saint Jean Eudes* (Paris: Bloud & Gay, 1964), 48–51. See also Brémond, *Histoire littéraire*, vol. III, 1313–39; and John Abruzzese, *The Theology of the Heart in the Writings of St. Francis de Sales* (Rome: Institute of Spirituality, Pontifical University of St. Thomas Aquinas, 1985).

242. John 14:6.

243. That is, Claude Martin and Marie Buisson.

fill them with his spirit and that they be eternally yours under the auspices of this adorable heart. I go on to remember some people with whom I have spiritual connections, as well as the benefactors of our house and of this new Church. I then address myself to the sacred Incarnate Word and say to him: *You know, my beloved, all that I want to say to our Father by your divine heart and by your holy soul. In saying it to him, I say it to you because you are in your Father and your Father is in you.*[244] *Therefore, make it so that all this is fulfilled and join yourself to me in order to sway through your heart that of your Father. Make it, in accordance with your word, that just as you are one with him, all the souls that I present to you are also one with him and with you.* Here is the exercise of the sacred heart of Jesus.

Then I envision what I owe to the Incarnate Word and in order to give him thanks, I say to him: *What shall I give back to you, O my divine spouse, for the surfeit of your graces upon me? It is through your divine Mother that I want to acknowledge them.*[245] *So, I offer you her sacred heart, this heart, I say, that loved you so much. Allow me to love you by this same heart, to offer you the sacred breasts that nursed you and this virginal womb that you wanted to sanctify, by dwelling therein before appearing in the world. I offer it to you in thanksgiving for all your blessings—both of grace and nature—upon me. I offer it to you for the amendment of my life and the sanctification of my soul, and so that it may please you to grant me the gift of final perseverance in your grace and in your holy love.*[246] *I give you thanks, O my divine spouse, for having chosen this very Holy Virgin for your Mother, for giving her the graces commensurate with such an eminent dignity, and finally for giving her to us as our mother. I adore the sacred moment of your incarnation in her very pure womb and all the divine moments of your itinerant life on earth. I give you thanks for wanting to make yourself not only our exemplary life by means of your divine virtues, but also our cause meritorious by means of all your works and the shedding*

---

244. John 14:10–11.

245. In this passage, Marie exemplifies the interweaving of Christocentric and Marian devotional threads typical to the French School; see Brémond, *Histoire littéraire*, vol. III, 963–9; Thompson, *Bérulle and the French School*, 47–54. The Mariological tendencies of the French School find particular expression in the work of Eudes; see Milcent, *Saint Jean Eudes*, 41–3.

246. The distinction between grace and nature is one fundamental to Catholic theology. Well developed in the work of Aquinas, the precise relationship between grace and nature was the subject of heated debate in Reformation Europe and into the seventeenth century and beyond; see Aquinas, *Summa Theologiae*, I, 1, viii, and I, 95. On the gift of final perseverance, see A. Michel, *Dictionnaire de théologie catholique*, ed. A. Vacant et al., vol. 12 (Paris: Letouzey et Ane, 1903–50), 1256–304. I am grateful to Bill O'Brien for his help with these references.

*of your blood.*²⁴⁷ *I want to live neither my life nor even for a moment, except by your life. Therefore, purify my impure and flawed life by the purity and perfection of your divine life and by the holy life of your divine Mother.* Then I say to the very Holy Virgin what love compels me to say, but always along the same lines as the aforementioned, and with that I bring my evening retreat to a close. At other times my heart and spirit are attached to their object and follow the inclination grace gives them. In the devotional exercise of which I just gave an account, I am an attribute of the spirit and this is only an expression of my interior, for I can't recite vocal prayers except the psalmody, my obligatory rosary being likewise fairly difficult.²⁴⁸

For the past twenty-three years, I have worn a little iron chain around my neck as a symbol of my commitment to the holy Mother of God. I have no other practice in this regard apart from kissing it to offer myself as a slave to this divine Mother.²⁴⁹

I beg you to accommodate yourself to my simplicity, my very dear son, and to excuse my informality. I can say like Saint Paul that I am making a fool of myself, but I will also say with him that it is you who are making me do it.²⁵⁰ I also composed a prayer that one of my friends translated into Latin for me, in order to honor the double beauty of the Son of God in both his divine and human natures. Here is how it goes: *Domine* Jesu-Christe, *splendor paternae gloriae, et figura substantiae ejus. Vota renovo illius servitutis qua me totam geminae pulchritudini tuae promisi reddituram: omnemque gloriam quae hic haberi aut optari potest rejicio, praeter eam qua me vere ancillam tuam in aeternum profitebor. Amen, mi* Jesu.

What inclined me toward this devotion to the double beauty of the holy Incarnate Word was this: One day in our house in Tours, while in the midst of an extraordinary transport, I had a vision of the eminence and transcendence of this double beauty of the two natures in Jesus Christ. While in this transport, I took

---

247. On the suffering and sacrificed Jesus Christ as the meritorious cause of justification, see "Decree on Justification," sess. VI, in *The Council of Trent*, ed. Waterworth, 34; see also Aquinas, *Summa Theologiae*, III, 48, i–vi.

248. Nicholas Paige contrasts the "eloquent transparency" of the medieval mystics with the "problematized communication" of their seventeenth-century counterparts, suggesting that the authenticity of interior experience was guaranteed by its inexpressibility. As Paige puts it, "the sense of interiority could only be provided if full exteriorization remained impossible" (Paige, *Being Interior*, 106, 158–61). See also Letters 109, 243, 267, and 274.

249. Here again, Marie's devotional practice resonates with the theology of Bérulle, who courted controversy for recommending vows of servitude to Jesus and Mary as a means of achieving *anéantissement*; see Thompson, *Bérulle and the French School*, 41–7. See also Raymond Deville, *L'école française de spiritualité* (Paris: Desclée, 1987), 42–4. In the Latin prayer cited below, Marie alludes to such a vow of servitude.

250. 2 Corinthians 12:11.

up my pen and wrote vows in conformity with what my spirit suffered. I have since lost this paper. When I came to, I found myself committed in a new way to Jesus Christ, although whatever one writes, one can never describe what happens in the soul when it is united in its depths to this divine object. In this single phrase *figure of the substance of the Father*, the spirit comprehends inexplicable things. The soul experienced in the ways of the spirit understands it to the extent of its grace. And in this renewal of vows to this double beauty, the soul, which is one and the same with its beloved, understands this secret as it understands that of its servitude to him.

I have spoken to you before about the devotion to Saint Francis of Paola, for I believe that you are aware that it was our great-grandfather who was sent by King Louis to ask for him from the pope and to bring him to France.[251] I often heard people speak about it to my grandfather. Even my aunt, who died when I was fifteen, had seen her grandmother, the daughter of this great-grandfather. He often took her to Plessis to visit this holy man who, with a pious affection, blessed this little one, making the sign of the cross on her face. Thus, our family has always been deeply devoted to this great saint. My grandfather recounted this to us quite often in order to preserve the memory of it and the devotion as he had received it from his grandfather.

This is the account of some of my devotions, which I am giving you with the same simplicity with which you asked me for it. Remember me in your own devotions, since for my part, I do nothing of which you do not have a goodly share.

Letter 196: September 16, 1661

My very dear son,

Finally, after having waited for a long time for the ships, they appeared at our port in the month of September, and they brought Monsieur the Baron du Bois d'Avaugour who is coming here to be our governor.[252] I had already learned your news from a fishing vessel. Without that, I would have been worried about you.

---

251. Francis de Paula, founder of the Order of Minims, was born in Paola, Italy, in 1416. According to legend, while on his deathbed, Louis XI sent for Francis to visit him from Italy. By the order of the pope, Francis reluctantly arrived in France and attended Louis XI at the moment of his death. He rather unwillingly remained in France, having been detained there by Louis XI's successors, Charles VIII and Louis XII, who wanted to keep him near their courts. Francis died in Plessis in 1507; see Anna Jameson, *Legends of the Monastic Orders as Represented in the Fine Arts* (London: Longmans, Green, 1872), 335–6.

252. Pierre du Bois, Baron d'Avaugour, served as governor of New France from 1661 to 1663.

But blessed be God for the fact that your news is good and that I know you are disposed as the Divine Goodness asks.

I don't doubt that you had been worried about us on account of the bad news that was brought to France last year concerning the persecution of the Iroquois.[253] They did even worse this year than in all the preceding ones, having killed and taken captive more than one hundred Frenchmen, from Montreal where they began their assault, to Cap Tourmente, which is the last of the French settlements. They came onto the Isle d'Orléans where almost all the settlers had retreated in order to avoid the carnage they witnessed among their neighbors. From there they went past Tadoussac to pursue our new Christians, who, in more than eighty canoes, had gone to trade with the nation of the Crees (who are said to be quite numerous), accompanied by two of our Reverend Fathers and some Frenchmen. On their way, these good neophytes and especially our Reverend Fathers encountered a great number of Indians to whom they proclaimed the word of God. But they weren't able to go further, for since the Iroquois had reached that nation, they scattered and fled just like the others to places still unknown. It was on account of a quite particular protection of the Divine Goodness that our Fathers and our Christians were preserved, for those barbarians went from place to place in order to stake them out and surprise them. Our people found their tracks fresh and their fires still glowing, but despite all these dangers they arrived safely. They were extremely fatigued from their travails, not the least of which was hunger, for they thought they would die for lack of food, not daring to hunt because of the enemy.

Of the French who were killed, Monsieur le Sénéchal, eldest son of Monsieur de Lozon, is the most notable. He was a very generous man and always ready to pursue the enemy. All the young people followed him enthusiastically. When the news broke about the murders on the Isle d'Orléans and at Beaupré, he wanted to go there in full force to hunt down the enemy, but he was stopped for good reason. The sister of Madame his wife, however, concerned that her husband was near the Isle, where he had gone hunting, had no rest until she had found someone to rescue him. Monsieur le Sénéchal wanted to take this opportunity to show his affection for his brother-in-law. He was the seventh to leave in a rowboat, which was opposite Sieur Maheu's house, which is in the middle of the island and had been abandoned for several days. He grounded it at low tide between two rocks which made a pathway to this house. He sent two of his companions there to discover if there were Iroquois. One of them entered through the open door and found eighty Iroquois lying there in ambush. They killed him and ran after the other one who, after having put up a good fight, was captured alive. They then went to

---

253. Thwaites, *Jesuit Relations*, vol. 46, 205–19; Thwaites, *Jesuit Journal*, 304–5.

besiege the rowboat, in which there were only five men left, who defended themselves to the death. Monsieur le Sénéchal, whom they did not want to kill, so as to take him alive to their country, defended himself to the last breath. He was found with his arms completely mangled and hacked up by the blows they had given him to make him drop his weapons. But they couldn't manage to do it and were never able to capture him. After his death, they cut off his head, which they carried away to their country. Thus were our seven Frenchmen killed, but they killed an even greater number of Iroquois, whose bones were found when the bodies of our own were taken away, their people having burned the bodies of their dead according to custom and left those of our Frenchmen whole.

After this expedition these barbarians withdrew in haste, seeing that help from Monsieur our Governor was coming, but too late. For he got wind of this encounter only through Monsieur de Lespinay, who is the one for whom they had put themselves at risk and who, having heard the sound of the shotguns, set sail for Quebec in order to warn of the disturbance. But when he realized that it was on his account that these men had exposed themselves to danger, he thought he would die of grief. His brother was among the seven, and the others were leading settlers who wanted to do a favor on this occasion for Monsieur le Sénéchal.

Since that time, there have been nothing but massacres. The son of Monsieur Godefroy, having left Trois-Rivières to go to the Attikameks, and the group of Algonquins with him were attacked and killed by the Iroquois, after having valiantly defended themselves and killed a great number of enemies.

These barbarians struck many other similar blows, but Montreal was the principal theater of their carnage. Madame d'Ailleboust traveled here and gave me an account of utterly awful things. She told me that a number of settlers were taken by surprise and killed in the woods, without anyone knowing where they were or what had become of them. No one dared to go looking for them nor even to leave, lest they run into similar trouble. At last, the place was discovered by means of dogs that were seen coming back drunk and covered in blood every day. This suggested that they were scavenging dead bodies, which deeply afflicted everyone. Everyone took up arms to go determine what had happened. When they had arrived at the spot, they found here and there some bodies cut in half, others hacked up and wasted away, with heads, legs, and hands scattered all around. Each one took it upon himself to give to the dead what they needed for a Christian burial. Madame d'Ailleboust, who told me this story, chanced upon a man who had fastened to his stomach the carcass of a human body, and whose hands were full of legs and arms. This spectacle so shocked her that she thought she would die of fright. But it was something else altogether when those who carried what remained of the bodies came into town, for then one heard nothing but the pitiful cries of the wives and children of these poor departed ones.

We have just learned that a cleric of the society of the Messieurs of Montreal, having just said mass, retired a short distance away (though nevertheless fairly close to seven of their domestics who were working) to recite his hours in silence and contemplation.[254] When he was least expecting it, sixty Iroquois who were lying in ambush opened fire on him. Although riddled with bullets, he still had the courage to run and warn his people to retreat, and thereupon he fell dead. The enemies were right behind him and got there at the same time. Our seven Frenchmen defended themselves as they were retreating, but not well enough, such that one was killed and another captured. Then these barbarians whooped and hollered as a sign of the joy they felt upon having killed a black robe. A renegade of their group stripped the cleric and dressed himself in his robe, and having put a shirt over it like a surplice, he made a procession around the body, in mockery of what he had seen done in the Church during funerals for the dead. Finally, they cut off his head, which they took with them, withdrawing in haste lest they be pursued by the soldiers of the fort. This, then, is how these barbarians wage war. They strike their blow and then retreat into the woods where the French can't go.

We had had awful portents of all these misfortunes.[255] Since the departure of the ships in 1660, signs appeared in the sky, which quite terrified everyone. A comet was seen, the beams of which were pointed toward the earth. It appeared at about two or three o'clock in the morning and disappeared at about six or seven with daybreak. A man on fire, totally enveloped in flames, was seen midair. A canoe of fire was seen in midair and also a great crown of fire near Montreal. On the Isle d'Orléans, a child was heard crying in its mother's womb. What's more, the confused voices of women and children together with pitiful cries were heard in the air. In another incident, a thunderous and horrible voice was heard. All these phenomena caused such terror as you can imagine.

What's more, it was discovered that there are sorcerers and magicians in this country. This became apparent on an occasion regarding a miller who had come

---

254. Thwaites, *Jesuit Relations*, vol. 46, 215–19.

255. Thwaites, *Jesuit Relations*, 202–4. Belief in the preternatural (events that occurred beyond the ordinary course of nature like meteorological phenomena, comets, and the like) was alive and well in seventeenth-century Europe, particularly in France; see, Lorraine Datson, "Marvelous Facts and Miraculous Evidence in Early Modern Europe," *Critical Inquiry* 18, no. 1 (Autumn, 1991): 93–124; Lorraine Datson and Katherine Park, *Wonders and the Order of Nature, 1150–1750* (New York: Zone Books, 1998), 135–72 and 215–54. For an excellent analysis of the place of the preternatural in seventeenth-century New England, see David D. Hall, *Worlds of Wonder, Days of Judgment: Popular Religious Belief in New England* (Cambridge, MA: Harvard University Press, 1990), 71–116 and 221–5. Marie's description of the mid-air canoe resonates with the Canadian narrative tradition of the *chasse-galerie*; see, for example, Honoré Beaugrand, *La Chasse-Galerie: Legends Canadiennes* (Montreal, 1900), 9–34.

from France at the same time as Monsignor our Bishop. Our bishop had made the miller abjure his heresy because he was a Huguenot.[256] This man wanted to marry a girl who had come over with her father and mother in the same ship, saying that she had been promised to him. But because he was a man of bad morals, no one ever tended to listen to him. After he was refused the girl, he attempted to get his way by means of the ruse of his diabolical art. He summoned demons or goblins to the girl's house, along with ghosts, which caused her a great deal of grief and fear. No one, however, knew what was causing this novelty. Until the magician appeared, there was reason to believe that this scoundrel had cast a spell, for he appeared to her day and night, sometimes alone and sometimes accompanied by two or three others, whom the girl named, although she had never seen them. Monsignor sent some Fathers to the girl's house and went there himself to chase away the demons by means of the prayers of the Church. However, the situation didn't improve, and the commotion continued more than before. Phantoms were seen, drums and flutes were heard playing, stones were seen falling out of walls and flying here and there. And always, the magician and his companions were there for the purpose of harassing the girl. Their plan was to make her marry this wicked man who, indeed, wanted it too but wanted to corrupt her first. The place where this happened is far away from Quebec, and it was a great travail for the Fathers to go so far to perform the exorcism. This is why Monsignor, seeing that the devils were trying to tire them out by this work and exhaust them by their antics, ordered that the miller and the girl be brought to Quebec. The one was put in prison and the other confined in the house of the Hospitallers. This is where things sit. A good many extraordinary things happened during the course of this affair which I am not mentioning, so as not to run on too long and so as to bring this matter to a close. As for the magician and the other sorcerers, they are still unwilling to confess to anything. No one says anything to them either, for it isn't easy to convict people of crimes of this nature.

After this pursuit of the sorcerers, the whole country was afflicted by an epidemic, which these sorcerers are thought to have caused.[257] It was a variety of whooping cough or flu which spread like a contagion in every family, such that no one was exempt from it. Almost all the Indian children and a significant

---

256. *Jesuit Journal*, 312. For a study of sorcery in Quebec, see Robert Lionel Séguin, *La sorcellerie au Québec du XVIIe au XIXe siècle* (Montreal: Leméac, 1971). See also Cliche, *Les Pratiques*, 65–74, who argues for the general compatibility between Catholic devotion and belief in sorcery in seventeenth-century Quebec.

257. For a discussion of beliefs about sorcerers, witches, and other metaphysical beings in seventeenth-century France, see Euan Cameron, *Enchanted Europe: Superstition, Reason, and Religion, 1250–1750* (Oxford: Oxford University Press, 2010), 247–315. See also Jan Machielsen,

number of French children died from it. Such mortality had never been seen before, for these maladies became pleurisies accompanied by fevers. We were all attacked by it—our pensioners, our seminarians, and our domestics were all *in extremis*. Ultimately, I don't think there were twenty people in all of Canada who were exempt from this disease, which was so widespread there was good reason to believe that these scoundrels had poisoned the air.[258]

So, these were two scourges by means of which it pleased God to test this new Church. The one is what I just spoke of, for no one had ever seen so many people die in Canada as died this year. The other is the persecution of the Iroquois. They keep the whole country in a state of continual fear. For I must confess that if they were as skillful as the French, and if they knew our weakness, they would already have exterminated us. But God blinds them on account of his good will toward us, and I hope he will always favor us by protecting us from our enemies, whoever they might be. I beseech you to pray for it.

Letter 204: August–September 1663

My very dear son,[259]

I decided to write you a separate account of the earthquake that happened this year in our New France, which was so prodigious, so violent, and so terrifying,

---

"Thinking with Montaigne: Evidence, Scepticism and Meaning in Early Modern Demonology," *French History* 25, nos. 427–52 (2011).

258. Marie's description of the epidemic as the effect of sorcery and her ascription to the epidemic of religious meaning (a scourge sent by God to test the Church in New France) testifies to a decidedly early modern construction of death and disease, which privileged etiologies focused on individual and collective sinfulness and remedies of repentance and Christian conversion. It is worth noting, as Laurence Brockliss and Colin Jones do, that the social construction of death and disease of the sort suggested in this letter does not prove a feature of popular interpretations alone but reflects beliefs about sickness and health shared across a spectrum of social and professional classes, including early modern medical practitioners themselves; see Laurence Brockliss and Colin Jones, *The Medical World of Early Modern France* (Oxford: Clarendon, 1997), 40–84. See also Toby Gelfand, "Medicine in New France," in *Medicine in the New World*, ed. Ronald L. Numbers (Knoxville: University of Tennessee Press, 1987), 64–100, for a discussion of the relationship between medical theory and practice in early modern France and New France.

259. Claude began a new three-year term as prior of Saint-Serge d'Angers in 1663. Oury contends that this letter is an amalgamation of extracts from a number of different letters in which Marie offers accounts of and reflections on the earthquake. For a brief discussion of the sources upon which the present letter relies and Claude's hand in editing the same, see Lettre CCIV, *Correspondance*, 699–700, n. 1. In his edition of the correspondence, Oury follows the text of Claude's *Lettres spirituelles et historiques*, but presents portions of this letter with the texts of the *Vie* and the *Lettres* in parallel. In my translation of Letter 204, I have opted to follow the text of the *Lettres* throughout for the sake of consistency.

I have no words strong enough to describe it.[260] And I even fear that what I will say about it will seem unbelievable and fabricated.

On the third day of this year 1663 an Indian woman, but a very good and excellent Christian, was awake in her cabin while everyone else was asleep, when she heard a clear and distinct voice say to her, "In two days, quite astonishing and marvelous things will happen." And the next day, the same woman was in the forest with her sister, gathering her daily supply of wood, when she distinctly heard the same voice say to her, "Tomorrow, between five and six o'clock in the evening, the earth will be shaken and it will tremble in an astonishing manner." She reported what she had heard to those in her cabin, who responded with indifference, thinking that she was describing a dream or a figment of her imagination. Meanwhile, the weather was fairly calm that day and still calmer the next day.

On the fifth day, the feast of Saint Agatha virgin and martyr, at five-thirty in the evening, a person of esteemed virtue and one who has extensive interactions with God saw that he was extremely irritated by the sins committed in this country. At the same time, she felt herself compelled to ask him for justice for it. She offered her prayers to the Divine Majesty for this purpose and also for the souls who were in mortal sin, so that his justice would not be without mercy. She also supplicated the martyrs of Japan whose feast day was being celebrated, asking God to intercede if it would be most conducive to his glory. While praying, she had a presentiment, or rather, an infallible certitude, that God was about to punish the country for the sins committed there and above all for the contempt in which the ordinances of the Church are held. She couldn't help desiring this punishment, whatever it might be, since it was ordained by divine decree without her having any idea of what it could be. Immediately after that and shortly before the earthquake began, she saw four furious and enraged demons at the four corners of Quebec who were shaking the earth so violently that it seemed as if they wanted to knock everything down. And, in fact, they would have succeeded but for a figure of admirable beauty and delightful majesty. She saw this figure among the demons, a figure who, from time to time, gave free rein to their furor, only restraining them when they were on the brink of destroying everything. She heard the voice of these demons who said, "Now many people are frightened, and we

---

260. For accounts of the earthquake of 1663 in New France contemporary with this one, see Thwaites, *Jesuit Relations*, vol. 47, 263–5; vol. 48, 25, 39–71, 185–221. Marie's account of the earthquake substantially follows that given by Charles Simon in the *Jesuit Relation* of 1663 (vol. 48). See also Lynn Berry, "'Le Ciel et la Terre nous ont parlés': Comment les missionnaires du Canada français de l'époque colonial interprétèrent le tremblement de terre de 1663," *Revue d'histoire de l'Amérique française* 60, no. 1–2 (Summer–Fall 2006): 11–35.

can see clearly that there will be many conversions, but which will last only a short while. We will indeed find a way to take back the world. Meanwhile, let us continue to shake the earth and do everything possible to knock everything down."

The weather was quite calm and tranquil, and her vision had not yet ended, when a frightening rumbling noise was heard from afar, as if a great number of carriages were rolling over the cobblestones with speed and fury. This noise had no sooner caught people's attention than they heard underground and above ground and on all sides something that sounded like a confusion of torrents and waves, which horrified them. Everywhere people heard what sounded like stones hailing on the roofs, in the granaries and in the rooms.

It seemed as if the marble stones that almost entirely comprise the foundation of this country, and out of which our houses are built, were going to split open into pieces and swallow us up. Thick dust was flying everywhere. Doors opened of their own accord and others that were open, closed. The bells of all our churches and the chimes of our clocks rang all by themselves, and the bell towers as well as our houses shook like trees in the wind, and all that in the midst of a terrifying confusion in which furniture toppled over, stones fell down, floors spilt apart, walls cracked open. In the midst of all that, the domestic animals were howling, some going out of the houses and others going in. In a word, people were so frightened that they thought judgment day was nigh, since they were seeing signs of it.

Such an unforeseen event, at a time when the young people were preparing to celebrate carnival in excess, was a clap of thunder upon everyone's heads when they were least expecting it. Or rather, it was a blow of the mercy of God upon the whole country, as indicated by its effects, about which I will speak elsewhere. From the moment of that first tremor, there was universal consternation. Since no one knew what it was, some cried out "fire," thinking it was a conflagration, while others ran to get water to extinguish it. Others grabbed their weapons, thinking it was an Iroquois army. But since it was nothing of the sort, the lucky ones went outside to avoid the destruction of the houses, which looked as if they were about to collapse.

It was no safer outside than inside, for by the movement of the earth which rippled beneath our feet like moving water under a rowboat, we immediately realized that it was an earthquake.

Several people grabbed ahold of trees, which knocked against each other, causing them no less terror than the houses they had fled. Others held on to stumps, which thrashed about so much that they beat the people harshly about their chests. The Indians, extremely frightened, said that the trees had beaten them sorely. Some of them said that this was the work of demons, and that God was using these demons to punish them for the excesses they had carried out while drinking the brandy that the bad French had given them. Other less educated Indians, who had come to hunt in these parts, said that it was the souls of their ancestors who wanted to return to their former dwelling place. On the basis of this error, they took their guns and shot them into the air against a band of spirits who were passing by, according to what they said. But in the end, our settlers as well as our Indians, finding no comfort on the land or in their houses, for the most part became incapacitated and, deciding on a better course of action, went into the churches for the consolation of dying there after having made their confessions.

Once this first tremor passed, which lasted nearly a half hour, people began to breathe again but only for a short time, for at eight o'clock in the evening the quake began again and the tremors repeated twice over the course of the hour. We were saying Matins in choir, reciting them partly on our knees in humility and abandoning ourselves to the sovereign power of God. The tremors repeated thirty-two times that night, according to what someone who had counted them told me, but I counted only six because some of them were weak and almost imperceptible. But at three o'clock in the morning there was quite a violent one, which lasted a long time.

These tremors continued over the space of seven months, although unevenly. Some were frequent but weak, while others were rarer but strong and violent. Thus, the evil did not abate except to rain down upon us more intensely, and we hardly had the leisure to reflect on the misfortune that was menacing us when it surprised us all of a sudden, sometimes during the day but more often at night.

If the earth caused us such alarm, the heavens caused us no less, both by the howls and roars heard lingering in the air and by the distinct voices which gave us fright. Some were saying, "Alas," others, "Let's go, let's go," and still others, "Let's dam the rivers." People heard noises that sounded sometimes like bells, sometimes like cannons, sometimes like thunder. They saw fires, flames, and burning globes, which sometimes fell to the ground and sometimes vanished in the air. A fire in the form of a man who shot out flames from his mouth was seen in mid-air. Our domestics, who had to go out at night in order to fetch us wood, saw these sorts of fires five or six times a night. Terrifying ghosts were seen and since demons sometimes mix in with thunder, although this is but an effect of nature, it was easily believed that they mixed in with this earthquake in order to heighten the fears that turbulent nature meant to cause us.

In the midst of all these terrors, no one knew how it was all going to turn out. At the end of each day, we prepared to be swallowed up by some abyss during the night; when day came, we were constantly expecting to die, seeing not a single moment in which our lives were assured. In a word, people withered away in the expectation of some universal misfortune. Even God seemed to take pleasure in confirming our fears.

On one occasion, a contemplative person went before the holy sacrament, in order to try and appease the wrath of God and to offer herself to him wholeheartedly as the victim of all the evils that were menacing her people.[261] She was suddenly seized with fright, as happens when one is approached by someone of great majesty, and immediately she perceived an extremely formidable figure clothed in a habit on which were written these words:

Quis ut Deus?[262]

He held in his left hand a balance, the basins of which were full, the one with steam and the other with writings, which said:

Loquere ad eos Jerusalem, quia completa est malitia et dimissa est inquitas illius.[263]

In the right hand he had three arrows, at the tips of which she read these words:

Impiety, impurity, lack of charity.

With that, redoubling her prayers, she saw these two words come out of the angel's mouth:

Deus non irridetur.[264]

The vision disappeared, and she found herself overcome by a strong desire to ask God to wait a bit longer to punish his people.

But meanwhile, we were constantly hearing the enemy rolling beneath our feet, seeing ourselves on the edge of the precipice between life and death, between fear and hope, according to the starts or stops of the tremors. One day, a holy soul, who was strongly inclined to prayer, glimpsed in her room a dim light shaped and

---

261. Some years later, Marie would reveal to Claude the identity of this visionary as Catherine de Saint-Augustin; Lettre CCXXXVIII, *Correspondance*, 813.

262. This Latin phrase—a literal transcription of his Hebrew name—identifies the figure as Saint Michael the Archangel upon whose shield this phrase is traditionally inscribed.

263. Isaiah 40:2.

264. Galatians 6:7.

shining like a naked sword, and at the same time she heard a ringing voice which said, "On whom, Lord, on whom?" She didn't hear the response, but only a great confusion of complaints and howls which followed this first voice.

A whole month went by like this, with people fearful and uncertain about what would happen, but finally the tremors began to abate, becoming less frequent and less violent, except on two or three occasions when they were very strong, and people began to notice the usual effects of violent earthquakes: namely a number of crevasses on the ground, new torrents, new springs, and new hills where there none had been before, the earth flattened where there had been mountains before, new chasms in some places which emitted sulphrous vapors, and elsewhere great plains entirely bare, which had been full of woods and brush before. Rocks were knocked over, ground raked up, forests destroyed, trees partly upended and partly sunk down in the ground to the tips of their branches. Two rivers disappeared and two new springs were discovered, one white like milk and the other red like blood. But nothing astonished us more, I say, than to see the great Saint Lawrence river (which because of its prodigious depth never changes—neither on account of the thaw of the snows which usually causes rivers to change course, nor on account of the confluence of more than five hundred rivers that disgorge there, not to mention the more than six hundred springs, which are for the most part very big) change, turn the color of sulfur, and stay this way for eight days.

A few Indians, who had fled the woods in fear and wanted to return to their cabin, found it destroyed in the middle of a lake that had formed there. A barn near us was seen flattened first on one side, then on the other, and finally put back in its original position. At the church of Beaupré, which is that of Château-Richer, the earth shook so roughly on Ash Wednesday that the walls were seen trembling as if they were made of cards. The holy sacrament which had been exposed likewise trembled, but didn't fall, held up by a little crown of artificial flowers. The lamp, which had been put out, fell three times, but the cleric who was in charge of that church lit it again and set it back in its place, and it fell no more.

We have learned from those who came from Tadoussac that the earthquake caused an extraordinary commotion there. For six hours, so much ash rained down that it was an inch thick on the ground and in the canoes. It was thus inferred that the fire contained underground activated some mine and that out of the opening it created, it spewed out these ashes, which were like burned salt. These gentlemen say that the first earthquakes greatly horrified them by their strange effects, but that what terrified them the most and seemed, as well, to be the most extraordinary, was that the sea, which rises and falls at regular times, and whose tide had just gone out, rose up again all of a sudden with a frightful noise.

Three young men went together to look for some Indians in order to trade some brandy with them. When one of them was apart from the others for some reason, a terrifying ghost appeared to him. His only thought was that he would die of fright. He immediately returned, although with difficulty, to join the other two, who saw how frightened he was and began to taunt him. One of them, however, pulled himself together and said, "Yet, this is no laughing matter. We are bringing liquor to the Indians against the prohibition of the Church, and perhaps God wants to punish us for our disobedience." With these words, they retraced their steps. That evening, they had barely taken shelter when the earthquake swept away their cabin right before their eyes, such that they could hardly escape themselves. This incident along with the former convinced them that heaven was persecuting them and meant to foil their plan.

Midway between here and Tadoussac there were two large capes which made it so windy that it was quite hard for the ships to sail. Now, they have been destroyed and have sunk down to sea level. And what's marvelous is that they extended farther out into the great river than the Loire is wide during the times of its greatest floods. The trees and foliage are still there, and today the land is flat. I do not know, however, who will dare to walk there first, although it looks stable. A young man, one of our neighbors, was on his way to trade and wanted to go down to the bank of a river which had not yet appeared, curious to see what had happened. With his first steps, he sank in so far that he thought he would die unless someone pulled him out, which someone did with difficulty.

Here is the lieutenant of Monsieur the Governor who is arriving from Tadoussac. He reports that the tremors are still as frequent and as furious there as in the beginning. They occur several times a day and several times a night. Meanwhile, I am writing this on the tenth of June, which is to say that this scourge has been going on for four and a half months already.

The rowboat that arrived at our port a few days ago, after having left the big ship at Gaspé in order to go ahead, found itself in quite a bit of trouble near Tadoussac. We learned from the secretary of Monsieur the Governor and one of our young neighbors, who was returning from France, that it leaped and shook in a strange manner, soaring up at regular intervals as tall as a house, which frightened them all the more since they had never experienced anything of the sort during navigation. Terrified, they looked to the land, where there was a big and tall mountain. They saw it suddenly move and whirl around as if pirouetting, and all of a sudden sink into the ground and break apart such that its summit was flat against the earth like a sheet of glass. This incident made them run away quickly to the river lest debris fall on them.

Sometime later, the big ship followed the same route and was surprised by the tremors. A respectable man who was traveling therein told me that everyone on the ship believed themselves dead, and, unable to hold themselves upright because of the agitation, fell upon their knees and prostrated themselves on the upper deck in order to prepare for death. They couldn't understand the cause of such an unprecedented phenomenon, for the whole great river, which is as deep as an ocean in that spot, shook like the earth. As an indication of how strong the tremor was, the big cable of the ship broke and they lost one of their anchors, which was a notable loss for them. I learned from those who arrived in these ships that in more than twelve places from here to Tadoussac, which is thirty leagues away from Quebec, the great commotion caused by the earth's tremors split apart rocky mountains in several places, principally near the two capes I mentioned above. They saw some small hills or protuberances, which had split off from their foundation and disappeared, forming little coves where small crafts and rowboats could find shelter during storms. This is so surprising that it almost defies the imagination, and every day one hears of similar prodigious things. People were afraid that such upheavals on the shores of the great river would impede navigation, but ultimately, they probably won't cause any harm provided one doesn't sail at night, for then it would be dangerous.

If the wreckage was so terrible near Tadoussac, it was no less so near Trois-Rivières. A person of faith, one of our friends, wrote us some astonishing details about it. And I would not know how to more faithfully recount what he told us than to report in his own words. Here they are:

The first and roughest tremor happened here on the fifth of February at five-thirty in the evening. It began with a rumbling, like a muffled roll of thunder. The houses shook like trees in a storm, making such a noise that many believed that fire was crackling in the granaries. The stakes of our palisade and individual fences seemed to dance, and what frightened us most was that, to the naked eye, the ground seemed to rise up more than a good foot above its usual level, bouncing and rolling like rough waters. This first shock lasted a good half hour. Everyone believed that the earth would open up and swallow us. However, since the houses are all made of wood, for there is no stone in Trois-Rivières, the only exterior effect was that some chimneys collapsed. But the most significant effects which, fortunately, are still continuing, occurred in people's consciences. Moreover, we have observed various symptoms of this disease of the earth, if one must speak thus. Just as the tremors are practically relentless, so also they are not equal in magnitude. Sometimes they imitate the rocking of a great ship that moves slowly at anchor, making many dizzy; sometimes the tremors are regular and precipitated by sudden shocks, which make the houses crack, especially at night, such that many get up and pray. The most common sort of movement is a trembling vibration, which could be attributed to underground fires. These underground fires have yet another effect, for since they are fueled by bituminous and sulphrous matter which they consume, they simultaneously form great cavities under our feet, which echo like vaults when one knocks upon the ground. This is what was written to us from Trois-Rivières.

We have been assured, too, that a ghost was seen in the air carrying a torch in its hand and passing from west to east above the great redoubt of this village of Trois-Rivières.

What is beyond doubt, according to the reports of our Indians and French from Trois-Rivières, eyewitnesses, is that five or six leagues from here, the hills on both sides of the river, which are four times higher than those here, were removed from their foundations and flattened to the water's level, extending about two leagues in length and more than ten *arpents* in depth into the countryside.[265] They had been overturned with their forests up to the middle of the canal, forming a formidable dam there, which will force the river to change direction and cause the water to spread out over these newly exposed great plains. Nevertheless, this river is wearing away and ceaselessly beating at this strange island by means of its rapid current, eroding it little by little with its water, which is still so roiled and muddy today that it is no longer potable. This violent disruption caused so much damage that hardly a tree has survived, most having been split lengthwise like the masts of a ship.

The first waterfall, so well-known, no longer exists, having been totally flattened. The destruction is still more extensive and has had more surprising effects near the river of Bastican. There were fifty people—French as well as Indian—living in the places where the earthquake caused the greatest destruction and created the deepest abysses. Since they were all afraid and constrained to move away in order to keep themselves from falling into the chasms that were opening beneath their feet, I will mention only some details which I gleaned from some individuals, for everyone was concerned only with himself and with how to escape from the fissures opening up all around them.

These natural mines thus began to act up there just as they had here at sunset on the fifth of February, and they continued to wreak their havoc all night long until daybreak, sounding like an army of canons and terrifying thunder claps which—in conjunction with the noise the trees of the immense forests made when they banged together and fell by the hundreds from all sides to the bottom of these abysses—made the hairs of these poor refugees stand on end. An Indian among them was partly trapped in an opening that was made in his cabin, and was pulled out with much difficulty by his companions. A Frenchman escaped a

---

265. As a unit of length, the *arpent* as it was used in seventeenth-century New France measured 180 French feet (or approximately 58 meters). As a unit of area, the *arpent* measured 32,400 French feet (or approximately 3419 square meters).

similar fate and was going back to get his gun which he had forgotten in his fear; he was obliged to wade through water up to his waist in the place where they had built their fire before. He exposed himself to this danger because his life depended on his gun. The Indians, so they said, attributed all these disorders to demons flying about in the air, and so fired their guns from time to time and howled in order to scare them and chase them away. That evening and all night long they felt the waves of stifling heat. Others assured me that they had seen mountains knocking against each other and disappearing before their eyes. Others saw sections of stone rising up in the air to the tops of the trees.

I spoke to someone who ran all night long, as he saw the land splitting open. Those who were far away and beyond the great wreckage attest that upon returning, they walked alongside the chasm for more than ten leagues without being able to tell where it began, where it ended or how deep it was. And they add that as they walked alongside the river of Bastican, they noticed dramatic changes—waterfalls were no longer where they had been before and the hills were sunk down into the earth. A tall mountain that was there before is now destroyed and reduced to flat land, as smooth as if the harrow had passed over it. In some places, one can see the tips of trees that have sunk into the ground and in others roots suspended in mid-air, the tree tops having broken apart on the ground.

The head of a family from the Beaupré coast, having sent one of his domestics to his farm, suddenly saw a great fire, which spread out like a city. Although it was broad daylight, he thought he would die of fear, and all the neighbors who saw the same thing were extremely frightened, convinced that they were all going to die. However, this great fire rolled down the bank of the river and crossed it, going to burn out on the Isle d'Orléans. A man who saw it assured me that this was true, and he is a trustworthy person.

The land has not yet firmed up although it is already the sixth of July, for I am writing only intermittently and as I find things out. The burning emissions that seep constantly from the ground had caused such a severe drought that all the seeds had yellowed, but for the past few days there have been whirlwinds and furious storms near Cap Tourmente, which took everyone by surprise, for they happened at night.[266] There was a terrifying noise caused by a flood of water, which cascaded from the mountains with an unbelievable abundance and fury.

The mills were destroyed and the trees of the forests uprooted and carried off. These new waters changed the course of the river, its former bed left sandy and dry. A quite beautiful barn, which was brand new, was carried off in its entirety two leagues away, where it ultimately broke apart on the rocks. All the livestock from

---

266. Thwaites, *Jesuit Relations*, vol. 48, 159.

these parts, which were numerous on account of the beautiful and vast prairies of this country, were carried off by the rushing waters. Several, however, were saved owing to the trees among which they were found entangled. They were extracted once the torrent had ebbed. The green wheat was entirely ruined. And not only the wheat, but also a piece of land measuring twelve *arpents*, was lifted up such that only a completely bare rock was left. One of our neighbors, a respectable man who had been there, assured us that over the course of the six days he stayed there, he didn't sleep two hours because he was so frightened by the tremors and storms.

The earthquake began everywhere at the same moment it began in Quebec and produced the same effects. Everyone from the mountains of Notre Dame to Montreal felt it, and everyone was equally terrified by it.[267]

New Holland was not exempt from it and the Iroquois, their neighbors, were just as alarmed by it as the Indians here. Since they had never experienced such earthquakes before and couldn't determine the cause of so much commotion, they asked the Dutch about it. The Dutch responded that it meant that the world wouldn't last for more than three years. I don't know where they got this prophecy.

On July 29th, a small boat from New England arrived at our port of Quebec. The people who disembarked from this ship say that in Boston, which is a beautiful city that the English have built, on Lundi Gras at five-thirty, they had tremors like we had here, and that it happened several times. They are reporting the same from Acadia and Port-Royal, which previously belonged to Monsieur the Commander of Razilly and has since been taken by the English. The other coast of Acadia, which belongs to the Messieurs de Cangé and Denys of our city of Tours felt the tremors, just like everywhere else. This boat was carrying five of our French prisoners, who were captives among the Iroquois Mohawks and escaped with the help of the Dutch, who treated them quite humanely, as they do all who take refuge with them.

Some Indians of a very distant land were urged to take refuge here in order to receive instruction and assure their consciences rather than to escape the tremors following them everywhere. They discovered something that had been sought after for a long time, namely the entry to the great sea of the north, in the vicinity of which there are numerous peoples who have not yet heard about God. This will be a great field in which the gospel workers will work to satisfy their zeal and fervor. It is believed that this sea leads to China and Japan. If that's so, the way to those lands will be made much shorter.

---

267. The Notre Dame Mountains run along the southern edge of the Saint Lawrence River valley, marking the present-day border between Quebec and Maine.

I return now to our quarters where we are constantly in fear, although we're beginning to get used to it. One of our friends, a respectable man, had built a house with a quite beautiful mill on top of a marble rock. In the midst of the tremors, the rock split open and the mill and the house were pushed into the abyss that formed. Last night, on the thirteenth of August, we felt the earth shake here quite roughly. Our dormitory and our seminary experienced a strong tremor from it, which woke us from our sleep and revived our fear.

I am closing this relation on the twentieth of the same month, without knowing how all this commotion will end, for the tremors are still continuing. But what is admirable amidst such strange and universal destruction is that no one has died, nor has anyone been injured. This is a clearly visible sign of God's protection of his people, which gives us just reason to believe that he is angry with us only for the purpose of saving us. And we hope that he will draw his glory from our fear, by means of the conversion of so many souls who were asleep in their sins and could not awaken by the simple movements of an interior grace.

Letter 207: September–October 1663

My very dear son,

A ship that just arrived and is preparing for a prompt return obliges me to write you a word, although I have not received news from you nor from any of our monasteries in France. I believe you know that the king is now master of this country.[268] When Messieurs of the Company learned that he intended to remove it from them, they went before him and offered it to him.[269] He took them at their word and promised to compensate them and thus this change was effected without much trouble. The king's ships brought back Monsignor our prelate who we were told had much to sort out in France concerning the liquor given to the Indians and which people feared would ruin this new Church entirely.[270]

---

268. The French crown took possession of New France from the Compagnie des Cents Associés in 1663, recognizing the colony as a royal province. For a classic account of this period of Canadian history, see W. J. Eccles, *Canada under Louis XIV* (New York: Oxford University Press, 1964).

269. That is, the Compagnie des Cents Associés. Created by Cardinal de Richelieu in 1627, the Compagnie des Cents Associés received the title to the totality of lands in New France (and assumed the obligation to settle the lands) in exchange for a fifteen-year monopoly on trade within the colony. By the middle of the seventeenth century, however, the trading partnership was in bad shape, having suffered under the aggressions of the English, who had succeeded in obstructing two of its first expeditions to New France and ultimately in occupying Quebec from 1629 to 1632. The Compagnie was dissolved in 1663 by Louis XIV.

270. The struggle against the brandy trade would prove an enduring one during Laval's episcopacy, pitting the bishop (and his concern for the success of the missionary enterprise) against

He made the trip in the company of a new governor that His Majesty is sending us, his predecessor (who served for only two years) having departed before his arrival. The king sent with them an intendant as well, who has put all the affairs of the country in order since his arrival.[271] He has established officers to administer justice according to the rules of law. He has also established a police for commerce and for the maintenance of civil society.[272] He has won the confidence and, generally, the respect of all the settlers of the country who admitted taking him for a king because of his castle in Quebec. In the regulations that have been made, Quebec is named a city and New France a province or kingdom. A mayor and municipal councilors were elected, as well as all the officers generally, who are people of honor and probity. There is a great union among all, and Monsignor the Bishop and Monsieur the Governor are named heads of the council. There is talk of building a courthouse, and prisons to lock up criminals, since the current accommodations are too small and ill-suited. Monsieur our Governor is named Monsieur de Mézy and is a very pious and wise gentleman from Normandy. He is an intimate friend of the late Monsieur de Bernières, who, during his life, played an important role in winning him to God.

The use of tithes has likewise been established, which are destined for the maintenance of a seminary founded by our bishop, who thus intends to build churches wherever they are needed and to support the priests who serve them. These churches will be like parishes, but those who preside there will be called superiors instead of *curés*, and their head will be the bishop. What's left from the

---

the civil authorities, the merchants, and the utility of alcohol within the context of commercial relations with the Amerindians. Laval's sojourn to France resulted in a temporary boon for the bishop's cause: Louis XIV agreed to prohibit the sale of brandy in the colony and on September 28, 1663, the Sovereign Council issued a decree against the same. For a concise history of the brandy trade with the Amerindians of New France, see George F. G. Stanley, "The Indians and the Brandy Trade during the Ancien Regime," *Revue d'histoire de l'Amérique française* 6, no. 4 (1953): 489–505.

271. Under the auspices of Minister Jean-Baptiste Colbert, the administration of New France was shared by a governor (in charge of the military and external affairs of the colony) and an Intendant (in charge of the departments of justice, the interior, the police, and finance). M. de Mézy, Charles-Auguste de Saffray, arrived in Quebec as the first governor of New France under the direct authority of the king, together with Louis Gaudais-Dupont, commissioned by Louis XIV to take possession of and collect information on the colony. The first Intendant, Jean Talon, would not arrive until 1665. For a discussion of the administrative organization and policy developments in the colony under Colbert, see Eccles, *Canada under Louis XVI*, 2–38. For a discussion of colonial administration in New France more generally, see, James Pritchard, *In Search of Empire: The French in the Americas, 1670–1730* (Cambridge, UK: Cambridge University Press, 2004).

272. For a discussion of the concept of "police" in early modern New France, see John Dickinson, "Réflexions sur la police en Nouvelle-France," *McGill Law Journal* 32, no. 3 (1987): 497–512.

tithes will go to aid the poor.²⁷³ This worthy prelate has already had a house built in Quebec for the bishop and for the purpose of lodging the majority of his seminarians. Well, all this sounds impressive and is off to a good start, but God alone knows how it will turn out, since experience teaches us that what actually happens is often quite different than what is intended.

The terrifying earthquakes that were felt all over Canada are doing much to bring people together, for just as they are keeping everyone in fear and humiliation, so also everyone is keeping the peace. It's hard to believe what a great number of conversions God has brought about, both among the infidels who have embraced the faith, and among Christians who have left their bad lives behind.²⁷⁴ At the same time that God rattled the mountains and the marble rocks of these lands, it is said that he took pleasure in rattling consciences. The days of carnival became days of penitence and sadness. Public prayers, processions, and pilgrimages were constant, fasts of bread and water quite common, and general confessions more sincere than they would ever have been in the extremes of disease. A single cleric who runs the parish of Château-Richer assured us that he himself heard more than eight hundred general confessions. I leave you to imagine what the Reverend Fathers, who were in the confessionals day and night, have been able to do. I do not believe that there is a single settler in the whole country who hasn't made a general confession. There were some inveterate sinners who, in order to assure their consciences, began their own again more than three times. Admirable reconciliations were seen, enemies kneeling before each other in order to ask for pardon, with so much grief that it was obvious these changes were strokes of heaven and of God's mercy rather than his justice. At the Fort of Saint Xavier, belonging to the parish of Sillery, there was a soldier of the garrison who had come from France in the king's ships—the meanest and most abominable man in the world. He insolently boasted about his crimes as another might do with regard to an action worthy of praise. When the earthquake began, he was seized by such a strange fright that he cried out in front of everyone, "Look for no other cause for what you see than me. God wants to punish me for my crimes." He then

---

273. Introduced to the colonial church by Laval in 1663, the tithe was initially set at a rate of one-thirteenth. Resistance by settlers, however, resulted in the reduction of the tithe the following year to one-twentieth and then one-twenty-sixth (which remained fixed for a twenty-year period). For a brief discussion of the institution of the tithe and the reorganization of the Church in New France under Louis XIV, see Cornelius Jaenen, "The Role of the Church in New France," *Historical Booklet* no. 40 (Canadian Historical Association, 1985): 26–7. See also Pierre-Paul Viard, "La dîme ecclésiastique dans les colonies françaises aux XVIIe et XVIIIe siècles," *Revue d'histoire moderne* 3, no. 15 (May–June 1928): 220–26.

274. Thwaites, *Jesuit Relations*, vol. 48, 57–71. See also Letter 204.

began to confess his sins aloud, with no regard for anything but the justice of God, who, he thought, was about to push him into the fires of hell. This fort is one-quarter league from Sillery, where he crawled on all fours to make his confession, crippled by his fear. God wrought such a happy and complete conversion in him that today he is a model of virtue and good works.

See herein the state of Canada both spiritual and temporal, to which I will add that the king has not sent us troops, as he had made us hope, to destroy the Iroquois. We are told that the conflicts with which he is engaged in Italy are the reason for it.[275] But he did send in their place one hundred families consisting of five hundred people.[276] He is paying their expenses for one year so that they can establish themselves easily and then subsist without hardship, for when one can have a year's advance in this country, one can clear the land and build a foundation for the coming years.

Letter 208: 18 October 1663

My very dear son,

The delay of your letter, which only just reached me, does not permit me to converse with you at length. I will only tell you, so that you may have compassion for me, that our elections have been carried out and that responsibility for the community has fallen on my shoulders.[277] The burden is heavy and difficult to bear in a country like this one, but ultimately one must consume oneself to the end. I will be sixty-four years old on the twenty-eighth of this month. Therefore, did I not have a reason to resist my election so as to remain at rest and prepare myself for death? But I needn't say more. What is the most perfect is to keep silent and to submit to the orders of God and those who hold his place for us.

---

275. Despite numerous requests from the colony, royal troops would not reach New France until 1665, when the Carignan-Salières regiment arrived. For a recent study of the regiment and its sojourn in Canada, see Jack Verney, *The Good Regiment: the Carignan-Salières Regiment in Canada, 1665–1668* (Montreal: McGill-Queen's University Press, 1991). Most historians, like Marie de l'Incarnation, attribute Louis XIV's unwillingness to heed the appeal of the beleaguered Canadians to France's military engagements in Europe. Following the Corsican guard incident (in which the pope's Corsican guards attacked and killed several members of the French ambassador's guard in Rome), relations between Louis XIV and the Holy See in particular soured; see H. G. Judge, "Church and State Under Louis XIV," *History* 45, no. 155 (October 1960): 217–33. For a history of war in the colony, see Louise Dechêne, *Le Peuple, l'état et la guerre au Canada sous le régime français* (Montréal: Boréal, 2009).

276. For a discussion of the colonial settlement program initiated by the crown in 1663, see Eccles, *Canada under Louis XIV*, 39–58; and Peter Moogk, "Reluctant Exiles: Emigrants from France in Canada before 1760," *William and Mary Quarterly* 46, no. 3 (July 1989): 473–87.

277. Marie's third and final term as superior lasted from 1663 to 1669. See also Letter 135.

I sent you the account of the terrifying earthquakes which happened all over Canada and which made men tremble no less than the earth.[278] As for me personally, I was no longer unsettled by it, our Lord having given me feelings quite other than those of fear, for I will tell you in passing that for more than two months not a day went by that I didn't prepare myself to be swallowed up alive in some abyss, because we knew neither where nor when such a violent quake would rupture the earth. It happened in various places, as you will see in the account I'm giving you about it. Nevertheless no one was wounded, our good God having wanted to show mercy toward his people and give them time to repent. Since I have begun to tell you about my interior dispositions in the midst of these events, I will plainly admit that I have never experienced anything which put me in such a state of deprivation of life and all worldly things. In my spirit I had an impression of these words of the Son of God: *Wisdom is justified by her children.*[279] I felt at the same time an emotion in my soul, which made me approve of what God was doing and moved me to sing in this same depth something great, in order to praise and bless him for a calamity that was threatening to destroy everyone. I again felt an inclination with my whole being, which led me to offer myself to His Divine Majesty as the victim for all the sins of men which had obliged him to carry out the punishment we were seeing before our eyes.[280] For this reason, I desired to be held responsible for all these sins as if they had been my own, so as to alone receive punishment for them. I had even wanted that all these abominations should appear before the eyes of men as my own crimes. My whole being was overcome by this inclination and this desire, such that I could do nothing other than bless the sovereign power of His Divine Majesty over all of nature and every heart, when he wants to rattle them. The big mountains and whole massive marble foundation that make up these lands are but bits of straw for him to move, and so many people who couldn't be swayed by the wrath of the Church were softened and transformed in a single moment. At the same time that he was terrifying us by shaking the things that bear us up and surround us, we had the consolation of seeing stubborn and hardened hearts soften and become as supple as these marbles when they moved about.[281] But let's turn from my dispositions to your own.

---

278. See also Letters 204 and 207.

279. Luke 7:35.

280. For an analysis of the theme of victimhood in Marie's spirituality, see Mali, "L'état de victime."

281. Here and elsewhere, Marie's interpretation of the earthquake of 1663 as an event of moral significance comports with a more general post-Tridentine move away from the spectacular (exterior) and toward the spiritual (interior); see Peter A. Goddard, "Science and Skepticism in the Early Mission to New France," *Canadian Historical Association Journal* 6 (1996): 43–58;

I bless God for the health and strength he's giving you, since you are using them to serve him. As for your interior dispositions, they seem to me conformed to the state to which he is calling you. Take care, however, not to want to advance prematurely. When he wants you to not lose sight of him, notwithstanding your exterior occupations, he will see to that himself. And moreover, when his spirit has become the master of your own and when he has seized your depths in order to keep you in the intimate and ongoing union with His Divine Majesty through a vision of love, none of your occupations will be able to distract you from this divine interchange. I say in these depths because it is impossible to deal with temporal affairs in this world without applying oneself to them, with an attention suitable to judgment and reason. In this state of union and interchange with God in the supreme part of the soul, one continues to enjoy his holy presence and this divine interaction with him, but it is necessary to make this distinction—that there are two ways of interacting and enjoying. In the one, in which one is completely at rest, the union is freer (not that it isn't always so) because its author and engine is the Holy Spirit, principle of true liberty. By contrast, when one is engaged in exterior affairs, part of the soul is occupied with external things, and the judgment and other faculties necessary to deal with these exterior affairs are obliged to apply themselves there and are in some sense distracted. Nevertheless, the cardinal virtues are useful in these situations and always despite the degree to which the soul is distracted from whatever sort of union. The difference between these two sorts of union and interaction with God is that when one is occupied with outside things, the union consists of a simple gaze directed at one's divine object, and one converses with him only sporadically as he permits and when he attracts one to it. But when the soul is completely at rest and entirely disengaged from the turmoil of exterior affairs, it is purged of the senses to a greater extent and then it deals and converses with God as a friend does with a friend.[282]

You are right to say that your perfection consists in doing the will of God. You will always be engaged in the turmoil of exterior affairs appropriate to your state, and in the midst of this turmoil he will give you the grace of this ongoing union if you are faithful to him. His Holy Spirit will give you the gift of advice concerning everything he wishes to commit to your care, such that you won't be able to want anything other than what he makes you want, nor do anything other than what

---

and Peter Burke, *The Historical Anthropology of Early Modern Italy: Essays on Perception and Communication* (Cambridge, UK: Cambridge University Press, 1987), 48–62. See also Hall, *Worlds of Wonder*, for a discussion of the various meanings—providential, punitive, and otherwise—attributed to natural wonders in Puritan New England.

282. Exodus 33:11. *Relation de 1654*, 257–62.

he makes you do. That is where his spirit is calling you and where you will arrive according to the extent of your fidelity.

And don't be surprised if you find faults in your actions. It is this state of union to which the spirit of God is calling you that opens your eyes. The more this spirit enlightens you, the more impurities you will see there. You will try to correct these, then others, and still others, but you will notice that these impurities are more and more subtle and of a different quality, for they are not like those sorts of impurities or faults—like those of vice or imperfection—that one committed in the past, whether out of attachment or surprise or habit.[283] They are much more interior and subtle, and the spirit of God, which can't tolerate anything impure, allows the soul no respite unless it labors only to progress from what is pure to what is even more so. In this state of greater purity, yet new faults are discovered, more imperceptible than the preceding ones, and the same spirit relentlessly prods the soul to hunt them down and ceaselessly purify itself. Nevertheless, the soul recognizes that it is powerless to safeguard this purity for itself, but the spirit of God does so by means of certain purgations or interior privations and by means of crosses conformed—or, rather, contrary—to the state it purifies. I often suffer from such a cross in the midst of the turmoil of external affairs in which I almost constantly find myself engaged. Be mindful of such a cross and you will find it within yourself.

I would take a singular pleasure in discussing these spiritual matters with you according to the questions you ask about them, but when I think about it or want to do so, work steals the time away from me. I write quite quickly, but I have been working on this letter for more than two hours. I am constantly pulled away, and so many times have I resumed writing without being able to finish.

Why do you have so much repugnance for going to live in your own country?[284] That is an imperfection. One must fly there if God wants it thus. It's not that I don't excuse you on account of the considerable difficulties you say must be endured there, but the gift of strength awaits you if God wants you there. I am pressed by time and must finish in spite of myself. Farewell, my very dear son.

I sent you the account of the earthquakes that happened in Canada by another way. They shook up a good four hundred leagues of this country. I wrote it in the form of a journal, so don't find it strange if it doesn't seem to follow in some places—it's just that I ordered it according to time rather than subject matter. There is nothing therein that isn't true.

---

283. *Relation de 1654*, 378–81, 418–21, 461–6.

284. See Letter 211.

Letter 211: August 16, 1664

My very dear son,

I received two of your letters this year. The first speaks to me about your particular dispositions, and the other gives me an account of the translation of the body of Saint Benedict, your glorious father and my own, because I have had a personal devotion to him my whole life. It is to the latter that I am responding here, and I feel compelled to tell you that even though I was far away, I had just as tender a devotion as if I had been there. I was not alone in feeling the sweetness of this sentiment—our whole community and our Reverend Fathers, with whom I shared your letter, felt the same. They even found the engraving of this magnificent reliquary so beautiful and so sumptuous that they wanted to keep it. We all blessed the Divine Goodness for having given to this holy patriarch such good children, who made such a sumptuous and worthy sanctuary for their father. A good Benedictine religious from Reims sent a cross made from the coffin of this great saint to Madame D'Ailleboust, her sister, who is with us.[285] You tell me that you are sending me a piece of his shroud, but I haven't received this holy relic which I was planning to put with those we already have. If it is lost this privation will cause me a great deal of sadness, although I don't deserve to have it, since I am not worthy to possess it. Finally, I praise your congregation for the effort it made with regard to this magnificent reliquary, as well as those good commendatory abbots who wanted very much to contribute to it. It was fitting that they gave a little for the great deal they receive from the monasteries of this great patriarch.

People in Tours expected that when your chapter came to an end, you would be sent to one of two monasteries. I'm not angry at you for the repugnance you have for it, for the proximity of one's relatives often causes difficulties and sometimes turns one away from God, but when divine providence orders as much and when we ourselves don't seek after it, we must lower our necks and submit.[286] If we are thereby mortified, we must endure it patiently. But ultimately, since the repose that you find at Angers makes you love that place, I am quite glad that you have returned there. Ah! My very dear son, who would ever have imagined—or

---

285. The body of St. Benedict was translated to the abbey of Saint-Benoît-sur-Loire in 1663, which presented the opportunity for the distribution of a number of the saint's relics.

286. Claude was sent to Saint-Serge d'Angers in 1663—not to the abbey of Saint-Julien in Tours as he had feared. Claude was not, of course, alone in imagining the close personal relationships to which the ties of blood give rise as sideshows that distract from the spiritual life. Not only had his own mother abandoned him to enter religious life, but Christ himself famously—and on multiple scriptural occasions—subordinated the biological family to a spiritual one; see, for example, Matthew 8:21–2, 10:35–7, 12:46–50, 19:29–30; Luke 11:27–8, 14:26.

even believed—that, you and I remaining alone after the death of your father, the Divine Majesty would have favored you from that point on, granting you the great and inestimable happiness of the religious profession? And even that he brought you into being for such honorable charges and such dazzling occupations? It is assuredly because I abandoned you out of love for him, and because I asked of him neither gold nor riches for you or for me, but only the poverty of his son for us both.[287] If he is providing for you as you experience it, it's because his generosity is as certain as his goodness. His promises do not go unfulfilled for those who hope in him. Do you remember what I said to you some time ago, that if I abandoned you he would take care of you and that he would be your Father? It is because of this that I never did anything with such generosity and with so much confidence in God as when I left you out of love for him, being grounded in his holy gospel, which was my guide and my strength. And when I embarked for Canada, and saw how I was again abandoning my life out of love for him, I was of two minds—the one having to do with you and the other with me. As far as you were concerned, it seemed to me that my bones were breaking apart and becoming disjointed, because of the pain that my natural sentiments felt on account of this abandonment. But as far as I was concerned, my heart melted with joy in the fidelity that I wanted to render to God and to his son, giving him life for life, love for love, all for all, since His Divine Majesty was rendering me worthy of it and giving me the opportunity—me, who was but the scum of the earth.

I return to the holy shroud you sent me. I regret its loss, fearing that it will fall into the hands of those who will not honor it as it deserves. Accept the respectful greeting of our community and our very humble thanks for it.

Letter 216: July 29, 1665

My very dear son,

Last year I received a letter of confidence from you to which I was not able to respond because of a great illness which it pleased the Divine Goodness to visit upon me. It lasted nearly a year and I am not yet entirely healed, but I am feeling much better than I was. His Divine Majesty prepared me in such an extraordinary and friendly way that I was not taken by surprise. You will perhaps be glad to know how it began and what happened after. I will tell you about it so that you help me praise his divine mercy.

---

287. *Relation de 1633*, 270–75, 288–93; *Relation de 1654*, 272–3, 281. See also Letters 56, 153, and 155.

Before falling ill, I dreamed I saw our Lord attached to the cross, still alive but completely covered in wounds over his whole body. He was moaning quite pitifully while being carried by two young men, and I had a strong impression that he was going to look for some faithful soul to ask for relief in his extreme pain. It seemed to me that a respectable lady presented herself to him for this purpose, but shortly after she turned her back on him and abandoned him to his suffering. As for me, I followed him, continually contemplating him in this pitiful state and looking at him with eyes of compassion. I saw nothing more, but with that my illness began, and there remained in my mind such a strong and vivid impression of this crucified divine savior that it seemed as if he was constantly before my eyes, but that he was sharing only part of his cross with me, although my pains were most violent and unbearable.[288]

The illness began with a bloody flux and a discharge of bile by all my members to the depths of my bones, such that it seemed to me that my whole body was being stabbed, from head to foot. Along with that, I had a constant fever and colic which gave me relief neither day nor night such that if God had not sustained me, I would have lost patience and would have cried out aloud. I was given last rites and these were repeated several times later, because of a relapse which began by a pain on the side like pleurisy, together with renal colic and a lot of vomiting, accompanied by a retraction of nerves which shook my whole body all the way to my fingertips. And to top off all these ills, since I could only tolerate one position in bed, stones formed in my kidneys which caused me unusual pains. Those who were taking care of me thought that this was a new illness until the condition was made apparent by my inability to pass urine. Finally, I passed a big stone the size of a pigeon egg and then a great number of little ones. The doctor had resolved to extract this stone from me, but when I heard that he wanted to put his hand inside of me, I had recourse to the very Holy Virgin by means of a *Memorare* which I recited faithfully and just then this stone came out on its own and the others followed after.

---

288. Marie's dream-vision of the suffering Christ not only recalls a medieval tradition of affective piety, but also raises intriguing questions about the interpretation of dreams within the context of an early modern New France in which Amerindian and European religious cultures coexisted in uncomfortable tension; see Dominique Deslandres, "Dreams Clash: The War over Authorized Interpretation in Seventeenth-Century French Missions," in *Empires of God: Religious Encounters in the Early Modern Atlantic*, ed. Linda Gregerson and Susan Juster, 143–53 (Philadelphia: University of Pennsylvania Press, 2011). For a discussion of the medieval tradition of affective piety, see Clarissa W. Atkinson, *Mystic and Pilgrim: The Book and World of Margery Kempe* (Ithaca: Cornell University Press, 1983), 129–56.

This long illness didn't bother me at all, and by the mercy of our good God, I was not in the least inclined toward impatience.[289] I owe this glory to the company of my crucified Jesus, whose divine spirit didn't permit me to wish for a moment of relief in the midst of my sufferings, but rather put me in a state of sweetness which kept me ready to endure them until judgment day. The remedies were only making my illness worse and intensifying my pains, which made the doctors resolve to leave me in God's hands, saying that the combination of so many illnesses was extraordinary and that the providence of God had sent them only to make me suffer. Since I was thus abandoned by men, all the good souls of this country prayed to God and said novenas for my health. I was urged to pray with them, but I couldn't, wanting neither life nor death but according to God's good pleasure. Monsignor our worthy Bishop urged me as well, and I responded to him that I was powerless to do so. This very good and very charitable prelate gave me the honor of visiting me several times. The Reverend Father Lalemant rendered me all the assistances of a good father. Even though she was put in charge of the whole house in my absence, Mother de Saint-Athanase, our assistant, wanted to be my nurse, and by the mercy of God, neither she nor any of my sisters fell ill or became indisposed, although they tirelessly watched over me day and night.

At present, I am feeling much better. The fever has left me, although it comes back periodically as do my pains. I am still quite weak and continue to suffer from a lack of appetite, along with a constant colic and the bloody flux which has not yet completely gone away. But all that seems like roses to me in comparison with my past sufferings. I walk about the house with the help of a cane. I attend the observances, except at the prayer that is recited at four o'clock in the morning, because my ills act up a bit at that hour.

I give thanks to God for having given you your health, too, and for the patience he gave you in your illness.[290] During the course of my own, His Divine

---

289. The spiritual—indeed, salvific—significance of suffering in the Christian tradition has been well studied. See for example: Peter Brown, *The Body and Society: Men, Women, and Sexual Renunciation in Early Christianity* (New York: Columbia University Press, 1988); Caroline Walker Bynum, *The Resurrection of the Body in Western Christianity 200–1336* (New York: Columbia University Press, 1995); Ariel Glucklich, *Sacred Pain: Hurting the Body for the Sake of the Soul* (New York: Oxford University Press, 2001); and Beverly Kienzle and Nancy Nienhuis, "Battered Women and the Construction of Sanctity," *Journal of Feminist Studies in Religion* 17, no. 1 (Spring 2001): 33–61. For a provocative analysis of the valorization of the suffering sick and, in particular, of the virtues demanded of the suffering sick within the context of Catholic culture, see Robert Orsi, *Between Heaven and Earth: The Religious Worlds People Make and the Scholars who Study them* (Princeton: Princeton University Press, 2005), 19–47.

290. See Letters 188 and 195.

Majesty, always amiable and always full of goodness toward me, gave me the grace and honor of remaining a faithful companion to me in my sufferings, just as he does when I am healthy and in the midst of the external affairs he desires of me. When a soul faithfully surrenders itself to his plans, he sometimes leads it to a state in which nothing can distract it, where all things are equal to it, and where, regardless of whether it must suffer or act, it does so with a perfect liberty of the senses and the mind, without losing this divine presence. But let's come to what concerns you.

In your letter, you shared with me some issues of confidence having to do with your interior crosses. I am obliged to you for this, for I will tell you that this information served me in helping a soul who contacted me and who has suffered for five years from similar troubles. They began under the same circumstances as yours, but I don't know if she will as faithfully struggle against them and persevere in her struggle, because her biggest problem is that her will is attacked, and so violently that she falls fairly often without knowing what she's doing. This greatly troubles her director, who, in order to avoid greater indispositions, often deprives her of communion and sometimes for a fairly long time. This makes her inconceivably agitated, for she takes it out on God by means of cries and words which make me tremble. What I find good about this person is that she faithfully reveals her wounds to the doctor of her soul, which makes me hope that God will have mercy on her; and besides there is no one more humble, more gentle, more charitable, more obedient. N.'s troubles are not like this.[291] They are in her imagination and her understanding, where she imagines that one or more demons are constantly speaking to her. These thoughts sometimes bother her so much that she thinks she is responding and acquiescing to them, which she isn't, because her will is so united to God that the demon can't breach it. This weighty cross will be without doubt the cause of her sanctification, for from morning to evening she interacts with God, showing him signs of her fidelity by acquiescing to his spirit and to his operation upon her. Monsignor our Bishop is not afraid for her, nor is Reverend Father Lalemant, on account of her fidelity with regard to temptation, and her submission to the orders of God—and, I would add, on account of the lowly sentiments of her spirit, for she considers herself the most miserable person on earth.[292] She recommends herself to your prayers and I recommend her personally to you.

---

291. Catherine de Saint-Augustin; see Paul Ragueneau, *La Vie de la Mère Catherine de Saint Augustin* (Paris: F. Lambert, 1671).

292. The spiritual torments suffered by Mother de Saint-Augustin are suggestive of what Sluhovsky argues is a distinctively early modern anxiety about possession, whether divine or demonic. As, over the course of the sixteenth and seventeenth centuries, possession both divine

As for you, I bless God for the graces he is giving you in the interior life. Oh, what a happy share it is to be called there and to render oneself faithful there! Let's take courage up to the very end. The troubles you have experienced have done you good, and what's more, they can be of great service to you in the guidance of souls. God operates in this way fairly often, making those he wants to use in the guidance of others pass through major ordeals so that they understand the illnesses of their inferiors by means of their own experience and apply more appropriate and suitable remedies to them.

In the same letter to which I am responding, you speak to me about several points of prayer which are fairly delicate. I will respond to them to the extent my weakness permits. I will tell you therefore, in my humble opinion, that with regard to supernatural prayer (for it is this sort that you discuss with me) I notice three states, which follow from each other, each of which has its particular perfection. There are souls that do not progress beyond the first; others are elevated to the second; others ultimately and happily reach the third. But in each of these states there are various degrees or operations, in which the Holy Spirit elevates them according to what pleases him for his greatest glory and for their particular perfection, and always with caresses which are characteristic only of a God of an infinite goodness.[293]

The first state is the prayer of quietude where the soul, which in the beginning customarily occupied itself in reflecting on the mysteries, is elevated by a supernatural attraction of grace. This attraction of grace astonishes the soul, because without any effort its understanding is carried away and enlightened in the divine attributes to which it is so strongly attached, nothing can separate it from them.[294]

---

and demonic became an increasingly interior affair (divorced from physical symptoms and somatic expressions), the process of spiritual discernment came to focus almost exclusively on "the personal traits of the visionary/possessed," one of the most telling of which was humility; see Sluhovsky, *Believe Not Every Spirit*, 204. See also Letter 204.

293. Here, as in the *Relation de 1654*, Marie (like a whole host of Christian mystics before her) describes the numerous stages, or "states of prayer," of the mystical journey. See also Letter 153. Although "those looking to slot [Marie] into an existing niche of [mystical] tradition can do so easily," Anya Mali argues that the conditions of life in New France affected Marie's spiritual itinerary, stamping it with the imprint of a theology of victimhood such that Marie's mystical journey cannot ultimately be captured by the traditional threefold pattern of purgation, illumination, and union; see Anya Mali, "Strange Encounters: Missionary Activity and Mystical Thought in Seventeenth-Century New France," *History of European Ideas* 22, no. 2 (1996): 75–85.

294. *Relation de 1633*, 157–8; *Relation de 1654*, 200–203. Marie's description of the prayer of quietude (effortless, experiential, and ineffable) strikes a curiously resonant chord with the spiritual teachings of Madame Guyon, whose *Les torrents spirituels* and *Le moyen court* were at the center of the Quietist controversy in late seventeenth-century France. It is interesting to note—as many have—that despite Guyon's condemnation by Bossuet and the papal censure

It remains in this state of enlightenment without being able to do anything on its own, but it receives and endures what God does to the extent it pleases His Divine Goodness to act in it and through it. After that it finds itself like a sponge in this great ocean, where it no longer sees the distinctions between the divine perfections, but all these distinct insights are suspended and arrested in it such that the soul no longer knows anything but God in his simplicity, who keeps it attached to his divine breasts.[295] The soul thus attached to its God, as to the center of its repose and pleasures, easily attracts all his powers to itself in order to make them rest with it. From there it passes into silence, where it doesn't even speak to he who holds it captive, because he gives it neither the permission nor the power to do so. Then it sleeps sweetly and softly on these sacred breasts. Its aspirations, however, do not rest, but rather grow stronger while everything else rests, and they light a fire in its heart which seems as if it will consume it.[296] At this point, the soul enters into a state of inactivity and remains as if overcome by he who possesses it.

At first this state of prayer, that is to say the prayer of quietude, is not so permanent that the soul doesn't sometimes go back to contemplate the mysteries of the Son of God or the divine attributes. But if it does go back, its aspirations are much more refined than in the past, because the divine operations that it underwent in its quietude gave rise to a deep intimacy with God, brought about not by work, effort, or study, but only by the attraction of his divine spirit. If the soul faithfully practices the virtues God asks of it, it will progress still further and enter into a more profound divine commerce with its beloved. This prayer of quietude will last as long as it pleases he who acts upon the soul. In the aftermath of this state God will make the soul go through various operations, which will build in the soul a foundation that will render it learned in the knowledge of the saints,

---

of the fundamentals of the Quietist movement, Marie's "pre-Quietist" (to borrow Sluhovsky's term) spirituality not only escaped criticism but even elicited Bossuet's approbation. For studies that compare Marie de l'Incarnation and Guyon, see: Bruneau, *Women Mystics*; Goldsmith, *Publishing Women's Life Stories*, 12–41, 71–97; and Paige, *Being Interior*. For an argument for the distinction between Marie's spirituality and the Quietism of late seventeenth-century France, see Dominique Deslandres, "Augustinisme," 29–42.

295. The image of divine breasts—with all its attendant gender ambiguity—has a rich history in the Christian tradition; see Elaine Pagels, "What Became of God the Mother: Conflicting Images of God in Early Christianity," *Signs* 2, no. 2 (Winter 1976): 293–303; and Carolyn Walker Bynum, "Jesus as Mother and Abbot as Mother: Some Themes in Twelfth-Century Cistercian Writing," *Harvard Theological Review* 70, no. 3/4 (July–October 1977): 257–84. See also de Sales, *Treatise*, V, ii; VI, ix; VII, i.

296. I have retained the ambiguity of the word "aspirations" here, which in French supports meanings of both physical inhalation and spiritual striving of the soul toward God.

although it cannot distinguish between them on the basis of their speech, and although it is difficult for the soul to describe what's happening in it.

The second state of supernatural prayer is the prayer of union, in which God, after having intoxicated the soul with the pleasures of the prayer of quietude, *encloses it in his wine cellars in order to introduce in it the perfect charity*.[297] In this state, the will governs the understanding, which is completely astonished and delighted by the riches it sees in it, and thus there are, as before, various stages that render the soul one in spirit with God.[298] These are the touches, the interior speeches, the caresses from which are born ecstasies, raptures, intellectual visions, and other very sublime graces which can be better experienced than described, because the senses are idle there, as the soul does nothing but suffer and endure what the Holy Spirit carries out within it. Although the senses do not labor in this state as they did in the interior occupations that preceded the prayer of quietude, one is nevertheless not entirely free there, because if it happens that the soul wants to speak externally about what it's experiencing internally, the spirit that keeps it occupied so overcomes the soul that words fail it and the senses sometimes stray.[299] A divine interaction between God and the soul again comes about, through the most intimate union imaginable, this God of love wanting to be the exclusive and absolute master of the soul that he possesses and is pleased to caress and honor in this way, unable to tolerate that anything else share in this pleasure. If the person has significant exterior occupations, she works at them without ceasing to suffer what God does within her. Such occupations even give her relief because since her senses are occupied and distracted, her soul is more liberated from them. At other times, worldly affairs and life itself are extremely painful for her because of

---

297. Song of Solomon 2:4. *Relation de 1633*, 159–61; *Relation de 1654*, 213–16.

298. In her elevation of the will over the understanding (or intellect) in the process of mystical union, Marie echoes de Sales who distinguishes the contemplation brought about by a movement of the will from the meditation "which almost always is performed with difficulty, labour, and reasoning"; see de Sales, *Treatise*, VI, vi, inter alia. Elsewhere, de Sales connects the intellect to a dangerous love of self and renders the intellect an obstacle to the cultivation of humility. For de Sales (reminiscent of a Christian mystical tradition which imagines mystical union as the coincidence of the mystic's will with God's will) the will submitted in perfect obedience to God and in imitation of Christ proved, against the intellect, the antidote to self-love and an aid to humility; see Francis de Sales, *Les vrays entretiens spirituels, in Œuvres de Saint François de Sales*, Tome 6 (Annecy: J. Niérat, 1892), 160–61, 427. See also Jantzen, *Power, Gender*, 145, 155.

299. Marie's subordination here of the physical senses to the spiritual interior reflects what Moshe Sluhovsky identifies as the pre-Quietist climate of "passive interiority" in early modern Europe; Sluhovsky, *Believe Not Every Spirit*, 97–136. For a discussion of the role of the senses in the discourse of mystical experience, see Bernard McGinn, "The Language of Inner Experience in Christian Mysticism," *Spiritus* 1, no. 2 (Fall 2001): 156–71; and McGinn, *The Foundations of Mysticism* (New York: Crossroad, 1994), 121–4. See also, Letters 68, 109, 128, 208, and 267.

the interactions they oblige her to have with creatures. The soul complains about it to her beloved in the words of the sacred spouse: *Let us flee, my beloved, let us go away.*[300] These are the amorous laments that win the spouse's heart and persuade him to caress his spouse in new ways that can't be explained. And it seems that the spouse confirms the soul in his most excellent graces and that the words he said to his apostles in the past are accomplished in it, as they are in fact in the depths of the soul: *If someone loves me, I will love him and my Father will love him; We will come to him and will make our resting place there.*[301] The soul, I say, experiences this truth, which gives rise to the third state of prayer, namely, spiritual and mystical marriage.[302]

This third state of passive or supernatural prayer is the most sublime of all. The senses are so free there that the soul that has reached this state can carry out the tasks in which its condition engages it without distraction. Nevertheless, it must have great courage because nature is bereft of all real help on the part of the soul, God having so taken over the soul that it is as if he is the depths of its substance. What happens is so subtle and so divine that one can't speak about it as one ought. It is a permanent state in which the soul remains so calm and tranquil that nothing can distract it. Its sighs and breaths are directed toward its beloved in a state as purified of all mixing as possible in this life, and with these same breaths it speaks easily to him about his mysteries and anything it wants. It is impossible for the soul in this state to meditate and reflect as usual because it sees things simply, which gives rise to its happiness, in which it can say: *My resting place is in peace.*[303] The soul experiences genuine spiritual poverty, being able to want only what the divine will wants of it. Only one thing makes it groan, which is to see itself subject to imperfection in this life and obliged to bear such a corruptible nature, although this is what reduces it to humility.

I return to the subject that prompted this digression and say that when a soul has reached this last state, neither activity nor sufferings can distract it or separate

---

300. Song of Solomon 8:14, 7:11.

301. John 14:21, 23.

302. *Relation de 1633*, 208–11; *Relation de 1654*, 213–16. Although here Marie identifies the third and final state of prayer as that of spiritual and mystical marriage, her *Relation de 1654* describes thirteen states of prayer—or stages of mystical ascent—the seventh of which is spiritual marriage. See Letter 153 (in which Marie provides the index to the *Relation de 1654*). It is this, argues Anya Mali, that distinguishes Marie from Teresa of Ávila (and others), for whom spiritual marriage represented the apex and end of the mystical experience. For Marie, spiritual marriage marked the mid-point of the mystical itinerary which culminated in the experience of true poverty of spirit; Mali, *Mystic in the New World*, 87–8.

303. Psalm 75:3, Vulgate.

it from its beloved. If it must suffer the pains of illness, the soul is as if elevated above the body and endures them as if this body was separated from it or as if it belonged to someone else.[304]

These seem to me, my very dear son, the points that you have raised with me and to which I am responding according to my limited experience. However, I don't know if what I have said about this is indeed appropriate, owing as much to my ignorance as to the little leisure I have, and my extreme infirmity, which prevents me from applying myself earnestly and seriously to anything.

Letter 217: August 30, 1665

My very dear son,

I have already informed you by my previous letters that I received three of your letters this year. I was quite consoled to learn about your improved health. And as for me, I report that I am emerging from a mortal illness that lasted an entire year. Only our Lord, who extricated me by his goodness, knows whether this will last. At present as I write, I am feeling so much better that I attend the regular exercises. I am still weak, but since I have a good temperament, I overcome difficulties without finding myself any the worse for it. To the contrary, I feel that my strength is returning by means of these small efforts.

In the long letter I wrote you a short while ago, I give you an account of my interior dispositions during this illness.[305] I also respond to you on several points of prayer about which you spoke to me last year. Since I was not able to satisfy you at that time because of my illness, I am trying to do so now to the extent my health permits. If I was close to you, I would often pour my heart out into your own, discussing with you the grandeurs of our beloved, for I can't express the consolation my soul feels in knowing that you want to love only him, and that the

---

304. The relationship between body and soul in Marie's spirituality is an intriguing one and deserves further study. By the time Marie migrated to New France, she had abandoned the corporeal mortifications she had practiced in her youth, arguably under the influence of the real material conditions of the seventeenth-century colony. In her more mature spiritual writings, the body emerges as, if not the cooperative partner of the soul, at least a neutral companion, which is neither hostile to the soul nor presents an obstacle to its progress toward God (although perhaps a more robust argument for the place of the body could be made, given the ways in which Marie's spiritual life culminated in the active service of others *in imitatio Christi*). For a discussion of the role of the body in Marie's spiritual writings, see Monique Dumais, "Relation au corps," in *Femme, mystique et missionnaire: Marie Guyart de l'Incarnation*, ed. Raymond Brodeur, 301–6 (Quebec: Presses de l'Université Laval, 2001). See also Mali, *Mystic in the New World*, 78.

305. See Letter 216.

interior spirit keeps you bound to him so tightly. I love you more as a poor religious than if you were monarch of the whole universe. You tell me that if the statute calling for separate cells for those religious who want to live alone is enforced in your congregation, you will be among the first who offer to fill them.[306] I don't think God is asking that of you. For now, you must abandon yourself to his guidance at the expense of your repose. Since God has permitted your congregation to progress so nicely and since there are so many monasteries in need of reform, your congregation needs a good number of workers. And since he is giving you the gift of leadership, you must turn a profit from this talent as often as obedience requires. However, govern by humility and command by obedience.

In the midst of your progresses, you are suffering persecution. Perhaps this is what makes you prosper. Don't let these sorts of persecutions demoralize you. As long as God has servants on earth, the world will be against them. We are here at the ends of the earth and yet we still experience this reality. You wouldn't believe how many calumniators there are against Monsignor our prelate, against the Reverend Fathers, against us, and against a number of meritorious people—and mostly for worldly reasons. Someone wrote defamatory letters which reached the king, who discovered the guile of the calumniators and the innocence of God's servants. When Monsieur de Tracy, who bears the name of Viceroy of America, arrived, he understood these matters so clearly that he gave a second opinion about them to the king. After this, those who had been degraded out of pure envy were esteemed more than ever, and their enemies humiliated by being removed from their posts.[307]

We were not exempt from these crosses, for some wanted to make us lose our concessions, saying that our titles, as well attested as they were, were but deceptions.[308] This matter was being debated during the time when I was nearly *in*

---

306. See also Letters 68 and 267.

307. The events to which Marie alludes here are those concerning the conflict over the configuration of the Sovereign Council between Laval and Governor de Mézy. The previous year (1664), de Mézy had succeeded in dismissing three council members who had earlier been appointed by Laval on the grounds that they were acting to protect the interests of the bishop and the clergy rather than the crown and the people. Laval, however, refused to sanction either the dismissal or the members' replacements until the arrival of Lieutenant-General de Tracy, keeping colonial affairs at an impasse until the following spring. The conflict between the two only intensified later that summer when a dispute arose over the election of Quebec's syndic, a body intended to represent the interests of the people and thus elected by popular vote. For an account of de Mézy's term as governor, see Raymond Dubois Cahall, *The Sovereign Council of New France: a study in Canadian Constitutional History* (New York: Columbia University, 1915), 22–36.

308. According to an ordinance of August 8, 1664, the crown would take possession of all colonial lands not yet cleared, even if already conceded. *Édits et ordonnances royaux et arrêts du conseil d'état du Roi concernant le Canada* (Quebec: E.R. Fréchette, 1854–56), I, 33. The Ursulines

extremis. Nevertheless, our Lord gave me the grace of giving me enough strength to write against these gentlemen. I sent my papers to Monsieur the Governor, begging him to defer this matter until the arrival of Monsieur de Tracy who was putting things in order after having informed himself about them. He granted me this grace despite these gentlemen who protested vociferously against me. Once Monsieur de Tracy had informed himself about this matter, he promised us his protection and is waiting for Monsieur the Intendant to arrive in order to put everything in order. You see, my very dear son, that God's servants suffer everywhere, but that the Divine Majesty takes their side and in time grants them success.

I will tell you before finishing this letter that our Lord made manifest some extraordinary effects of his omnipotence this year by means of miracles, or at least miraculous effects that it pleased him to work through the invocation of the Holy Family.[309] And as some redounded to the benefit of some French soldiers, you wouldn't believe how much devotion to this Holy Family has spread throughout the whole army. I will hold off telling you the details until another letter where I hope to speak to you about the preparations for war against the Iroquois.[310] Meanwhile, I beg you to ask God to give me the genuine dispositions which I need for eternity.

Letter 220: October 29, 1665

My very dear son,

If the letters I wrote you this year reached you, this one is the fifth that you should have received from me. But I seriously doubt that the great number I wrote to various towns of France arrived there, because the vice-admiral of the king's fleet which was carrying our most significant responses and the papers having to do with our most important affairs was shipwrecked two hundred leagues from

---

had, however, retained the titles to their various concessions and these were reissued to them in 1670.

309. Reference to the Holy Family here coincides with the growing popularity of the devotion in New France. First established in Montreal in 1642, the Confraternity of the Holy Family came to Quebec in 1665 at Laval's invitation and tended, unlike its counterpart in France, toward the ends of the moral reform of the Christian family. For a discussion of devotion to the Holy Family in New France, see Marie-Aimée Cliche, "La Confrérie de la Sainte-Famille à Québec sous le régime français, 1663–1750," *La société canadienne d'histoire de l'Église catholique* (1976): 79–93, who argues that the devotion in New France was one of the distinguishing features of colonial Catholicism. See also Cliche, *Les Pratiques*, 158–165. See also Letter 220.

310. See Letter 220.

here.³¹¹ What we know for certain about this event is that the ship was not yet in open water when it shattered upon the rocks. Nevertheless, everyone survived except for one sailor. Likewise a good part of the baggage was saved, which gives me some hope that our letters and our memoires have escaped the wreck. This accident happened at night when everyone except the helmsmen was in bed and resting, and all of a sudden the ship sank to the bottom between two rocks. On this ship were three respectable ladies who were going to France on business. They had to be rescued from danger by pulleys, which were attached to the top of the mast and then, with tremendous effort, pulled up by ropes and set upon the rocks. Everyone retreated to the Notre-Dame Mountains, which is the most barren and coldest place in America, having salvaged from the wreckage only enough provisions for twelve days. Monsieur de Tracy ordered three of the king's ships, which left, to pick up all these people as they passed by, or, in case they couldn't reach them and were constrained to leave them to spend the winter on the rocks, to send them provisions for eight months. He also sent people to give them aid. No one has come back yet. We are waiting for news about it.

We were distraught over this event, but we weren't surprised, because in all the years we've been in this country, we had never seen such severe storms, whether at sea or on the great river, as we did this year. The twelve ships that arrived thought they were going to perish. The thirteenth, which was Monsieur de Tracy's frigate, sank to the bottom at the mouth of the river where it had been seen. All his people, all his provisions, all his baggage was lost, which set him back a bit in his affairs because of the great expenses he is obliged to make and the extensive retinue he must maintain. See, my very dear son, the accidents of human life, which teach us that nothing is for certain in this world and that we ought to attach our hearts only to the spiritual goods of eternity.

Money, which was rare in this country, is at present quite common here, these gentlemen having brought a lot. They pay in cash for everything they buy, whether food or other necessities, which suits our settlers quite well.

The hundred girls whom the king sent this year have only just arrived and already almost all of them are provided for.³¹² He will send two hundred more

---

311. Juchereau de la Ferté Saint-Ignace, *Les annales de l'Hôtel-Dieu de Québec, 1636–1716*, ed. Dom Albert Jamet (Quebec: l'Hôtel-Dieu, 1939), 147; *Jesuit Journal*, 357.

312. *Jesuit Journal*, 356–7. Between 1663 and 1673, more than 800 young women known as the *filles du roi* migrated to New France as part of the crown's settlement program. Mostly orphaned and under the age of twenty-five, these *filles du roi* were intended as a means of redressing the gender imbalance that distinguished the colony in the earlier part of the century and persuading *engagés* to remain in the colony even after the expiration of their terms of service. For a recent study of the *filles du roi*, see Yves Landry, *Les Filles du roi au XVIIe siècle: Orphelines en France, pionnières au Canada* (Montreal: Leméac, 1992). See also Letters 246 and 254.

next year and a similar number in the following years. He is also sending men to be married and this year five hundred came, in addition to those who make up the army. In this way, it is astonishing to see how the country is populating and growing. It is said, too, that His Majesty wants to spare no expense here, animated by these seigneurs who are here and who find the country and the journey delightful in comparison to the American islands where they're coming from, and where the heat is so extreme that it's hard to live there. That country is rich because of the sugars and tobacco it exports, but wheat cannot be imported there, and their bread is made from a certain root which necessity obliges them to do without. But here wheat, vegetables, and all sorts of grain grow in abundance. The land is suitable for wheat and the more it is cleared of woods, the more fertile and abundant it is. Its fertility was aptly on display this year because the army's flour spoiled at sea, and there was enough wheat here to meet its needs without taking away from the provisions of the settlers. Despite this abundance, however, there are a great number of poor people here, and the reason is that when a family begins a settlement, it takes two or three years before they have enough to feed themselves, let alone clothing, furniture, and an infinity of little things necessary to support a household. But once they have made it through these first difficult years, they begin to live comfortably, and if they are prudent they become rich over time, to the extent one can in a new country like this one. At first, they live on their grains, their vegetables and the yield of their hunts, which is abundant in winter. And for clothing and other household goods, they make boards to cover their houses and cut the wood into frames, which they sell at a high price. Having thus met their own needs, they begin to trade, and in this way they get ahead little by little.[313]

This small economy so impressed these gentlemen officers that they bought land to have cultivated here. It is thus unbelievable how this country is developing and becoming populated all over. But what people most earnestly seek after is the glory of God and the salvation of souls. It is for this that they work, as well as to inculcate devotion in the army, making the soldiers see that they are fighting a holy war where there is more profit to be made for heaven than fortune for earth. There are a good five hundred soldiers who have adopted the scapular of the Holy Virgin, and many others who say the rosary of the Holy Family daily. They have so much devotion to this Holy Family that God has agreed to work miracles in order to reward their faith and increase their fervor. I have spoken to you elsewhere about this, which is why I am not repeating it here.

---

313. For a discussion of the seventeenth-century agricultural economy, see Greer, *The People of New France*, 27–42.

I told you in another letter that part of the army went ahead, in order to seize the river of the Iroquois and establish forts in the most strategic locations on the shore.[314] To this, I add that our Algonquin Christians went to camp with their families in the shelter of the forts and those who guard them. They go on great hunts where their enemies used to go hunting and there they get the better part of their pelts. Their hunt is so successful that it is said they trap more than a hundred beavers a day, not to mention moose and other wild animals. The French and Indians help each other in this enterprise: the French defend the Indians and the Indians feed the French with the meat of the animals they trap, after having removed the skins from them, which they bring to the country's trading posts. Monsieur de Tracy told me a few days ago that he had reported all this to the king, advising him as well of the other advantages of waging war on the sworn enemies of our faith. Join your prayers to ours, so that God showers his blessings upon an enterprise so conducive to his glory.

Letter 223: October 16, 1666

My very dear son,[315]

I am extremely obliged to you for the sumptuous gift of holy relics you sent me. We will keep them carefully and with veneration in a place designated for this purpose, where we have four reliquaries, which we expose on the altar during solemn feasts. In the course of the translation of the holy bodies of Saint Flavian Martyr and Saint Felicity, which our Holy Father gave to Monsignor our Bishop for this country, we had a part, as did the two other religious houses. Never had such a beautiful ceremony been seen in these lands.[316] In the procession were forty-seven clerics in surplice, copes, chasubles, and dalmatics. Since the relics had to be brought into the four churches of Quebec we had the consolation of seeing this magnificent ceremony. Viceroy de Tracy and Governor de Courcelle, together with two of the most notable of the nobility, carried the dais. The most dignified of the clerics carried the four great reliquaries on magnificently ornamented stretchers. Upon exiting a church, the procession left a reliquary there. The music never ceased, neither in the streets nor in the stations. Monsignor

---

314. Thwaites, *Jesuit Relations*, vol. 49, 251–3.

315. Claude was appointed prior of Notre-Dame de Bonne-Nouvelle in Rouen in 1666.

316. The ceremony described by Marie here took place on August 29, 1666, following the dedication of the parish church to the Immaculate Conception. The relics were distributed between four churches—those of the Jesuits, the Hospitallers, the Ursulines, and the parish; *Jesuit Journal*, 368.

followed the holy relics and the procession in his pontifical habits. A few days earlier he had consecrated and dedicated the cathedral church with magnificent pomp, and he hopes to consecrate our own next year. I would never have dared to hope to see such great magnificence in the Church of Canada where, upon my arrival, I had seen nothing but ignorance and barbarity. It is delightful to see Monsieur de Tracy so marvelously exact in being the first to arrive at all these holy ceremonies, for he wouldn't want to miss a moment of them. He was seen in the church for more than six whole hours without leaving. His example has so much influence that everyone follows him like children follow their father. He favors and sustains the Church by means of his piety and the influence he has over everyone, which makes us fear that the king will call him back next year, as we have in fact been informed that His Majesty is having a magnificent ship equipped, in order to take him back to France with the honor that he earned in his great commissions.

He has left in order to go fight in person against the Iroquois of New Holland, who are keeping the other nations from believing. He did everything possible to win them over with kindness, but these people are brutes who couldn't let themselves be conquered by this charm that wins over anyone who has anything left of reason. According to estimates of the army's progress, the battle in the first village must have been carried out during these past three days. If God blesses this initial effort, the two other villages will be attacked next. They have good forts, they have cannons, they are brave, and without doubt they will put up a good fight. But our French soldiers are so fervent that they fear nothing, and there is nothing that they don't do or undertake. They undertook to carry cannons on their backs through the waterfalls and really difficult portages. They even carried their rowboats, which is unheard of. It seems to everyone in this militia that they are going to besiege paradise and that they hope to take it and enter within, because it is for the good of the faith and religion that they are going to battle. We heard this news a few days ago and we are assured, moreover, that the whole army is in good health, that Monsieur the Governor is leading the advance guard and Monsieur de Chambly holds the rear guard. Monsieur de Salières is the colonel of the regiment and Monsieur de Tracy, as generalissimo, commands the whole body. Our new Christian Indians follow the French army along with all our young Canadian French, who are very brave and run through the woods like Indians. We won't have any news of their combat for two more weeks. Meanwhile this whole new Church is at prayer, and we are reciting the forty-hours prayer which is continuing in the four Churches one by one, because the fate of the whole country depends on the outcome of this war.[317] This is the third time that our Frenchmen have

---

317. Marie's conviction of the cosmic dimensions of the struggle against the Iroquois is apparent

gone to their country since February, to the great astonishment of the English and the Iroquois alike, who can't understand how only the French have dared to undertake this voyage.[318] Monsieur de Tracy departed from here with the majority of the army only on the day of the Exaltation of the Holy Cross, and it is assumed that they arrived there after one month's journey. I will give you news about this expedition at greater length once they return, or as soon as we learn something about it from reliable sources. For now, I beg you to let me finish so that I might rest a bit, as I am quite fatigued from having written a great number of letters. I don't have more than forty left to write, which I hope to send by the last ship. Do not cease to pray for us.

Letter 234: October 30, 1667

My very dear and beloved son,

I have given myself the consolation of writing you by several ways. This letter is only to reiterate my sincere affection for you, as the person dearest to me in the whole world.

On account of my sincere affection for you and yours for me, I advise you to you procure as many masses as possible for me from the reverend Fathers of your holy congregation when you learn of my death. I am awaiting this grace from their goodness and from yours, not because I have presentiments of my death, but because a person of my age can reasonably believe that she is not too far from death. In addition, my considerable illnesses, which come and go from time to time, ought to serve as a clock to warn me to be at the ready to soon give an account to the Divine Majesty of my whole life, and especially for the inadequate use I have made of his great graces, to which I have so poorly corresponded that I will burn for a long time in purgatory unless divine mercy relieves me through the intercession of the Church. It seems to me that I am quite rich to have you and in you, all your good Fathers. Thus I expect that you will think seriously about

---

here. Writing to Claude in 1660, Marie defended the plan to exterminate the Iroquois—against Claude's misgivings—whom she elsewhere renders agents of the devil and enemies of God and the Church; See Lettre CXCII, *Correspondance*, 649. For Marie and others in the colony, the war against the Iroquois was a holy one, a regrettable but necessary means to the end of the success of the missionary project and the survival of the New World colony. For an analysis of the ways in which Marie's reflections on the Iroquois draw on the rhetoric of crusade popular in mid-seventeenth-century France, see Robert Sauzet, "Mission et croisade: La rencontre des Iroquois," in *Femme, mystique et missionnaire: Marie Guyart de l'Incarnation*, ed. Raymond Brodeur, 25–36 (Quebec: Presses de l'Université Laval, 2001).

318. Thwaites, *Jesuit Relations*, vol. 50, 139–45.

this, so that by means of your sacrifices and theirs, I will soon be able to go and enjoy he whom my heart and my soul want to love and bless eternally.³¹⁹ Ah! How content we will be when we see each other thus engaged!

About forty years ago, His Divine Majesty gave me the grace of indicating to my soul that he wanted me to praise him from then on, like the angels and saints praise him in heaven, and His Goodness put me in the position to do so, whereupon followed very great and magnificent favors.³²⁰ But without a doubt I mixed my own self in with that, by means of my imperfections and confusions, which makes me repeat to him incessantly this verse from Psalms: *Delicta quis intelligit? Ab occultis meis munda me.*³²¹ It's not that I have major well-known and manifest faults, but I have an innumerable number of secret and hidden ones, and for those—as well as for all the faults I have committed in my spiritual life by my infidelity and inadequate correspondence to his adorable plans—I will be rigorously punished unless you remember to obtain remission for me by means of your holy sacrifices at the holy altar.

The purity God demands of a soul to whom he gives the honor of allowing access to His Divine Majesty by means of a constant union is of an inestimable grandeur, and it is the esteem I have for it that makes me fear, although in the midst of this fear my soul enjoys an inexpressible peace.³²² Obtain for me, again, the authenticity of this peace, because sometimes the peace we experience in our spiritual lives is counterfeit, and I leave it for God to judge of what sort is this peace I enjoy.

When I took up my pen to begin this letter, I didn't have the least thought of discussing all this with you, but our good God moved me to do so, in order to have recourse to you for the security of my soul's affairs, His Goodness giving me a great confidence in the sacred treasures of his Church, rich with the precious blood of his son, our divine spouse and most adorable savior.

This letter is the last you will receive from me this year. So I must bid you farewell.

Letter 235: August 9, 1668

My very dear son,

Here is the response to your third letter. I thank you as much as I possibly can for the holy and precious relic you sent me.³²³ It will be placed in a beautiful

---

319. See also Letter 155.

320. *Relation de 1654*, 264–7.

321. Psalm 18:13, Vulgate. See also Letter 155.

322. *Relation de 1654*, 400–404.

323. This was a relic of Saint Wulfram of Fontenelle, archbishop of Sens (c. 640–703).

reliquary from which we had removed the relics in order to put them in the altar of our church when it was consecrated. You have obliged me in sending me their attestations, because it is to be exposed to the public. When I saw this holy relic, my heart was moved with devotion and I thanked this great saint for honoring this country with his venerable remains. I thank you once again, my very dear son.

You think that I'm going to die. I don't know when this happy moment will arrive, which will give me over completely to our divine savior. My health is in some ways better than in years past, although since I don't have much strength it wouldn't take much to carry me off, especially because I am not completely free of the bloody flux that has lasted such a long time and always preserves a bitterness in my mouth, making everything I eat taste like absinthe. I have gotten used to it; otherwise I would die of weakness. Nevertheless, my spirit is content in this infirmity, which constantly reminds me of our Lord's bitterness on the cross. Despite these inconveniences, I keep my rules. I fasted during Lent and observed the other fasts of the Church and the rule, and in a word I do my duty, thanks to our Lord. I sing in such a low voice that I can hardly be heard, but I still have enough strength to recite spoken prayers in a proper voice. Kneeling during mass is painful for me. I am weak on this point, and people are astonished that I am not more so, considering the nature of my illness which has lasted such a long time along with a high fever.

We were hoping that this ship would bring my dear Mother Cécile de Reuville de l'Enfant Jésus, religious from Rouen, and I was preparing to teach her the Algonquin language, persuading myself that she would be suited for it and dedicated to it, for these barbarous languages are difficult and one must be of a constant character to commit oneself to the task. I am occupied on winter mornings by teaching them to my young sisters. Some carry on until they know the basic principles and grammatical rules, provided I translate the Indian words into French for them. But learning a number of words from the dictionary is troublesome for them and a thorn in their sides. Of our young sisters, only one is making a real effort. The assistant Mother and the Mother de Saint Croix know these languages fairly well, because in the beginning we learned the dictionary by heart. As these things are very difficult, I am determined to leave as many writings as I can before I die. From the beginning of last Lent to Ascension Day, I wrote a big Algonquin book about sacred history and holy things, along with a dictionary and an Iroquois catechism, which is a treasure. Last year I wrote a big Algonquin dictionary in the French alphabet. I have another one in the Indian alphabet.[324] I am telling you this so that you can see that the Divine

---

324. Among Marie's works in Amerindian languages are three Algonquin dictionaries (at least one of which was in the Algonquin alphabet and one in the French) composed between 1662

Goodness is giving me the strength in the midst of my infirmity, to leave my sisters something with which to work in his service for the salvation of souls. As for the French girls, they need study nothing other than our rules. But ultimately, after we will have done what we can, we must believe that we are only useless servants and small grains of sand at the foundation of the edifice of this new Church.[325] I am writing you by all the ships, but since my letters can get lost, I will repeat here what I told you elsewhere about our tasks since you want me to discuss them with you.

First, we have seven choir sisters employed in the instruction of French girls every day, not including two converse sisters who take care of exterior affairs. The Indian girls live and eat with the French girls, but for their instruction, they must have their own mistress, and sometimes more than one, depending on how many of them we have. To my great regret, I just refused seven Algonquin seminarians because we don't have adequate provisions, the officers having taken everything away for the king's troops, who needed it. For as long as we've been in Canada, we had never refused anyone, notwithstanding our poverty, and that we had to refuse these seminarians deeply mortified me, but I must put up with it and humiliate myself in our powerlessness, which also obliged us to give some French girls back to their parents. We are limited to only sixteen French girls and three Indian girls, among whom are two Iroquois and a captive to whom we want to teach the French language. I am not mentioning the great number of poor, with whom we must share part of what we still have. Let's get back to our pensioners.

We are quite assiduous in this country in instructing French girls, and I can assure you that if there were no Ursulines their salvation would be in constant danger.[326] The reason is that there are a great number of men, and parents who don't want to miss mass on a feast day or a Sunday will leave their children at home with several men to watch them. If there are girls among them, of whatever age, they are in evident danger and experience shows that they must be put somewhere safe. Finally, I can say that the girls in this country are for the most part more knowing in many dangerous matters than those in France. Thirty resident girls give us more work than sixty in France. The externs give us a lot of work, but we do not watch as closely over their morals as we would if they were in the

---

and 1667, three Algonquin catechisms (1662), a collection of Algonquin prayers (1662), a collection of "sacred history and holy things" in Algonquin (1668), a Huron catechism (1662), and an Iroquois dictionary (1668) and catechism (1668). These texts have unfortunately been lost.

325. Luke 17:10.

326. See Letter 142.

cloister. They are docile, they have good character, they are committed to the good when they are aware of it, but since many are only pensioners for a short while, the mistresses must apply themselves assiduously to their education and teach them sometimes in a single year to read, write, and count, prayers, Christian morals, and everything a girl should know. There are some whose parents leave them with us until they are old enough to be provided for, whether in the world or in religious life. Eight of our professed as well as our novices didn't want to return to the world and are doing very well, having been raised in great innocence, and there are still more among us who don't want to return to their parents' houses, finding themselves well in God's house. Two of these are the granddaughters of Monsieur de Lauson, who is well known in France. They are only waiting for the return of Monsieur de Lauson-Charny to enter into the novitiate. They were given to us so that we could prepare them for their first communion, and thus they are staying in the seminary for two or three months.

As for the Indian girls, we take them at all ages. Sometimes it happens that some Indian—whether Christian or pagan—does what he shouldn't and kidnaps a girl of his nation, keeping her in violation of God's law. This girl is given to us, and we instruct her and keep her until the Reverend Fathers come to take her back. Others are like fleeting birds and stay here only until they are sad, which the Indian humor cannot tolerate. As soon as they are sad their relatives take them out lest they die.[327] We give them the liberty to do this, for they are rather won over in this way than by retaining them by force or prayers. There are others who take off out of fancy or caprice. Like squirrels they climb our palisade, which is as high as a fortress wall, and go running off into the woods. Some persevere and these we raise as French girls. They are provided for then and they do very well.

---

327. European accounts of Amerindian practices of child-rearing tended to emphasize what European observers concluded was a deplorable culture of indulgence toward children. Gabriel Sagard, for example, notes at once the great affection Huron parents showed their children and, at the same time, their reluctance to discipline or otherwise exercise authority over their offspring. The result, Sagard concludes, is that Huron children are "for the most part very naughty, paying [their parents] little respect, and hardly more obedience...and parents, for failure to punish their children, are often compelled to suffer wrong-doing at their hands, sometimes being beaten and flouted to their face...Bad example, and bad bringing up, without punishment or correction, are the cases of all this lack of decency" (James Axtell, ed., *The Indian Peoples of Eastern America: A Documentary History of the Sexes* [New York: Oxford University Press, 1981], 7, citing Gabriel Sagard, *Le grand voyage au pays des Huron* [1632]). See also Denise Lemieux, *Les petits innocents: L'enfance en Nouvelle-France* (Quebec: Institut québécois de recherche sur la culture, 1985); Trigger, *Children of Aataentsic*, 47; and Cornelius Jaenen, "Amerindian Views," 285–6. Differences between European and Amerindian attitudes toward children, as Marie suggests here, presented challenges to the Ursuline educational mission and ultimately compelled the order to focus its energies on the education of French, rather than native, girls in the colony.

One of them was given to Monsieur Boucher who has since become Governor of Trois-Rivières.[328] Others return to their Indian relatives. They speak French well and know how to read and write.

These are the fruits of our small labors, some details of which I have longed to tell you, in order to respond to the rumors you say are being spread, namely that the Ursulines are useless in this country and that the *Relations* don't mention anything they do here. Our Reverend Fathers and Monsignor our prelate are delighted with the education we are providing to the young girls. They give our girls communion as soon as they turn eight years old, finding them as well instructed as they can be. If it is said that we are useless here because the *Relations* don't talk about us, one must likewise say that Monsignor our prelate is useless, his seminary is useless, the seminary of the Reverend Fathers is useless, Messieurs the clerics of Montreal are useless, and finally that the Hospitaller Mothers are useless because the *Relations* say nothing about all that. And yet this is what supports and gives strength and even honor to the whole country. If the *Relations* don't say anything about us or about the societies or seminaries I just mentioned, it's because they only discuss the progress of the gospel and what relates to it and, even then, many things are edited out of the *Relations* once the copies sent from here arrive in France. Madame de la Duchesse de Senneçay, who has given me the honor of writing to me all these years, told me last year how displeased she was about something that had been edited out, and she told me something similar this year. M. C. who prints the *Relations* and who has a strong affection for the Hospitallers here, inserted therein upon his own initiative a letter that the superior had written him, which caused quite a commotion in France.[329] My very dear son, what we are doing in this new Church is seen by God and not by men. Our

---

328. In the middle of the seventeenth century, colonial policy toward the intermarriage of Amerindian and French was not only one of tolerance, but active encouragement as a means to the end of assimilating the Amerindian into French culture. By the end of the century, however, official policy reversed course as it became clear that the attractions of native life all too often meant that assimilation went the other way. See Guillaume Aubert, "'The Blood of France': Race and Purity of Blood in the French Atlantic World," *William and Mary Quarterly*, Third Series 61, no. 3 (July 2004): 439–78; and Sara E. Melzer, "The Underside of France's Civilizing Mission: Assimilationist Policies in 'New France,'" in *Classical Unities: Place, Time, Action*, ed. Erec R. Koch, 151–64 (Tübignen: Narr, 2002).

329. Marie's suggestion here that there was more to the *Jesuit Relations* than met the eye raises important—and ongoing—issues of interpretation and strategies of reading with regard to this rich body of seventeenth-century mission history. For an insightful discussion of ways of reading the *Jesuit Relations*, see Blackburn, *Harvest of Souls*, 3–20. The letter to which Marie alludes, written by the superior of l'Hôtel-Dieu, was inserted by the editor of the *Jesuit Relations* in a limited number of copies from 1665 and 1666 that were intended for potential donors to the Hospitaller mission.

enclosure covers everything and it is difficult to talk about what can't be seen. It is wholly otherwise with the Hospitaller Mothers. The Hospital is open and the good works carried out there are seen by everyone. Thus, their exemplary charity could reasonably be praised. But ultimately, we are both awaiting the reward for our services from he who penetrates the most hidden places, and who sees as clearly in darkness as in light—that is good enough for us.

Letter 243: October 16, 1668

For me, my very dear son,

I have nothing more to say at the feet of the Divine Majesty.[330] My prayers consist of only these words: My God, my God, blessed are you, O my God. My days and nights pass thus, and I hope that His Goodness will make me expire with these words and make me die as he makes me live. What I have said in these words, I will say better in these breaths, which don't permit me to do any activity. I don't know how to speak about things as naked and simple as these, which consume my soul in its sovereign and unique good, in its simple and unique all.

I saw myself prone to so many infirmities and thought, according to the course of nature, that they would consume me and end only with death. Love, which is stronger than death, put an end to these infirmities, and by the mercy of God here I am, just about as healthy as I was before such a long illness, although I don't know how long it will last. It doesn't matter to me, provided that the very holy will of God is done; but I don't think my end is too far off, given that I turned seventy this year.[331] My days and minutes are in the hands of he who gives me life, and all things are equal to me provided that they all happen according to his good pleasure and adorable plans for me.

God has never guided me by a spirit of fear, but by one of love and trust. Nevertheless, when I think about what a sinner I am, and that on account of the misfortune of this condition I could be deprived of my God's affection, I am more humiliated than one can imagine, and I am seized by the fear that this misfortune will befall me. If this fear was a constant one, I could neither live nor subsist, because it separates me from a God of love and goodness from whom I have received more grace and mercy than there are grains of sand in the sea. But trust, with a single glance, dispels this fear, turning my gaze away from such an awful

---

330. Marie's struggle to articulate her interior experiences only becomes more acute during the last few years of her life, suggesting an inverse relationship between spiritual progress and communicability. See also Letter 267.

331. Marie would not, in fact, turn seventy years-old until October 28, 1669.

object and making me abandon myself in the arms of my celestial spouse in order to rest there.

Again, I feel myself powerfully strengthened by the protection of the very Holy Virgin, who is our divine superior according to the special choice and solemn vow that our community made in this regard several years ago.[332] This very divine Mother assists us substantially. She continually helps us in our needs and preserves us as her eye's pupil. It is she who supports our family in a secret but efficacious manner. It is she who manages all our external affairs. It is she who raised us up from our fire and from an infinity of other calamities, under the weight of which we ought naturally to have been crushed. As we were not able to have religious from France, she gave us six novices, who are all very good subjects capable of helping us bear the weight of our duties, which increase from day to day. Who can I fear under the wings of such a powerful and lovable protector?

Thank the Divine Goodness and this Holy Mother for their assistance of our little community, and of me personally, who am the most infirm and the most imperfect of all.

Letter 246: October 1668

My very dear son,[333]

Monsieur Talon is leaving us at last and returning to France, to the regret of everyone and to the loss of all of Canada, for since he has been Intendant here, the country is more developed and its affairs more advanced than ever before.[334] In his place, the king is sending someone named Monsieur Boutroue, whose nobility and merit I know nothing about yet.

This year, the ships did not bring sick people. The ship that arrived here was laden as if with merchandise of mixed quality. There were Portuguese, Germans, Dutch, and others from I know not what nations. There were also women—Moors,

---

332. The Virgin Mary occupied a central place in Marie's spiritual universe, playing a leading role in her 1633 vision about Canada and the subsequent development of her mystical experience. See *Relation de 1654*, 303–6, and Letters 56, 195, and 216, inter alia. See also Henri de Lubac, "Marie de l'Incarnation et la Sainte Vierge," in *Maria, Études sur la Saint Vierge*, ed. Hubert du Manoir, vol. 3, 181–204 (Paris: Beauchesne, 1954).

333. Claude was appointed assistant to the Superior-General of the Congregation of Saint-Maur in 1668, a post he would retain until 1675.

334. Jean Talon was appointed Intendant of New France in 1665, a post he agreed to hold only until 1667. Talon's success in the colony was so substantial, however, that the king obliged him to remain in New France for an additional year. Talon therefore left the colony—much to the regret of Marie and others—in 1668. He was ultimately persuaded to return to Canada in 1670 to resume his post and remained there until 1673.

Portuguese, French, and those from other countries. A great number of girls came and still more are expected. The first to be married is the Moorish woman, who wed a Frenchman. As for the men, these are people who were terminated from the king's service and whom His Majesty wanted sent to this country. They were all put in Bourg Talon two leagues from here, in order to live there and populate it. When they have consumed the barrel of flour and lard that the king gives them, they will suffer extraordinarily until they have cleared the land. Only village girls, who can work like men, will be requested from now on, since experience shows that those who weren't brought up that way aren't suitable for such work here, and sink into a misery from which they can't extract themselves.

My praise in years past for the pumpkins of the Iroquois has given you an appetite for them. I am sending you seeds that the Hurons brought us from their country, but I don't know if your soil will change the taste. The pumpkins are prepared in various ways—in soup with milk, and fried in oil; they are baked like apples, as well, or braised like pears such that they truly taste like cooked Pippin apples. In Montreal, melons grow which are as good as the best in France. They grow only rarely here because we are not as far south. There is also a certain variety called the watermelon, which grows like the pumpkin. They are eaten like melons; some salt them, others put sugar on them. They are excellent and not toxic.[335] The other garden vegetables and legumes are like those in France. They are harvested like wheat so that they can be used throughout the winter, until the end of May, because the gardens are covered in snow. As for the trees, we have plum trees, which are well fertilized and cultivated and yield abundant fruit for three weeks. The plums are not baked, for then there is nothing left of them but a stone covered with skin, but they are used to make marmalade with sugar, which is excellent. We make ours with honey, and this seasoning suffices for us and our children. In addition, redcurrants are preserved in fat as are cranberries, which are Indian fruits that taste good with sugar. We are beginning to have Pippin and Calville apples, which grow very beautifully and nicely here, but these varieties came from France. Such are our domestic affairs and our delicacies, which would be counted for nothing in France but are much valued here.[336]

---

335. Curiously, the *Jesuit Relations* also allude to the benignity of the watermelon; see Thwaites, *Jesuit Relations*, vol. 65, 73.

336. For a study of the agricultural production of seventeenth-century New France, see Jacques Mathieu, *La Nouvelle-France: Les Français en Amérique du Nord, XVIe–XVIIIe siècle* (Quebec: Presses de l'Université Laval, 2001), 89–94. See also Pierre Boucher, *Histoire véritable et naturelle des mœurs et productions du pays de la Nouvelle-France* (Paris, 1664). See also Letters 142 and 143.

The bearer of this letter is Monsieur de Dombourg, who is going to France in order to accompany Madame Bourdon his mother. I beg you to receive them with demonstrations of affection, because I love and cherish this family more than any other in this country. They didn't want to leave without bringing you a word from me, so as to have the consolation of seeing you and talking to you. Monsieur Bourdon was the king's prosecutor, an office given to him on account of his probity and merit. He was a very particular conduit of spiritual goods for me, for under the cover of his secular habit he led one of the most orderly lives.[337] He enjoyed the constant presence of God and a continual union with His Divine Majesty. Once he risked his life to reach an agreement with the Dutch on behalf of our French captives, for this charitable man gave himself entirely to the public good. He was the father of the poor, the consoler of the widows and orphans, an example to everyone. In brief, ever since he came to this country, he has consumed himself in all sorts of spiritual goods and good works. He had four girls, all of whom he dedicated to the service of God, and in his generosity he performed this action with much pleasure and graciousness. Two were Hospitallers, one of whom died. The two older ones are Ursulines in our monastery and are very good religious. He was left with two sons. The youngest is studying in Quebec, and the elder is the one who is presenting you this letter. I think of them as my nephews and so I enthusiastically recommend this one to you.

As for Madame Bourdon, she is anxious to see you. This lady shines as an example of piety and charity in the whole country. She and Madame d'Ailleboust are united together, visiting prisoners, succoring criminals, and even carrying them to their site of burial on a stretcher. The one I am describing as the most vigorous and active is constantly occupied with these good works and in collecting for the poor, which she does successfully. In brief, she is the mother of the wretched and the example of all sorts of good works. Before coming to Canada, which she did on a principle of piety and devotion alone, she was the widow of Monsieur de Monceaux, a noble gentleman. Some time after her arrival Monsieur Bourdon was left a widower with seven children, none of whom was capable of caring for either their father or themselves. She had a powerful impulse to assist this family, and for this reason she resolved to marry Monsieur Bourdon, with whose virtue she was pretty familiar, but on the condition that they would live together as brother and sister. That was done and the condition has been assiduously observed. She submitted to this condition in order to carry out this act of charity. In France, where she was well known both in Paris and the countryside, this was considered a thoughtless act in view of the life she had led—one quite

---

337. See Letter 97.

unlike that of marriage. But people changed their opinions when they learned of all the good that came from this generous act, for she raised all Monsieur Bourdon's children with an unparalleled cheer and put them in the position where they are now. I went on so long, in order to honor the virtue of this lady and her pious family, and to show you that there are persons of honor and merit in this country. Show them affection. They deserve it.

Letter 247: July 30, 1669

My very dear son,

A ship from France arrived at our port toward the end of June, and since then no others have shown up. This one brought us your news, which gave me reason to praise God for his blessings upon you and upon me. It's true that my greatest worldly joy is reflecting on them, and I see that the joy you feel from experiencing them touches you keenly and is useful to you.

Are you not glad, my very dear son, that I abandoned you to his holy direction in leaving you out of love for him?[338] Have you not found a boon therein which cannot be expressed? Know, then, once more, that when I separated myself from you, I died while still alive and that the spirit of God, who was unmoved by the tender feelings I had for you, gave me no rest until I had delivered the blow. I had to go through that and obey him without reason because he doesn't want reason to play a part in the execution of his absolute will. Nature, which doesn't give up easily when its interests are at stake, especially when they concern the obligation of a mother toward her son, could not bring itself to do this. It seemed to me that in leaving you so young, you wouldn't be brought up to fear God, and that you could fall into bad hands or under some influence where you would be in danger of ruin, and thus that I would be deprived of a son whom I wanted to raise only for the service of God, staying with him in the world until he was capable of entering into some holy religious order, which was the end for which I had intended him.

This divine spirit who saw my struggles had no sympathy for my feelings, saying to me in the depths of my heart, "Quickly, quickly, it is time, delay no longer. There is no longer anything good left for you in the world." Then he opened

---

338. *Relation de 1633*, 270–76; *Relation de 1654*, 272–5; Martin, *Vie*, 168–79. Marie's invocation of the abandonment here, nearly forty years after the fact, betrays a lingering anxiety about the legitimacy of her decision. Despite professions of confidence that she had done the right thing in abandoning Claude for religious life, Marie's repeated allusions to the event suggest the durability of a substratum of doubt that resists her attempts to discursively put such misgivings to rest. See Letters 56, 109, 155, 195, 211, and 267.

the door to religion for me, his voice constantly urging me by a holy impetuosity that gave me no rest day or night. He took care of my affairs and so engagingly disposed what pertained to religion, that everyone opened their arms to me, such that even if I had been the most important person in the whole world and had brought great gifts, there wouldn't have been more of a consensus. Dom Raymond took care of everything he could with my sister and brought me himself where God wanted me.

You came with me and in leaving you, it seemed to me that my soul was being sundered from my body with extreme pains. Note, too, that since the age of fourteen, I had a very strong vocation for religion, which couldn't be realized because my parents didn't consent to my desire. But since the age of nineteen or twenty, my spirit has abided there and only my body remained in the world to raise you until the moment I could carry out God's will for you and for me.

After I had entered, I saw how you came to cry at our parlor and the grill of our choir, how you passed a part of your body through the communion rail, how seeing by chance the big convent door left open by the workmen, you entered into our court and being warned that you ought not to do this, you went out backwards to see if you could see me.[339] Some of the novice sisters cried about this, and told me that I was quite cruel not to cry and that I didn't even look at you. But alas, the good sisters didn't see the agonies of my heart for you, nor the fidelity that I wanted to render to the very holy will of God.

The assaults began again when you came to crying to the grill, asking that your mother be given back to you or that you be allowed to enter to become a religious with her. But the strongest blow was when a group of young children your age came with you to the windows of our refectory, crying out that I be given back to you, with your voice distinct from the others wailing pitiably that your mother be given back to you and that you wanted to see her.

The community, hearing all this, was keenly touched by grief and compassion, and although not a single one admitted to me that she was bothered by your cries, I thought that this was something the community wouldn't be able to bear and that I would be sent back into the world to care for you. After grace, I went back to the novice house and the spirit of God said to my heart that I must not trouble myself with all that, and that he would take care of you. These divine promises instilled a sense of calm in me and caused me to experience that our Lord's words are *spirit and life*.[340] I understood that he was true to his promises such that even

---

339. *Relation de 1633*, 288–93; *Relation de 1654*, 279–82.

340. John 6:64.

if the whole world had told me other than what he told me in this interior speech, I wouldn't have believed it. Since then, I have had no more sadness about this matter. My spirit and heart enjoyed such a sweet peace in the conviction that God's promises would be fulfilled in you. I saw all the things done to your advantage and what followed, to make you advance in the ways I had desired for your education. Immediately after, you were sent to Rennes to study, then to Orléans, the Divine Goodness giving me access to the Jesuit Reverend Fathers who took care of you. You know how God has helped in this matter. In brief, my very dear son, you and I alike have experienced the infinite mercy of such a good Father. Let's leave it at that. We will see many more things if we are faithful to him. Continue to pray for me.

Letter 254: October 1669

My very dear son,

I received your last letter by the hands of Madame Bourdon and her son, who at the same time were delighted to be able to tell me your news.[341] They feel satisfied by the good welcome you gave them, and since they are among my best friends and it was on my behalf that you rendered them this honor, I thank you for it with all my heart.

Madame Bourdon was given responsibility in France for one hundred and fifty girls whom the king was sending to this country on the Norman ship. They gave her quite a bit of work during the long trip, for since they come from all walks of life, some are very coarse and difficult to manage. There are others of better stock who are more respectable and gave her more satisfaction. A little earlier, a ship from La Rochelle had arrived, laden with men and girls and entire families. It is a prodigious thing to see how the population grows in this country. The ships have no sooner arrived than the young men go there looking for wives and a great number are married by the dozens. The most prudent begin establishing their households a year before marrying, because those who have households find better wives. This is the first thing about which the girls inform themselves, and they do so wisely because those who aren't established suffer a lot before becoming comfortable. In addition to these marriages, those who have been established in this country for a long time have so many children that this is marvelous and everything is flourishing. There are a number of beautiful towns, villages, and hamlets, not to mention the lone and isolated settlements. In addition, the king has sent captains and officers here to whom he has given forts so that they can

---

341. See Letter 246.

establish and provide for themselves here. They do as much, and many are already quite far ahead.

Monsieur Talon, whom the king is sending back to put the affairs of this country in order and to arrange them according to His Majesty's plans, is expected any day now. There are five hundred men with him and only two noblewomen with their servants. It is now the end of autumn, and we have reason to fear that some misfortune has befallen this ship and the other accompanying it, because two weeks ago, there was a horrible storm in which we fear they might have perished. Thus, there are three buildings positioned at the mouth of the sea, so that one can watch for the ships or some debris. The houses of the lower town of Quebec suffered quite a bit of damage, the sea having swelled so extraordinarily that it reached the third floor. There are quite a few battered houses in the upper town, too. The storm was so violent everywhere that our house shook as in the earthquake. The roof and rafters of our domestics' house were blown away. Our wooden fences and those of Monsignor the Bishop, the Hospitallers, the Reverend Fathers, and others of this sort were knocked down. The loss caused by this storm in Quebec is estimated at more than one hundred thousand *livres*. Here is the reason for our concerns with regard to Monsieur Talon, whose loss would do irreparable damage to the country, because since the king gave him total power, he is undertaking major projects without worrying about the cost.[342]

It's true that there are many people coming here from France and that the population is growing fast. But among the virtuous people there is much riff-raff of both sexes who cause a great deal of scandal. It would have been better for this new Church to have a few good Christians than to have so many who cause so much trouble. What causes the most harm is the traffic of wine and brandy. Those who give them to the Indians are reproved and excommunicated, and the bishop and the preachers proclaim from the pulpit that it is a mortal sin. Notwithstanding all that, many have developed a conscience that allows as much, and on the basis of this voluntary error, they go into the woods and bring liquor to the Indians so as to get their pelts for nothing when they're drunk. From this follow impurities,

---

342. As Intendant, Talon was responsible for the administration of the colony, a charge that included the supervision of the judicial system, colonial finances, and military operations, inter alia. By all accounts, Talon's energies were as extensive as his duties. Among the major projects he undertook during his first term as Intendant were a number designed to guarantee the colony a subsistence economy and to expand colonial production in the direction of trade. Talon succeeded in not only diversifying the colony's agricultural economy, but also in encouraging the development of a variety of industries—textile, fishing, lumber, and ship-building. Talon deserves credit, too, for founding and supporting Canada's first brewery, as well as coal, iron, and copper mines. See Thomas Chapais, *The Great Intendant: A Chronicle of Jean Talon in Canada, 1665–1672* (Toronto: Glasgow Brook, 1914).

violence, thefts, and murders. The disorder was so extensive this year that we were on the point of seeing all the Indian nations flare up against each other, or unite together to come and swoop down upon the French. Here's what happened.

Three French soldiers killed one of the most notable Iroquois chiefs of the nation, after having intoxicated him with brandy. After they hid his body, they stole his pelts. These assassins were discovered and imprisoned, and thus the matter remained dormant for some time. But it was revived by an incident more awful than the first. Three other wretched Frenchmen slaughtered in the same way and for the same purpose six persons of the Mohican nation who are friends of the French. This news inflamed the whole nation, and since they couldn't imagine that their friends the French were capable of such a great perfidy, they thought the Iroquois had done it because they were allied with a nation with which the Iroquois were at war. On the basis of this suspicion they took up arms and declared war against the Iroquois. When the assassins returned here with the pelts of those they had killed, which were worth a good three thousand *livres*, they wanted to make it seem as if they had reaped this profit by hunting. But the justice of God saw to it that one of the assassins who was not happy with his associates disclosed their crime to someone who revealed it to others, and when the word began to spread, they immediately took flight. The Indians got wind of it and were on the point of breaking the peace they had made with us and which was so costly for the king. What made the affair more complicated is that there was reason to fear that our Fathers, who were dispersed in all these nations, and all the Frenchmen with them, would have their throats slit. The conflagration that had ignited between the Mohicans and the Iroquois began to heat up against the French, these two nations feeling equally offended and joining together in order to avenge themselves. Here is one of the ways in which it began. Four warriors from the Mohican nation attacked a French house in which there were only two valets, the master being absent. They pretended to ask for brandy in order to determine how many people were there, and seeing that the house was not well defended, they pillaged it and stole the brandy and everything they could get their hands on. They wanted to kill the valets, but the valets were bold enough to seize the weapons of some of these Indians, with which they defended themselves for some time. Then, having seized their master's money, they went to find him to tell him what had happened. People went to those places where they discovered the house burned and three people dead, namely two Indians whom the two valets had knocked dead in self-defense and the mistress of the house, whom the other Indians had killed before retreating.

What made the situation still more bitter for the Iroquois is that when questioned, one of the three soldier assassins I mentioned testified that the two others had proposed to poison as many Iroquois as the opportunity would permit.

This rumor erupted and made us fear the worst—that the Iroquois would kill our Reverend Fathers and that they would destroy our distant settlements, as the Mohicans did to the one I just mentioned.

To add to the antagonism and misfortunes, the Ottawa, who are friends of the French, have carried out a major act of hostility against the Iroquois, having captured and killed nineteen of their people. It always offends the Iroquois to see themselves attacked by our allies and this makes us fear that the peace, in general, will be broken. But an opportunity arose which made it possible to restore things to where they had been. Six hundred Ottawa came here last July laden with pelts to trade. They gained much and our merchants still more. But it was not trade that brought them here as much as the desire to make peace with the Iroquois through the mediation of the two Fathers who came with them from their country, and it appears it was these two Fathers who satisfied their interests and convinced them to take this step.

In order to deal more directly with this matter and to diffuse the other situations which were menacing all of Canada, Monsieur the Governor went to Montreal where all the interested nations were meeting. Meanwhile, Monsignor our Bishop found the matter so important that he had public prayers said and the forty-hours prayer recited in each of the churches of Quebec in turn. Although all these people were in Montreal more for the purpose of hunting and trading than on account of a premeditated intention to discuss peace, Monsieur the Governor took the opportunity to bring them together. Reverend Father Chaumonot, who knows all the languages quite well, spoke so powerfully and so joyfully in the Indian style that by means of gifts offered to resuscitate the dead, wipe away tears, level out the roads, and alleviate the difficulties of commerce, both sides were appeased and the peace treaties renewed.[343] The Ottawa gave the Iroquois back three of their captives, promising to return twelve others whom they had left in their country, which the Iroquois wanted Monsieur the Governor to guarantee.

Matters having thus been brought to a close, Monsieur the Governor had the three soldier assassins put to death in the presence of all the assembled nations, so as to convince them that neither he nor the French had taken part in their crime. They were flabbergasted by what they took for a severe show of justice, for you'll note that among their own, when one Indian kills another they don't put him to death, but in order to bring the dead back to life they give the deceased's name to someone else selected by the interested parties, who assumes the position in the

---

343. For a study of the practice and significance of gift-giving among the Amerindians of New France, see J.R. Miller, *Compact, Contract, Covenant: Aboriginal Treaty-Making in Canada* (Toronto: University of Toronto Press, 2009).

family that the deceased held.[344] Thus, the Iroquois were astonished to see that three Frenchmen were put to death for one of theirs who had been killed. They even gave generous gifts in an effort to preserve the lives of at least two of them, and were unable to look upon the convicted without crying, out of compassion and sorrow. They were told that it was the custom of the French to do things in this way, and that in this case, two were put to death for the sake of justice and one for the sake of he who had been killed. In addition, all the pelts that the soldiers had stolen were given to the widow and with the matter thus settled, everyone returned to his own land. You see what results from these wretched drinks. In the past, the French had never been seen committing crimes like these, and so one can only attribute them to this pernicious trade.

I return again to Monsieur Talon. If God grants him the good fortune of reaching port, he will find new means of enriching the country. A beautiful mine containing lead or tin has been discovered about forty leagues past Montreal, as well as a slate mine and a coal mine. Monsieur Talon favors exploiting all that to the country's advantage. He has already established a large brewery at very great cost. He has done still more great works in Quebec and elsewhere, and if God inspires him to eradicate the trade in liquor, his memory will be immortalized in this new Church. I'm not saying anything about the Church here, its progress or the labors of those who cultivate it and try to extend it throughout all the nations of our America. I did that by another way, and if I left something out, you can learn about it in the *Relation*.

Letter 267: September 25, 1670

My very dear and beloved son,

Here is the response to your letter of April 25, 1670, which I read with a quite particular joy seeing therein the lovable operations of God upon you and upon me, for which I will praise him eternally. You obliged me in telling me about the progress of our holy order, which I love and honor more than I can say. I look upon it and think about it only with respect and veneration, and the praises I render to the Divine Goodness for having called you there are continual. I look upon

---

344. For the classic study of the Iroquois in early modern New France, see Daniel K. Richter, *The Ordeal of the Longhouse: The Peoples of the Iroquois League in the Era of Colonization* (Chapel Hill: University of North Carolina Press, 1992). See also José António Brandão, *Your Fyre Shall Burn No More: Iroquois Policy toward New France and its Native Allies to 1701* (Lincoln: University of Nebraska Press, 1997), 19–30. For an analysis of French perceptions of civic organization among the indigenous peoples of New France and the dissonance between French notions of law and order and native ones, see Blackburn, *Harvest of Souls*, 70–104.

all your customs and your conduct in this holy order, and I find nothing there but what's holy.[345] So, stop telling me that you would love solitude and the contemplative life more than responsibilities and occupations. Don't love them because they are dazzling but because they are in the order of God's will.[346] It is good, however, that you can see your imperfections, your incapacities, your deficiencies. It's God who gives rise to these feelings in you and keeps you humiliated in your own eyes, in order to sanctify you in the occupations where those who overestimate their own strengths lose themselves. I will tell you simply, my very dear son, that God directs me in the same manner that he directs you. I see myself full of so many infidelities and misery, and I am so often annihilated by them before God and so small in my own eyes (which I feel continually), that I don't know how to remedy it, because I see my imperfections in an obscurity that has neither a way in nor a way out. This is how I am at the end of my life, and I do nothing worthy of a soul who must soon go before her judge. However, as utterly imperfect as I am, and as annihilated as I am in his presence, I see myself lost by degrees in His Divine Majesty, who for many years has kept me in an interaction with him, in a relationship, a union, and an intimacy that I can't explain. This is a kind of spiritual poverty, which doesn't even permit me to converse with the angels about the delights of the blessed ones or the mysteries of the faith. Sometimes, I want to distract myself from my depth in order to focus on them and rejoice in their beauties as things I love much. But I forget them immediately, and the spirit who guides me puts me back more intimately in my depth, where I lose myself in he who pleases me more than all things. I see there his kindness, his majesty, his grandeurs, his powers, without, however, any activity of reason or research, but in a moment that endures always. I want to say what I can't express, and unable to express it, I don't know if I say it as I should. The soul bears in this depth immense treasures that have no limits. There is nothing material there, but a totally pure and naked faith which speaks of infinite things. The imagination, which plays no part in this state, tries to satisfy its hunger, and flutters about here and there to find its food, but that makes no difference to this depth. The imagination can't go there, and its activity ebbs without going further.[347] These, however, are attacks which, although weak and fleeting, are nonetheless disturbing and subjects of patience and humiliation. In this state the senses—whether interior or exterior—do not play a part, nor does the discourse of reason. All their operations are lost and overwhelmed in this depth where God himself acts and where his divine spirit

---

345. See Letter 68.

346. See Letters 68 and 217.

347. See also Letter 274.

operates.³⁴⁸ Faith reveals everything independently of the powers.³⁴⁹ In this interior disposition, one has no trouble following the exercises of the community. Temporal affairs are not harmful, because one does them with peace and tranquility, which is impossible when the senses are still operative.

By the little I have just told you, you can see the present state of God's operation upon me. It would be quite difficult for me to extend myself enough to give an account of my prayer and my interior disposition, because what God gives me is so simple and so disengaged from the senses, that in two or three words I have said it all. In the past, I was able to do nothing in my prayer except to say by a sort of breath in this interior depth, "My God, my God, my great God, my life, my love, my all, my glory."³⁵⁰ Today, I indeed say the same thing or rather, I breathe the same. But what's more, when uttering these very simple words and these very intimate breaths, my soul experiences the plenitude of their signification. And what I do in my current prayer I do all day long—when I go to sleep, when I wake up, and at all other times besides. Thus I can't undertake methodical exercises, since everything gives way to the interior operation of God upon me. I take only a short quarter-hour in the evening to present the heart of the Son of God to his Father for this new Church, for the workers of the gospel, for you and for my friends.³⁵¹ I address myself next to the Holy Virgin, then to the Holy Family, and all that is done by simple and short aspirations. The psalmody, which is a regulated exercise, does not inconvenience me but rather comforts me. I also follow and practice without trouble the regular exercises. My interior occupation doesn't distract me from them at all, but on the contrary it seems to me that my whole interior disposes itself to keep them perfectly.³⁵² But I'm dwelling too long on myself, my very dear son. Let's get back to what relates to you.

---

348. *Relation de 1654*, 452–61.

349. For a classic theological discussion of the powers of the soul, intellect, and appetite, see Aquinas, *Summa Theologiae*, I, 75–81.

350. *Relation de 1633*, 200–203; *Relation de 1654*, 243–6.

351. See Letter 195.

352. Marie's appeal to the interior (and the associated rhetoric of "depth") throughout her correspondence with Claude—of which this passage is an illustrative example—reflects the rise of interiorized subjectivity in the seventeenth century, elegantly charted by Nicholas Paige. Marie's repeated opposition between interior and exterior suggests what Paige argues was "a topos of baroque spirituality that the exterior did not reflect the interior—that the latter was the only important spiritual dimension, or, rather, that all spirituality was by definition inner" (Paige, *Being Interior*, 162). See also Goldsmith, *Publishing Women's Life Stories*, 26–8, who suggests that the material conditions of New France enhanced Marie's impulse toward spiritual interiority. Interior and exterior are not, however, inexorable antagonists in Marie's spiritual

Take your pleasure in the occupations God gives you. There you will find your sanctification, and God will take care of you through it all. Be raised up, be brought down; provided that you're humble, you will be happy and well always. I understand the occupations of your position and everything related to it. I see nothing there that isn't holy and which, consequently, isn't capable of sanctifying you.

Why do you ask my forgiveness for what you call your youthful follies?[353] Things had to happen thus so that what followed would give us genuine reasons to bless God. To speak frankly, I had regrets about having done you so much wrong, even after I came to Canada. Before God had called you to religion, I found myself in such extreme distress, fearing that my estrangement from you would lead to your ruin and that my relatives and friends would abandon you, that it was hard for me to go on.[354] One time the devil gave me a strong temptation that this had happened by means of certain incidents with which he filled my imagination. I believed that all that was real, such that I was constrained to go out of the house in order to remove myself from the company of others. I thought then that I would die of sadness. However, I had recourse to he who had promised me that he would take care of you. Shortly after, I learned about your retreat from the world into holy religion, which revived me like a dead person coming back to life. Admire the goodness of God, my very dear son. He gives me the same impressions he gives you, relating to the graces he gave me. I regard myself as continually in God's house, thanks to his mercy. I seems to me that I'm useless there, that I don't know anything, and that I don't do anything worthy in comparison to my sisters, that I am the most ignorant person in the world, and that although I teach others they know more about it than me. I have, thanks to God, neither thoughts of vanity nor a high opinion of myself. If my imagination tries to form such thoughts because of some small hint of good, the sight of my poverty smothers it right away. Let us admire, therefore, the goodness of God to have given us such similar sentiments. I notice it in everything you say to me in your letter.

As for the vow for the greatest glory of God, you have the same difficulties as Saint Teresa had. The vow she had made was general and without qualifications, which frequently troubled her conscience.[355] This obliged her director, who was

---

writings, but rather coexist in a tense harmony as Marie defends, repeatedly, the compatibility between activity and contemplation.

353. See Letter 247.

354. See Letter 56.

355. See *L'Histoire générale des Carmes déchaussés et des Carmélites déchaussées contenant les miracles que Dieu a faits en la personne de la séraphique Mère Sainte Thérèse de Jésus* (Paris: Sébastien Huré, 1655), 79–81.

no less troubled than Teresa herself, to write her a version of the vow that I am sending you and to which Reverend Father Lalemant has judged appropriate that I hold myself. I had also made a general vow, which obligated me to do and to suffer all that I would consider conducive to the greater glory of God and the greater perfection, as well as to cease to do and to tolerate what I considered contrary to it.[356] I intended the same with regard to my thoughts. I continued using this general vow for many years, and I found it fitting. But since this Reverend Father had seen this formula in the Chronicles of Mount Carmel, he wanted me to follow it. You see by this that someone must direct you in the practice of this vow, which isn't as extensive in the version I'm sending you as you think. Here is this version:

> *Vow for the greater perfection or for the greater glory of God, reduced in practice and given to Saint Teresa to exempt from all scruples both her and her confessors.*

To promise God to accomplish all that your confessor, after having interrogated him in confession, tells you and determines for you is the most perfect, and that you are then obliged to obey and to follow him.

But this obligation must assume three conditions: first, that your confessor is informed of this vow and that he knows you have made it; second, that you yourself propose to him the things that seem to you to be for the greater perfection, and that you ask him his opinion about them, which you will take as an order; third, that the thing specified for you is, in fact, the greater perfection for you. Thus conditioned, this vow will oblige you quite reasonably, whereas the one that you had made previously, in an excess of fervor, assumed too delicate a conscience and exposed you and your confessors alike to many troubles and scruples.

Here is, my very dear son, the general vow moderated and restrained by the above version. But I can easily see that in the way you undertook it, it would cause you anxiety, and thus I would counsel you not to do it. One must follow interior movements there with a great fidelity, and you are susceptible to the excesses and extremes you suggest.

Letter 274: October 8, 1671

My very dear son,

Since you want me to clarify what I told you in my writings about the mystery of the very holy trinity, I will tell you that when that happened to

---

356. See Letters 153 and 274. See also *Relation de 1654*, 408–9.

me, I hadn't yet been taught about this great and most adorable mystery.[357] Even if I had read and reread something about it, whatever men could have written or taught wouldn't have been able to give me the impression I had then and which has stayed with me since. That happened to me by a sudden impression which left me immobile on my knees. I saw in an instant what can only be described in speech or writing as if time passed between one thing and another. At that time, I was in the state of being attached to the sacred mysteries of the Incarnate Word. I spent five hours upon my knees without getting tired or thinking about myself, the love of this divine savior keeping me united to and transformed in him. In the midst of the attraction in question, I forgot everything, as my spirit was absorbed in this divine mystery, and all the powers of my soul were focused on and overwhelmed by the impression of the very august trinity with neither form nor figure perceptible to the senses. I'm not saying that this was a light, because that is still perceptible to the senses, and thus I am saying "impression," although that seems to me suggestive of something material.[358] But I can't express myself otherwise, the thing being so spiritual that words can't begin to describe it. The soul found itself in the truth and understood this divine interaction in an instant without form or figure. And when I say that God made me see it, I don't mean to say that this was an action, because actions can still be described and appear material, but this is something divine which is God himself. The whole contemplated itself in this impression and made itself visible to the soul by means of a fixed and purified regard, ineffably, and free from all ignorance. In a word, the soul was plunged into this great ocean where it saw and understood inexplicable things. Although it takes time to describe it, the soul saw the mystery of the eternal generation in an instant, the Father begetting his Son and the Father and the Son producing the Holy Spirit, without mixing or confusion. This purity of production and procession is so noble that although the soul was plunged into the whole, it wasn't able to do anything, because this immense light in which it

---

357. Over the course of her life, Marie experienced three visions of the Trinity—the first in 1625, the second in 1627, and the third in 1631. See *Relation de 1654*, 233–6, 251–5, and 295–9. Throughout this letter, Marie's makes a robust appeal for the authority of lived experience over theological training.

358. The distinction Marie draws here between "light" and "impression" reflects her concern to preserve a sense of divine transcendence and recalls the tradition of Pseudo-Dionysius who, like Marie, made use of the imagery of light to illustrate the illuminating goodness of God while at the same time carefully maintaining the distinction between "this visible image" of God and the transcendent God himself; see *Pseudo-Dionysius: The Complete Works*, ed. Colm Luibhéid (Mahwah, NY: Paulist Press, 1987), 75.

was absorbed rendered it powerless to speak to it. It bore in this impression the grandeur of the majesty which didn't permit it to speak to him. Although thus annihilated in this abyss of light as nothingness in the whole, in his immense and paternal goodness this most adorable Majesty instructed it, without his grandeur being held back by any obstacle of this nothingness, and he shared with it his secrets about this divine interaction between the Father and the Son, and between the Father and the Son and the Holy Spirit by means of their embrace and mutual love—and all that with a simplicity and purity that can't be described. In this same impression I was informed about what God does by himself in communicating His Divine Majesty to the supreme hierarchy of angels composed of cherubim, seraphim, and thrones, making known his divine will to this hierarchy directly and without the interposition of any created spirit. I understood distinctly the relationship between each of these three persons of the very august trinity and each of the choirs of this supreme hierarchy—the unshakable solidity of the Father's thoughts in those which are thus called thrones, the splendors and lights of the Word in the others who are named cherubim for it, and the ardors of the Holy Spirit in the others who for this reason are called seraphim, and finally that the very holy trinity, in the unity of its divine essence, communicated itself to this hierarchy, which then made known his will to the other celestial spirits according to their ranks.

My soul was completely lost in these grandeurs and my visions of these great things followed without interruption, one after the other. When one looks at a picture depicting several mysteries, one sees them all together, but to really consider them in detail one must interrupt oneself. But in an impression like this one, the whole is seen distinctly, purely, and without interruption. I finally experienced how my soul was the image of God, that it was connected to the eternal Father by the memory, to the Son the divine Word by the understanding, and to the Holy Spirit by the will, and that just as the very holy trinity was three in persons and one in essence, so also was the soul three in its powers and one in its substance.

I was also shown that even though the Divine Majesty subordinates some angels to others so that some receive illumination from others, he nevertheless illumines them himself when he wants to, according to his adorable will, just as he does with some chosen souls in this world. And although I am but mud and muck, my soul was certain that it was among this number. This was so clear to me that even though I was certain I was but a nothing, I had no doubt about it. Thus this great light came to an end, which transformed my spiritual state.

The rest of this vision is as I have described, but you will please note that these great things are never forgotten, and I still remember them as clearly as when they happened. As for the terms I have used, they are unstudied and signify only what my spirit supplies me, but they can never do justice to the things themselves, because there are no better terms for expressing them.³⁵⁹

After these lights and the others I have described in my writings, the Reverend Father Dom Raymond, with whom I wasn't always able to communicate, gave me the works of Saint Denis translated by a Father of his order, after they were printed.³⁶⁰ I understood them clearly in all their aspects and I was extremely consoled to recognize therein the great mysteries that God had communicated to me out of his goodness. But things are quite different when His Divine Majesty imprints them on the soul than they are in books, although what books say about them is genuine and accords with our holy faith. I have read some books about such matters since, and I have never seen anything that comes close to what Saint Denis said about them. This great saint outdoes them all, based on the impression that has stayed with me, and I am convinced that this great saint had the light of the Holy Spirit although he wasn't able to say more, for these are in fact inexplicable things. I was greatly consoled to see there what was reported about Saint Hierotheus, that he endured divine things, because often and almost continually by the operation of the eternal Word, I was in the transports of love, which maintained me in an indescribable intimacy with his divine person.³⁶¹ That made me fear from time to time that I was mistaken, although my confessors assured me that it was the spirit of God who was acting. This reading helped me and although I didn't see transports like those I endured described there, the sense of the text nevertheless satisfied me and allayed my fear, for at that time I didn't have the experience I do now.

As far as the second thing about which you ask me, having to do with my current state, I will tell you that even though I read or listen as attentively as possible, I forget whatever prayer I try to say. It's not that I don't envision the mystery when

---

359. Marie's protestations of ignorance here and elsewhere comport not only with a Teresian rhetoric of incompetence, but also with the early modern celebration of (feminine) experience at the expense of erudition. In the case of Teresa of Ávila, Alison Weber argues that Teresa's claim to theological illiteracy was part of a deliberate strategy intended to insulate her from Inquisition scrutiny; see Weber, *Teresa of Avila and the Rhetoric of Femininity*, 110–22. It is worth considering whether a similar rhetoric of incompetence—whether furnished by Marie's own pen or the heavy hand of her editorial son—functions in Marie's writings as a prophylactic of sorts within the context of a religious establishment that, by the end of the century, had proven itself hostile to the mystical current.

360. R. P. Jean de Saint-François, *Seconde traduction des œuvres de S. Denys Aréopagyte* (Paris: Adrian Taupinart, 1629).

361. Pseudo-Dionysius (here, Saint Denis) claims Hierotheus as his teacher in *The Divine Names*, where he reports that Hierotheus had been privileged with "mysterious inspiration, not only leaning but also experiencing the divine things" concerning the mystery of the incarnation; *Pseudo-Dionysius: Works*, 65.

I begin, for I am powerless to meditate, but in an instant and without reflecting I find myself in my usual depth where my soul contemplates God in whom it abides. I talk to him as he moves me, and this great intimacy neither permits me to contemplate him without speaking to him nor to speak to him without following his attraction. If the attraction is to his grandeur, and I see my nothingness at the same time, my soul speaks to him appropriately. I don't know if these are the sorts of actions that are called anagogies, for I don't focus on these distinctions.[362] If the attraction is to his sovereign domain, they are of the same sort. If it is to his kindness and to what is nothing but love in him, my words are addressed as if to my spouse, and I am powerless to speak otherwise to him. This love is never idle and my heart can breathe only in it.[363] I have said that these breaths that give me life are those of my spouse, who consumes me off and on in such a way that if mercy didn't adapt its grace to nature, I would succumb and this life would kill me, although none of that is perceptible to the senses nor impedes me from carrying out my regular duties. I notice that sometimes I stagger while walking about the house. I don't know if others notice. This is because my spirit is enduring a transport which consumes me. I can do almost nothing in these situations, because this consuming love doesn't let me.[364] At other times, my soul experiences the above and speaks in a language of love to its spouse that he alone can make it speak. But whatever intimacy he permits me, I don't forget my nothingness which is an abyss within a bottomless abyss. In these situations, I can't stay upon my knees without some support, for although my senses are free I am nevertheless weak, and my weakness prevents me from doing so, such that if I want to force myself not to sit down or support myself, the body suffers and worries, distracting me and obliging me to do one or the other, and I am calm again for a while. Since there is nothing material in this interior occupation, sometimes my imagination troubles me with trivialities which have no foundation and go just as easily as they come. The reason is that since the imagination plays no part in what's going on inside, it looks for a way to maintain its natural and fickle activity, but this makes no difference to my depth, which remains unchanging. In other situations, I feel

---

362. According to Antoine Furetière's 1690 *Dictionnaire universel*, the term "anagogie" derives from the Greek and refers to that which elevates the spirit to things celestial and divine.

363. The centrality of the "heart" in the rhetoric of seventeenth-century spirituality has been well studied: Mino Bergamo, *L'Anatomie de l'âme: de François de Sales à Fénélon*, trans. Marc Bonneval (Grenoble: Jerome Millon, 1994), 7–21; and Louis Cognet, "Le Coeur chez les Spirituels du XVIIe Siècle," *Dictionnaire de spiritualité ascétique et mystique* (Paris: Beauchesne, 1964), vol. II, col. 2300–307, who argues that understandings of the "heart" operative in seventeenth-century France are almost universally variations on a voluntarist theme.

364. See Letter 267.

as if I am crucified. My soul contemplates God, who meanwhile seems to take pleasure in holding me captive. I would like to embrace him and interact with him as usual, but he keeps me bound and in my binds I see that he loves me but I can't, however, embrace him. Ah, how tormenting this is! Nevertheless, my soul acquiesces to it because I cannot want to be in a state other than that where His Divine Majesty wants me. I consider this state one of purgation or a purgatory, for I can't call it anything else. Once this state passes, I find myself as usual.

When I said to you above that my soul experiences the signification of the actions it produces, I meant to say that my soul is pushed along by the spirit. The spirit guides me according to what I see and experience in its attraction, which doesn't permit me to do anything else. If what I see and experience are things of love, as the one that I love is only of love, the actions it makes me do are all actions of love, and my soul, which loves the love, understands that it is completely love in him. This is the explanation. I would like to be able to explain myself better, my very dear son, but I can't. If you want something from me, I will not neglect to respond to you about it, if I am alive and in a position to do so. If I was near to you, I would pour my heart into yours and take you for my spiritual director.[365] It's not that in my current state, which is a state of simplicity with God, I have a lot to say, for I would almost always say the same thing, but certain situations arise in which one needs to communicate. I do so with our good Father Lalement, for even though he is almost eighty years old, his senses and mind are as sound as ever.

You have reason to make the judgment you're making about Saint Teresa's vow of the greater glory of God and the greater perfection.[366] I drew the paper I sent you from the Chronicles of Mount Carmel, which say that at first she had made this vow absolutely and without qualification. As for the one I made, everything is included there and I have never understood it otherwise my whole life long. The Reverend Father Lalemant permits me to renew it from time to time, as we do our vows of religion. He wanted me to make the vow as it is recorded on this paper, but I try to hold myself to what I have done, and by the mercy of God it causes me no scruple. If I commit faults or imperfections without thinking about it, I hope that the all good and merciful God will not impute them to a breach of my vow. He helps me not to breach my vow knowingly, and does so mercifully because as for me, I am a poor woman and a great sinner, which is why you must pray for my conversion.

---

365. See Letter 195.

366. See Letter 267.

Index

Note: Letters of Marie de l'Incarnation are listed by date under main topics.

Abandonment
  September 4, 1641, 42, 43
  Summer, 1647, 90
  August 9, 1654, 130, 131
  August 16, 1664, 183
  July 29, 1665, 184
  July 30, 1669, 208–210
  letters as window into mother-son relationship, 1, 2, 4, 6, 7–8, 11n31, 32–40, 43n7, 49n23, 53n31, 208n338
Abbey of Saint-Vannes, 43n6
Abenakis, 59, 85
Abnegation of will, 27n84. *See also* Self-abnegation
Acadia, 173
Acarie, Barbe, 11n31, 25
Activity and contemplation
  September 1, 1643, 54
  October 13, 1660, 153
  commentary, 31, 54–55n35, 57n36, 216–217n352
Affected modesty, 123n176
Affection
  Summer, 1647, 90
  September 13, 1651, 104
  August 9, 1654, 130
  October 15, 1657, 139

  October 30, 1667, 198
  October 1668, 207
  commentary, 9, 10, 12n32, 35, 90n99
Affective piety, 90n99, 184n288
Agriculture, 195, 206, 206n336
Ahlgren, Gillian, 18n50, 107n141
Alcohol, 67, 67n64, 176n270
Algonquins
  September 4, 1641, 46, 47
  August 29–September 10, 1646, 79, 80, 81, 87
  August 30, 1650, 103
  October 18, 1654, 137
  October 4, 1658, 145
  September 16, 1661, 161
  October 29, 1665, 196
  October 30, 1667, 200
  conversion of, 15
  Jesuits and, 47n19
  language of, 15n41, 23, 46, 200–201, 200–201n324
Alterity, 22
Amerindians. *See also specific tribes*
  September 4, 1641, 45–46
  September 30, 1643, 57
  August 30, 1650, 100
  October 16, 1666, 197
  acculturation of, 23n67, 203n328

Amerindians (*Cont.*)
   alcohol and, 67, 67n64
   biblical worldview and, 20–21
   child-rearing practices, 202n327
   "civilizing," 46, 46n16
   conversion of, 21, 39
   earthquake and, 166–167, 169, 173
   economic relationships with, 16
   gift-giving's significance to, 213n343
   intermarriages with French, 203n328
   languages of, 200–201n324
   letters as anthropology of, 2, 20–24
   linguistic groups, 15n41
   piety of, 58n41
   rhetorical tradition, 77n80
   Sillery settlement for, 45n15
Andouesteronons, 102
Anéantissement, 27, 29, 30, 31, 48n21
Angélique (Algonquin neophyte), 59, 59n43
Antenhofer, Christina, 35
Apprenticeships, 9n22
Aquinas, Thomas, 71–72n69, 157n246
Arendarhonons, 15n41
Ariés, Philippe, 9
Aristotle, 71–72n69
Arnauld, Antoine, 155n239
Arnauld, Henri, 155n239
Artisans, 105
Attignawantans, 15n41
Attigneenongnahacs, 15n41
Attikameks
   September 30, 1643, 57
   August 29–September 10, 1646, 78
   September 1, 1652, 114
   September 16, 1661, 161
Augustinian anthropology, 46n16
Authorial agency, 93n111, 131n186
Autobiographical texts, 91n104, 107n141, 131n186

Baptism, 16, 57, 59, 62, 68, 77, 78
Baroque spirituality, 216n352

Benedict (Saint)
   September 4, 1641, 44
   August 30, 1644, 73
   August 30, 1650, 99
   August 16, 1664, 182
   relics, 182n285
Benedictines
   canonical visitations and, 134n195
   Claude as novitiate with, 33, 42n5
   reforms to conventual observance, 43n6
   scholarship on Marie, 3n5
   of Tiron, 55n36
   at Vendôme, 33, 42n5
Bernard of Clairvaux, 95n119
Bernières, Jean de
   September 4, 1641, 48
   September 9, 1652, 116
   August 24, 1658, 141
   September–October 1659, 148
   September–October 1663, 176
   commentary, 48–49n23
Bérulle, Pierre de, 27, 27n84, 28, 31, 48n21, 72n70, 73n73, 94n112, 155n239, 158n249
Bishops. *See also specific individuals*
   September 9, 1652, 118
   August 24, 1658, 141
   September–October 1659, 148
Body, 191n304
Boston, 173
Bourdon, Madame, 207, 210
Bourdon, Monsieur, 81, 208
Bourgeoys, Marguerite, 150n225
Boutroue, Monsieur, 205
Brandy, 67, 67n64, 175n270, 211
Breastfeeding, 8
Brébeuf, Jean de, 46, 51n27, 99n126, 100
Brewery, 214
Brienne, Countess, 43
Brockliss, Laurence, 164n258
Bruneau, Marie-Florine, 17–18, 19n50, 25, 35

Buisson, Marie, 41*n*1, 75, 75*n*78, 117–118, 156*n*243
Burning, allusions to, 50*n*27
Buteux, Father, 114

Calvinism, 73*n*73, 132*n*189
Canfield, Benoît de, 51*n*28
Captivity narrative, 146–147*n*219
Carignan-Salières Regiment, 15*n*41, 178*n*275
Carvajal, Luisa de, 93*n*110
Catherine de Saint-Augustin, 168*n*261, 186, 186*nn*291–292
Catholic Reformation, 24, 25, 26, 30, 31
Cayugas, 15*n*41
Cécile de Reuville de l'Enfant Jésus, 200
Centuries of Childhood (Ariés), 9
Chabanel, Noël, 99*n*126, 100
Chapels, 60
Charity, 70
Charles VIII (king), 159*n*251
Chastity, 75*n*77
Château-Richer, 177
Chaumonot, Father
  September 4, 1641, 46
  August 26, 1644, 70
  October 18, 1654, 136
  October 4, 1658, 145
  October 1669, 213
Child-rearing, 8–10, 9*n*22, 202*n*327
Choir nuns
  August 26, 1644, 66
  August 30, 1644, 74
  September 9, 1652, 118
  September 2, 1656, 138
  October 30, 1667, 201
  commentary, 66*n*61
Le Chrétien intérieur (Bernières), 49*n*23
Christocentric theology, 27, 27*n*84, 28, 29, 34, 72*n*70, 157*n*245
Clandestine Catholics, 85*n*92
Clergy as first estate, 113*n*155
Cliche, Marie-Aimée, 141*n*212

Clothing, 64–65, 64–65*n*58
Cognet, Louis, 121*n*173
Colbert, Jean-Baptiste, 14, 176*n*271
Colombage pierrotté architectural style, 63*n*54
Commerce, 110, 110*n*148, 147, 176*n*270
Communion, 51, 77
Compagnie des Cents Associés, 14, 85*n*92, 152*n*230, 175*nn*269–270
Condren, Charles de, 27, 29, 31, 44*n*12, 47*n*20, 95*n*117
Conflagration, 50*n*27
Confraternity of the Holy Family, 193*n*309
Conscience
  August 26, 1644, 69
  August–September 1663, 171
Consumption, language of
  Summer, 1647, 95
  October 16, 1668, 204
  October 8, 1671, 222
  commentary, 95*n*117
Contemplation, 31, 36, 54, 54–55*n*35, 189*n*298. *See also* Activity and contemplation; Interiority
Converse nuns
  August 26, 1644, 66
  August 30, 1644, 74
  September 9, 1652, 116
  September 2, 1656, 138
  October 30, 1667, 201
  commentary, 66*n*61
Cornerstones, 63
Corporeal mortification. *See* Mortification
Cosmological phenomena, 16, 162, 162*n*255
Council of Trent, 24, 134*n*195
Counter-Reformation, 42*n*4
Couture, Paul-Eugène, 26
Coûture, Sieur, 79, 80, 81
Crosses to bear. *See* Suffering

d'Aiguillon, Marie Madeleine de
 Vignerot du Pont de Courlay, 9n23,
 43, 44n9
d'Ailleboust, Madame
 September 16, 1661, 161
 August 16, 1664, 182
 October 1668, 207
d'Angers, Monsignor, 155, 155n239
Daniel, Antoine, 99n126
Daran, Father, 97, 99, 101
d'Argençon, Monsieur, 139
d'Argenson, Governor, 15
d'Argenson, Pierre Voyer, 152n230
Davis, Natalie Zemon, 17, 33
Death
 Summer, 1647, 93
 October 18, 1663, 178
 October 30, 1667, 198, 200
 October 16, 1668, 204
 commentary, 164n258
de Bretonvilliers, Monsieur, 150
de Certeau, Michel, 25, 26, 94n112
de Chambly, Monsieur
 October 16, 1666, 197
de Chantal, Jeanne, 11
de Courcelle, Governor, 196
de Dombourg, Monsieur, 207
de la Peltrie, Madeleine, 13, 63n54
de la Troche, Marie de Savonnières,
 48n22. See also Marie de Saint
 Joseph
de Lauson, Monsieur, 202
de Lespinay, Monsieur, 161
de Lionne, Father, 135
de Mézy, Charles-Auguste de Saffray,
 176, 176n271, 192n307
de Monceaux, Monsieur, 207
Demons and demonic forces
 September 1, 1643, 54
 August 29–September 10, 1646, 77
 October 4, 1658, 143
 August–September 1663, 164–175

 commentary, 58–59n42, 135n198,
  186–187n292
de Montigny, Abbé, 141
Denis (Saint), 221n361
 October 8, 1671, 221
de Noüe, Anne, 54n33, 82–84
de Paula, Francis, 65n59, 159n251
de Plessis, Monsieur
 September 1, 1652, 113
de Quen, Jean, 69, 77n79, 152
de Queylus, Thubières de Levy, 149–150,
 149n224
de Sales, Francis, 11, 96n121, 153n233,
 189n298
de Salières, Monsieur, 197
de Senneçay, Duchesse, 203
de Sévigné, Madame, 12n32, 123n176
Deslandres, Dominique, 30n99
de Tracy, Lieutenant General
 August 30, 1665, 192, 193
 October 29, 1665, 194, 196
 October 16, 1666, 196, 197, 198
 commentary, 15, 192n307
de Valence, Marie, 25
Devotional practices, 29, 155–158
Diefendorf, Barbara, 11n31, 27n84
Diseases
 September–October 1659, 152
 September 16, 1661, 163
 October 1668, 205
 commentary, 164n258
Divine breasts, 188, 188n295
Divine will. See Will of God
Dreams, 143n215, 184, 184n288
du Bois, Pierre, Baron d'Avaugour, 159,
 159n252
du Creux, François, 17
du Peron, Father, 146

Earthquake (1663), 16–17, 165n260,
 179n280
 August–September 1663, 164–175

September–October 1663, 177
October 18, 1663, 179
Ecclesiastical jurisdiction, 149*n*224, 150*n*226
Eckhart, Meister, 121*n*172
Écrits spirituels et historiques (Martin), 2, 3
Education. *See also* Teaching
    October 30, 1667, 203
    of Amerindians, 22, 202*n*327
    of children in France, 8, 9
Enclosure rules, 64*n*57, 204
L'Enfant et la vie familiale sous l'Ancien Régime (Ariés), 9
Epidemics. *See* Diseases
l'Ermitage, 48–49*n*23
Eudes, Jean, 27–29, 31, 73*n*73, 95*n*117, 156*n*241

Famines, 84
Farrell, Michèle, 123*n*176
Fatigue, 13, 61, 61*n*51, 105
Fear, 204
Felicitas, 43*n*7, 196
Feminine rhetorical strategy. *See* Rhetoric of femininity
Fénelon, Archbishop, 30*n*99
Filles de Notre Dame, 25
Filles du roi
    October 29, 1665, 194–195
    October 1668, 205–206
    October 1669, 210
    commentary, 194*n*312
Fire of 1651
    September 13, 1651, 104
    October–November, 1651, 106–107
    September 9, 1652, 119
    commentary, 32, 37
Fireplaces, 64
First estate, 113*n*155
Fishing industry, 211*n*342
Flavian Martyr (Saint), 196

Forgiveness, 217
Francis of Paola, 159
Françoise de Saint-Bernard
    September 4, 1641, 45
    September 30, 1643, 56
    October 26, 1653, 124
    September 2, 1656, 138
French School of Spirituality
    burning and conflagration allusions and, 50*n*27
    Christocentric theology, 28, 29
    commentary, 24, 31
    sacrificial theology, 44*n*12
    self-abnegation and, 73*n*73
Furetière, Antoine, 222*n*362

Gallicanism, 150*n*226
Garnier, Charles
    September 4, 1641, 46
    August 30, 1650, 100
    martyrdom of, 99*n*126
Gaudais-Dupont, Louis, 176*n*271
Ghosts, 167, 170
Goddard, Peter, 46*n*16, 59*n*42
Godefroy, Monsieur, 161
Goldsmith, Elizabeth, 19*n*53, 20, 131*n*186
Goupil, René, 51*n*27
Gourdeau, Claire, 23*n*67
Grace, 30*n*99, 73–74*n*73, 132*n*189, 157*n*246, 187
Greer, Allan, 68*n*66
Gres-Gayer, Jacques M., 119*n*165
Guyart, Marie. *See* Marie de l'Incarnation
Guyon, Madame, 30*n*99, 187*n*294

Hadrian (emperor), 52*n*29
Harrison, Jane, 13
Hierotheus (Saint), 221, 221*n*361
Histoire de la Nouvelle-France (Lescarbot), 17
Historia Canadensis (de Creux), 17

Holy Family
    August 30, 1665, 193
    October 29, 1665, 195
    September 25, 1670, 216
    commentary, 193n309
Hospitaller nuns
    August 26, 1644, 63, 66
    September 9, 1652, 117
    September–October 1659, 150, 152
    October 30, 1667, 203–204
    October 1668, 207
    commentary, 18, 25, 66n62, 150n225, 196n316
Hôtel Dieu (Quebec), 66n62, 203n329
Houses, construction of, 62–63, 177
Humility
    September 1, 1643, 56
    August 26, 1644, 62
    August 30, 1644, 73
    commentary, 18, 19n50, 65n59, 91n104, 107n141, 189n298
Hurons
    September 4, 1641, 46, 47
    September 30, 1643, 60
    August 26, 1644, 69–70
    August 29–September 10, 1646, 79, 80, 81, 82, 85, 86
    August 30, 1650, 97, 103
    October 18, 1654, 136, 137
    October 4, 1658, 146
    September–October 1659, 151
    October 1668, 206
    child-rearing practices, 202n327
    conversion of, 15
    hostilities with Iroquois, 15n41
    language of, 15n41, 23, 46, 47, 201n324
Hurtubise, Pierre, 22

Ignatius of Antioch, 154n236
Ignatius of Loyola, 93n110
Immolation, 27

Incompetence, 18
Indentured servitude, 63n56
Indians. *See* Amerindians; *specific tribes*
Indifference, 50
Infant mortality, 10
Informality, 158
Interiority. *See also* Contemplation
    Summer, 1647, 92–93
    October 26, 1653, 121
    October 18, 1663, 180
    July 29, 1665, 187
    September 25, 1670, 216
    baroque spirituality and, 216n352
    commentary, 31n101, 99n126, 131n186, 158n248
    inexpressibility of experiences, 204n330
Intimacy
    Summer, 1647, 92, 94
    October 8, 1671, 222
    commentary, 34–36
Introduction à la vie dévote (de Sales), 153n233
Iroquois
    September 4, 1641, 46
    September 30, 1643, 60, 61
    August 26, 1644, 62, 68, 70
    August 29–September 10, 1646, 79, 80, 81, 86
    August 30, 1650, 97, 102, 103
    September 1, 1652, 112, 113
    September 9, 1652, 116, 118
    October 18, 1654, 136, 137
    August 24, 1658, 141–142
    October 4, 1658, 145, 147
    September–October 1659, 150, 151
    September 16, 1661, 160, 161, 162, 164
    August–September 1663, 173
    October 16, 1666, 197
    October 1668, 206
    October 1669, 212, 213, 214

conversion of, 15
hostilities with Hurons, 15n41
language of, 15n41, 201n324
persecution by, 32, 38, 197–198n317
political stability and, 16n42
troops dispatched to subdue, 14–15, 14n39, 15n41
Isle d'Orléans, 160, 162

Jaenen, Cornelius, 21n56
Jamet, Albert, 2n2, 3n5
Jansenism, 30n99, 73n73, 132n189
Jantzen, Grace, 94n112
Jean Baptiste (chief), 86
Jesuits
  September 10, 1640, 42
  September 4, 1641, 46
  October–November, 1651, 109
  September 1, 1652, 110
  August 24, 1658, 141
  July 30, 1669, 210
  Amerindian anthropology and, 68n66
  Claude denied entrance among, 41n2
  Claude's education and, 9
  ecclesiastical jurisdiction and, 149n224
  Iroquois and, 16n42
  Marie's affection for, 30n99
  moral rigorism and, 141n212
  native languages learned by, 23
  neoscholasticism and, 59n42
  in New France, 14, 47n19
  relics and, 196n316
  Ursulines of Tours' beliefs about, 38–39, 109, 110
Jogues, Isaac
  September 30, 1643, 60
  August 26, 1644, 61, 62
  August 29–September 10, 1646, 79, 81
  martyrdom of, 51n27, 54n33
John of the Cross, 51n28

Jones, Colin, 164n258

Laborers, 105
Lalemant, Gabriel, 51n27, 99n126
Lalemant, Jérôme
  October–November, 1651, 108, 109
  October 26, 1653, 122
  September 2, 1656, 138
  August 24, 1658, 141
  September–October 1659, 149
  October 13, 1660, 154
  July 29, 1665, 185, 186
  September 25, 1670, 218
  October 8, 1671, 223
  commentary, 93n110, 123n177, 149n223
Laval, François de
  September–October 1659, 148
  appointment of, 148n221, 150n226
  brandy sales opposed by, 176n270
  character of, 15
  Confraternity of the Holy Family and, 193n309
  in l'Ermitage, 49n23
  material poverty and, 32
  Sovereign Council and, 192n307
  tithes established by, 177n273
Le Jeune, Father
  September 4, 1641, 45
  August 30, 1650, 103
  October 26, 1653, 129
Le Moyne, Father, 147
Lescarbot, Marc, 17
Louis XI (king), 159n251
Louis XII (king), 159n251
Louis XIV (king), 14, 149n224, 152n230, 175, 175n269, 176nn270–271, 178n275
Love
  August 30, 1665, 192
  October 16, 1668, 204
Lumber industry, 211n342

Maheu, Sieur, 160
Mali, Anya, 4n5, 19n50, 30, 31, 54–55n35, 187n293, 190n302
Manners, 66
Marian devotional threads
  October 16, 1668, 205
  September 25, 1670, 216
  commentary, 157n245, 205n332
Marie de l'Incarnation. *See also specific topics from letters*
  on abandonment, 1
  biographical background, 5–14
  Claude seen as spiritual peer, 37–38
  elected superior, 105n137, 178n277
  health of, 136, 183–186, 191, 198, 200, 204
  letters written in lifetime, 61n51
  reconfigured relationship with Claude, 34
  Trinity visions of, 218–221, 219n357
  vision which inspired her vocation in Canada, 12
Marie de Saint Joseph
  September 4, 1641, 47, 48, 49
  August 26, 1644, 69
  August 30, 1644, 76
  August 29–September 10, 1646, 86, 87
  Summer, 1647, 91
  September 1, 1652, 114
  September 9, 1652, 119
  Amerindians and, 24
  death of, 114, 119
Marmoutier monastery, 42, 42n6
Marshall, Joyce, 4n6
Martène, Edmond, 41n1, 135n197
Martin, Claude. *See also* Abandonment
  on abandonment, 7n18
  attempts to get Marie's writings, 33, 49n23, 50n26, 90–91, 91n104, 129n184, 131n186
  biographical background, 5–14

  in Blancs-Manteaux, 129n183
  denied entrance among Jesuits, 41n2
  entry into religious life, 33
  flight from boarding school, 6, 6n14
  health of, 153n232, 185, 191
  in Jumièges abbey, 61n52
  in Notre-Dame de Bonne-Nouvelle, 196n315
  as obstacle to Marie's entry into religious life, 6
  reconfigured relationship with Marie, 34
  in Saint-Corneille de Compiègne, 139n206, 154n238
  in Saint-Martin of Sées abbey, 97n123
  in Saint-Nicaire de Meulan, 109n145
  in Saint-Serge d'Angers, 153n231, 164n259, 182n286
  as Superior-General of Congregation of Saint-Maur, 205n333
  in Tiron abbey, 55n36
  in Vendôme, 103n133
Martin, Claude (the elder), 5, 5n7
Martyrdom
  September 4, 1641, 47
  September 1, 1643, 52
  August 26, 1644, 62
  August 30, 1650, 100, 101
  Catholic Reformation and, 51n27
  commentary, 22, 47n20, 52n29, 99n126
Massé, Annemond, 54n33, 82, 84–85
Material poverty, 32, 152
Maternal guilt, 34
Maternal love, 10. *See also* Affection
Maurists, 42–43n6, 121n173
McGinn, Bernard, 48n21, 72n71
Melons, 206
Michael the Archangel, 168n262
Minims, 65, 65n59, 159n251
Mining, 214
Miracles, 193

Mixed life. *See also* Activity and
contemplation
   September 1, 1643, 54
   August 9, 1654, 133
   commentary, 54–55*n*35
Mohawks
   October 18, 1654, 136, 137
   October 4, 1658, 147
   language of, 15*n*41
Mohicans, 212
Molinos, Miguel de, 51*n*28
Montagnais
   September 4, 1641, 47
   September 30, 1643, 57
   conversion of, 15
   Jesuits and, 47*n*19
   language of, 23
Montmagny, Monsieur de, 79
Montreal, 150*n*225, 161, 206
Moral discourse, 52*n*28, 148*n*222
Moral rigorism, 141*n*212
Mortification
   September 1, 1643, 56
   August 9, 1654, 130
   commentary, 11*n*31, 53*n*33, 135*n*197, 191*n*304
Mysticism
   October 26, 1653, 121
   August 9, 1654, 133
   anéantissement and, 48*n*21
   burning and conflagration allusions and, 50*n*27
   Claude's attraction to, 121, 121*n*173
   discernment of spirits, 116*n*161
   experience as primary source of spiritual authority, 73*n*71
   inexpressibility of experiences, 26, 94*n*112, 158*n*248, 204*n*330
   letters as spiritual itinerary of, 2, 24–32
   prayer and, 187*n*293
   reason and, 72*n*71, 117*n*161
   secularized, 55*n*35
   spiritual marriage and, 31, 95*n*119, 190*n*302
   suffering and, 30

Natural disasters, 16–17
Neo-Augustinianism, 73*n*73, 132*n*189
Neophytes
   September 30, 1643, 57, 59
   August 30, 1650, 102
   October 4, 1658, 146
   September 16, 1661, 160
Neoscholasticism, 59*n*42
Neo-stoic motif, 107*n*142
New France. *See also specific settlements*
   September–October 1663, 176
   letters as early history of, 1–2, 14–20
   Marie's travel to, 13, 32
   migration to, 194*n*312
   mission field perceived as battleground of divine and demonic, 22
   Ursulines in, 75*n*77
New Holland
   October 4, 1658, 147
   August–September 1663, 173
Nobility as second estate, 113*n*155
Nothingness, 94–95*n*116, 222
Notre Dame Mountains, 174, 174*n*267

Obedience
   August 29–September 10, 1646, 78
   Summer, 1647, 96
   October–November, 1651, 107
   August 9, 1654, 130
   commentary, 18, 19*n*50, 75*n*77, 107*n*141
Oblation, 27
Les Œvres spirituelles (Bernières), 49*n*23
Olier, Jean-Jacques, 27, 31, 31*n*101, 73*n*73, 95*n*116
Omens, 16, 162
Onandagas, 15*n*41

Oneidas, 15n41, 79–80
Onondagas, 136, 137, 145
Onontio, 80, 82, 146
Ophaned children, 11
Order of the Visitation, 25
Ottawa, 213
Ouinipeg, 85, 85n93
Oury, Guy-Marie, 2, 3, 3n5, 4, 5n7, 46n16, 63n54, 85n93, 153n233, 155n239

Paige, Nicholas, 72n71, 91n104, 107nn141–142, 131n186, 158n248, 216n352
Papal bull
  August 30, 1644, 75, 75n77
  August 30, 1650, 101
Passive interiority, 189n299
Passivity, 19, 19n50
Peltrie, Madeleine de la, 49n23
Penance
  August 26, 1644, 67
  August 29–September 10, 1646, 78
Perfection
  September 2, 1656, 138
  August 24, 1658, 140
  October 18, 1663, 180
  September 25, 1670, 218
  October 8, 1671, 223
  commentary, 93n110
Perpetua, 43n7
Personal agency, 93n111
Pijart, Father, 46, 97
Politesse, 66, 66n63
Pollock, Linda, 9, 10
Poncet, Joseph-Antoine
  September 4, 1641, 49
  August 26, 1644, 70
  August 30, 1644, 76
  October 26, 1653, 122
  commentary, 2, 122n174
Porete, Marguerite, 48n21

Port-Royal, 173
Possession, 186n292
Poverty. *See also* Material poverty; Spiritual poverty
  September 1, 1643, 53
  October 26, 1653, 121
  September–October 1659, 152
  commentary, 32, 75n77
Prayers
  September 30, 1643, 59
  August 26, 1644, 69
  August 29–September 10, 1646, 78
  October 26, 1653, 122, 124, 125–128
  September 16, 1661, 158
  July 29, 1665, 187–191
  September 25, 1670, 216
  commentary, 25, 29, 37
  states of, 31, 125–128, 187–191
Predestination, 30n99, 74n73
Prior, Father, 74
Protestantism, 25, 85n92
Providence. *See also* Will of God
  August 30, 1650, 98
  September 13, 1651, 105
Pseudo-Dionysius, 219n358, 221n361
Pumpkins, 206

Quebec. *See also* New France
  administration of, 176
  Marie's travel to, 13
  migration to, 1
  population of, 13, 195, 211
  structure and administration of, 18
Quentin, Father, 61
Quietist movement, 30n99, 121n173, 187–188n294
Quietude, 187–188, 187n294. *See also* Contemplation

Radler, Charlotte, 51n28
Ragueneau, Father, 97, 146

Rapley, Elizabeth, 44n9
Raymond, Dom, 43, 43n8, 49, 221
Reason
   September 1, 1643, 52
   August 30, 1644, 72
   October 26, 1653, 122
   commentary, 36, 72n71, 189n298
Redworth, Glyn, 93n110
Reformed Catholicism. *See* Catholic Reformation
Relics, 196, 196n316, 199, 199n323
Respect humain, 148n222
Revelation, 16
Rhetoric of femininity, 18, 18n50, 19, 123n176
Rhetoric of incompetence, 221n359
Rhetoric of obedience, 107n141
Ribera, Francisco de, 93n110
Richard of St. Victor, 55n35
Richaudeau, Abbé, 2n2
Richelieu, Cardinal, 44n9, 175n269

Sacraments
   September 10, 1640, 42
   September 1, 1643, 51
   August 26, 1644, 69
   September 1, 1652, 111
Sacrificial theology, 27, 44n12, 45n12, 47n20, 95n117, 154
Sagamite, 23, 58n40, 67
Sagard, Gabriel, 202n327
Saint-Athanase, Mother de, 185
Saint-Julien monastery, 42, 42n6
Sanctification
   September 1, 1643, 51, 56
   July 29, 1665, 186
   September 25, 1670, 217
Scarlet fever, 152
Seclusion, 11n31
Second estate, 113n155
Secularized mysticism, 55n35
Sedentary Indians

   September 30, 1643, 57, 60
   August 26, 1644, 63, 70
   commentary, 57n37
Self-abnegation
   August 30, 1644, 73
   commentary, 11n31, 27n84, 30, 30n99, 73n73, 93n111, 96n121, 107n142
Self-love
   September 1, 1643, 51
   August 30, 1644, 72
   August 9, 1654, 133
   commentary, 29, 36, 51n28, 52n28, 189n298
Self-purgation, 51n28, 121n172
Senecas, 15n41
Sénéchal, Monsieur le
   September 16, 1661, 160, 161
Senses, 189, 189n299, 190
Servitude, 72, 72n70, 158n249
Ships
   September 1, 1643, 53
   September 30, 1643, 57
   August 30, 1650, 101–102
   October 29, 1665, 194
   October 1668, 205
   seasonality of, 13
   ship-building industry, 211n342
Shoes, 65–66
Shorter, Edward, 9
Sillery settlement
   September 4, 1641, 45
   September 30, 1643, 57
   August 29–September 10, 1646, 78
   August 30, 1650, 103
   September–October 1663, 177
   commentary, 45n15
Simon, Charles, 165n260
Simpson, Patricia, 150n225
Sluhovsky, Moshe, 16, 30n99, 51n28, 186n292, 189n299
Social conformity, 148n222

Solitude. *See also* Contemplation
  September 1, 1643, 54
  August 24, 1658, 139
  September 25, 1670, 215
  commentary, 57n36
Sorcery
  September 30, 1643, 58
  August 29–September 10, 1646, 77
  September 16, 1661, 162, 163
  commentary, 163n256
Soul, 191n304, 199
Sovereign Council, 192n307
Specularity, 99n126
Spirit, 219
Spiritual advice, 36, 91–92, 181
Spiritual discernment, 187n292
Spiritual motherhood, 86n95, 103
Spiritual poverty
  October 26, 1653, 121
  September 25, 1670, 215
  commentary, 32, 121n172, 190n302
Suffering
  September 4, 1641, 42
  September 1, 1643, 50, 54
  August 30, 1650, 99, 101
  September 9, 1652, 119
  October 26, 1653, 124
  August 9, 1654, 134
  September–October 1659, 152
  October 18, 1663, 178, 181
  July 29, 1665, 186
  August 30, 1665, 192
  commentary, 30, 185n289
Superstition, 58
Symphorosa (Saint), 52, 52n29
Synderesis, 73n72

Tadoussac mission
  September 30, 1643, 57
  August 26, 1644, 67–68
  August 29–September 10, 1646, 76, 77

August–September 1663, 169
  commentary, 77n79
Tahontaenrats, 15n41
Talon, Jean
  October 1668, 205
  October 1669, 211, 214
  commentary, 18, 176n271, 205n334, 211n342
Teaching. *See also* Education
  September 4, 1641, 45
  September 25, 1670, 217
  commentary, 18, 25, 75n77
Teresa of Ávila
  September 25, 1670, 217
  October 8, 1671, 223
  commentary, 18, 18n50, 19, 19n52, 24, 71n67, 93n110, 107n141, 123n176, 190n302, 221n359
Textile industry, 211n342
Third estate, 113n155
Thomas Aquinas, 71–72n69, 157n246
Tithes, 176, 177n273
Trans-Atlantic travel. *See also* Ships
  September 30, 1643, 57
  September 9, 1652, 116
  dangers of, 14, 53, 194
Transcendence, 94n112, 219n358
Trinity
  October 8, 1671, 218–219
  commentary, 34, 34n110, 219n357
Trois-Rivières
  September 4, 1641, 46
  August 29–September 10, 1646, 78
  September 1, 1652, 114
  September–October 1659, 151
  August–September 1663, 171
  peace treaty (1645), 15n41, 79

Ultramontanism, 150n226
University of Paris, 119n165
Ursulines

of Arles, 75n76
Association of Avignon, 75n76
of Bordeaux, 75nn76–77
congregations of, 75n76
daily activities of, 18, 203, 207, 214
of Dijon, 2, 75n76
and fire of 1651, 37
food practices adopted from Amerindians, 23–24
of Lyon, 75n76
native languages learned by, 23
of Paris, 75nn76–77, 108
of Quebec, 1, 66, 75n77, 116n160
relics and, 196n316
of Saint-Denis, 2
of Toulouse, 75n76
of Tours, 2, 6, 32, 38–39, 48n22, 77n78, 103, 108, 110, 115, 138
of Tulle, 75n76
vows of, 75n77

Victimhood, 27, 30, 179n280
La Vie de la Vénérable Mère Marie de l'Incarnation (Martin), 3, 33
Visions, 218–221

Walker, Claire, 64n57
Wampum, 80n86
Watermelons, 206
Weber, Alison, 18, 18n50, 123n176, 221n359
Wet-nursing, 9, 10
Widows, 11
Wilkin, Rebecca, 4n5, 32
Will of God
  September 1, 1643, 53
  August 30, 1650, 98
  October–November, 1651, 107
  September 1, 1652, 109–110
  October 18, 1663, 180
Wine
  August 26, 1644, 67
  October 1669, 211
Winter
  August 26, 1644, 64
  October 4, 1658, 147
Word from New France: The Selected Letters of Marie de l'Incarnation (Marshall), 4n6
Wulfram of Fontanelle, 199n323

Zecher, Carla, 93n111